■ United States Holocaust Memorial Museum
Center for Advanced Holocaust Studies

Documenting Life and Destruction
Holocaust Sources in Context

SERIES EDITOR

Jürgen Matthäus

CONTRIBUTING EDITOR

Jan Lambertz

DOCUMENTING LIFE AND DESTRUCTION

HOLOCAUST SOURCES IN CONTEXT

This groundbreaking series provides a new perspective on history using first-hand accounts of the lives of those who suffered through the Holocaust, those who perpetrated it, and those who witnessed it as bystanders. The United States Holocaust Memorial Museum's Center for Advanced Holocaust Studies presents a wide range of documents from different archival holdings, expanding knowledge about the lives and fates of Holocaust victims and making those resources broadly available to the general public and scholarly communities for the first time.

BOOKS IN THE SERIES

1. *Jewish Responses to Persecution, Volume I, 1933–1938*, Jürgen Matthäus and Mark Roseman (2009)
2. *Children during the Holocaust*, Patricia Heberer (2011)
3. *Jewish Responses to Persecution, Volume II, 1938–1940*, Alexandra Garbarini with Emil Kerenji, Jan Lambertz, and Avinoam Patt (2011)
4. *The Diary of Samuel Golfard and the Holocaust in Galicia*, Wendy Lower (2011)

with major support from

The William S. and Ina Levine Foundation
The Blum Family Foundation

and additional support from

The Dorot Foundation

Documenting Life and Destruction
Holocaust Sources in Context

THE DIARY OF SAMUEL GOLFARD AND THE HOLOCAUST IN GALICIA

Wendy Lower

Advisory Committee:

Christopher R. Browning
David Engel
Sara Horowitz
Steven T. Katz
Aron Rodrigue
Alvin H. Rosenfeld
Nechama Tec

AltaMira Press
in association with the United States Holocaust Memorial Museum
2011

For USHMM:
Project Manager: Mel Hecker
Researcher: Greg Wilkowski
Translators: Monika Adamczyk-Garbowska, Tomasz Frydel, Jolanta Kraemer, Kathleen
Luft, Vladimir Melamed, Magdalena Norton, Alina Skibińska, and Leah Wolfson.

Published by AltaMira Press
A division of Rowman & Littlefield Publishers, Inc.
A wholly owned subsidiary of The Rowman & Littlefield Publishing Group, Inc.
4501 Forbes Boulevard, Suite 200, Lanham, Maryland 20706
http://www.altamirapress.com

Estover Road, Plymouth PL6 7PY, United Kingdom

Copyright © 2011 by AltaMira Press

Library of Congress Cataloging-in-Publication Data

Lower, Wendy.
  The Diary of Samuel Golfard and the Holocaust in Galicia / Wendy Lower.
    p. cm.
    "Project of the United States Holocaust Memorial Museum."
    Includes bibliographical references and index.
    ISBN 978-0-7591-2078-5 (cloth : alk. paper) — ISBN 978-0-7591-2080-8 (ebook)
    1. Golfard, Samuel—Diaries. 2. Jews—Ukraine—Peremyshliany—Diaries.
  3. Holocaust, Jewish (1939-1945)—Ukraine—Peremyshliany—Diaries. 4. World War,
  1939–1945—Ukraine—Peremyshliany—Personal narratives. 5. Jews—Persecutions—
  Ukraine—Diaries. 6. Peremyshliany (Ukraine)—Ethnic relations. I. Title.
  DS135.U43G634 2011
  940.53'18092—dc23
  [B]   2011018412

♾™ The paper used in this publication meets the minimum requirements of American
National Standard for Information Sciences—Permanence of Paper for Printed Library
Materials, ANSI/NISO Z39.48-1992.

Printed in the United States of America

"A month has passed again. Those who will endure will know perfectly well what such a period of time means in our life, they will be able to give testimony. One is in touch with death every moment, one trifles with it. It has become an everyday game, like bitter daily bread."

— Samuel Golfard, diary entry for February 1, 1943

CONTENTS

Preface   xi
Acknowledgments   xxiii
Editor's Note   xxv

PART I: Introduction to Samuel Golfard's Diary   1

Reading Jewish Diaries of the Holocaust   7

The Golfard Diary as a Source of Holocaust History in Poland
    and Ukraine   14

The Local Setting of Golfard's Diary: Peremyshliany (Ukrainian),
    Przemyślany (Polish), Peremyshlany (German)   28

Peremyshliany before the Nazi Occupation   33

The German Occupation of Peremyshliany, 1941–1944   37

PART II: Samuel Golfard's Diary, January to April 1943   49

PART III: Related Documents   97

Wartime Documents   97

Postwar Documents   116

Jacob Litman's Testimonies   123

Rescue in Peremyshliany: The Example of Tadeusz Jankiewicz
    and His Family   131

List of Documents   137
Place Names Mentioned in the Diary   139
Bibliography   141
Chronology of Events Related to the Diary   151
Biographies   161
Index   169
About the Author   177

PREFACE

DIARIES ARE among the most powerful sources penned by victims of the Nazi genocidal onslaught as it ravaged Europe. For the estimated 6 million Jews who did not survive to offer testimony in the courtroom, in the classroom, or in published memoirs, such intimate writings from the time are the only traces we have of their lives so brutally cut short. Yet not all written traces of the past that are unearthed merit publication. The rare ones often come to light not because a scholar knows precisely where to look but because of serendipitous events. Indeed, it was by chance that I "discovered" Samuel Golfard's diary.

In 2004, the director of the Jewish Studies Program at American University, Professor Pamela Nadell, telephoned me about the family of a Holocaust survivor she knew from the local Jewish day school. The survivor, Jacob Litman, possessed a 1943 diary from Ukraine that he had kept tucked away in his desk drawer. But this small, faded notebook that bore the markings of another era was not meant to remain hidden. As Litman, who was Golfard's wartime companion, explained in his unpublished manuscript, "Ever since the diary came into my possession, I have had the peculiar feeling that Samek [Samuel] 'willed' it to me, that it was somehow destined for my hands so that his intent in writing his testimony might be fulfilled."[1] With care and diligence Litman translated the diary from Polish in the early 1980s, but he doubted whether Golfard's story would fit in with the growing body of survivor memoirs. At the time, a greater perceived value was placed on official documents, mostly those created

---

1. "Samek" is the diminutive, affectionate form of Samuel.

by perpetrators. Litman's own deteriorating health and an intellectual climate that did not seem receptive to Jewish diaries discouraged him from pursuing a publisher for his manuscript.

Jacob Litman's children took it upon themselves to fulfill the diary's destiny and their father's wish. Shortly before Litman died in June 2004, I met with his son, Dr. Robert Litman, and Professor Nadell at a coffee shop in Washington, D.C. During our meeting, Robert pulled out from his briefcase what looked like an ordinary appointment book, weathered and worn. He placed the object on the table, and for a moment we fell silent. The existence of this artifact gave us reason to pause—and question. Who wrote it? Where was it written? What new insights, truths, facts, and understandings might we discover in its pages?

The diary had miraculously survived the ravages of Nazi-occupied Ukraine, though its rather mysterious creator, a Jewish forced laborer nick-named Samek, had not.[2] Less than 2 percent of the Jewish population in the territory of present-day Ukraine outlived the war, and most of the country's estimated 1.5 million Jewish victims of the Shoah perished without a trace. But here was evidence of one such victim's experience. This diary was the only physical remnant of Golfard, indeed, of the entire Golfard family's existence. After glancing at a few random entries, I realized that Golfard's notebook was not only a precious object, but also a revealing historical document. In the vivid blue ink of his fountain pen, he freely expressed his innermost thoughts about human behavior during war and carefully recorded events, persons, and dates on the lined page and along the margins. On the diary's back cover, he scrawled his last words, filling up every possible space. Having run out of pages and time, he concluded his testimony in mid-April 1943, approximately two months before he died.

Strictly as a source of information, the diary alone fills a significant gap in the historiography, for it documents how and when hitherto unknown camps and ghettos in rural Ukraine were destroyed in 1942 and 1943. It portrays heroic rescuers as well as those puzzling individuals who inhabited the "gray zone" of Holocaust history, in survivor Primo Levi's words, a human terrain "studded with obscene or pathetic figures (sometimes they possess both quali-ties simultaneously) whom it is indispensable to know if we want to know the

---

2. The diarist was a Polish Jewish refugee in eastern Galicia, a region that had belonged to interwar Poland and, after June 1941, fell within the boundaries of the part of Nazi-occupied Poland known as the Generalgouvernement. The territory was ethnically populated by a majority of Ukrainians; it had briefly been part of the Ukrainian Soviet Socialist Republic in 1939–1941 and was then reannexed to Soviet Ukraine after World War II. Today it remains within the borders of independent Ukraine.

human species [. . .]."[3] Above and beyond its empirical value, however, the diary has literary merit. Golfard carefully composed his testimony. Like any good writer, he struggled to find the words to express his feelings and describe his experiences. This is evident in the passages where Golfard crossed out words. But his text cannot be analyzed apart from the extreme circumstances in which he wrote. This writer had little time to write, had to write in secret, and had only one notebook. Obtaining a precious fountain pen was doubtless an enormous challenge. Golfard's Dantean images of the Nazi inferno show few signs of editing. He realized that this diary was his one and only chance to speak out. But could he imagine that scholars and students, generations removed from the horrific violence that consumed him, would actually read his text?

Who was this diarist? The only available biographical information about Samuel comes from his friend Jacob Litman's testimonies and a Polish rescuer's postwar recollections. To this day, we are unsure if the diarist's family name is Golfard, Goldfarb, or Golfarb. Golfard is an uncommon last name, but Goldfarb and Golfarb are not. Litman himself interchanged Golfard and Goldfarb in his written and oral statements. The Polish rescuer Tadeusz Jankiewicz referred to Samuel as Goldfarb in two letters that he sent to Litman after the war. In one (from 1981) he mentioned an enclosed photograph of "Goldfarb" posing with other persons mentioned in the diary. The photo was sent to Litman, but was somehow misplaced or discarded. Many survivors from Radom (Samuel's hometown) who were contacted and interviewed for this book recalled Goldfarb families in town but no Golfards. One Goldfarb, a journalist, is mentioned in Radom's memorial book to the Jewish community, but "Golfard" does not appear in the index of family names.[4] The name Golfard could not be found in the numerous registries and listings of Holocaust survivors and victims, including the available records of the Red Cross's International Tracing Service. The registry in the town hall of Radom reported in January 2009 that it had record of 141 birth certificates (from 1908 to 1940) bearing the name Goldfarb, but no names matched those in the diary. Scholars of Polish and Jewish history, as well as archivists in Poland, Germany, and the United States, all searched for a trace of Samuel Golfard or Goldfarb. This research might lead one to the conclusion that Golfard was not our diarist's last name.

Frustrated by our archival search and traditional database approach, we decided to go back to the actual artifact, to examine it more closely. Robert

---

3. Primo Levi, *The Drowned and the Saved* (New York: Vintage, 1989), 40.

4. Memorial books for the Jewish community of Radom are available online at www .jewishgen.org/yizkor/pinkas_poland/pol7_00530.html and http://yizkor.nypl.org (accessed May 10, 2011).

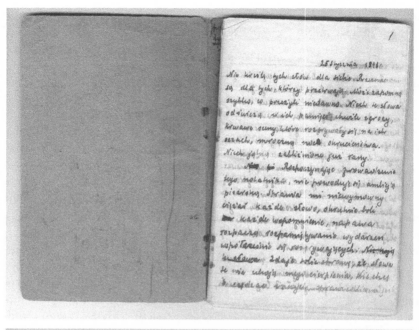

Pages from the diary of Samuel Golfard, 1943 (USHMMA Acc. 2008.316, Litman family collection).

Litman and I met with U.S. Holocaust Memorial Museum conservator Emily Jacobs. Aided by infrared light and magnifying goggles, we discerned handwriting impressions on the diary's cover. It was written in Polish and in pencil. We asked museum staff who work closely with Polish materials, Teresa Polin, Jacek Nowakowski, and Suzy Snyder, to help us decipher the handwriting. The script did not match that of the fountain pen entries on the pages within the diary. On the cover, we read, "Pana magistra spisał Samuela Golfarda." This roughly translates from Polish into "Mr. *Magister* Samuel Golfard wrote."

We deduced that this was probably written by Jankiewicz, who was among the very few who had the diary in his possession and who had a high regard for the diarist. He would most likely identify in Polish "Mr. *Magister* [holder of a degree] Golfard" formally and respectfully on the cover of the diary. He would also be knowledgeable enough to edit the original diary by penciling in the names of the towns that Golfard had designated cryptically with only a capital letter and period. Perhaps Jankiewicz did this shortly before he mailed the diary to Litman in the United States. When Litman received the diary, he used a ballpoint pen to number the pages and fill in other details. In his formal translation of the diary, Litman stuck with "Golfard." Given that Jankiewicz and Litman referred to the diarist as Golfard in these contexts, this family name seems most likely, but given the lack of other corroborating documentation, the mystery remains unsolved.

Why bother to search deeply for the diarist's surname? In Holocaust research, establishing the family name of the victim is essential. One needs it to determine whether family members have survived or whether the German documentation identifies the victim or the victim's family members in the wartime lists of registered prisoners, labor or deportation records, or population surveys. Postwar records of victims, such as those of the International Tracing Service and Yad Vashem's central database, are accessible by name, as are the vast oral history collections held in various archives in Europe, the United States, Canada, and Israel. Names are the primary means for recovering the lost history of who was victimized. By determining the full name of a victim, researchers and laypersons alike restore the identities and lives of those who perished for no reason other than their existence. The symbolic and memorial importance of this is best illustrated today in the common practice of the public reading of names on Holocaust Remembrance Day.

Why did Samuel leave us guessing about his own family name? Why did he not proudly write his full name on the cover of his diary or somewhere on its opening page? He intended his diary to be read in a post-Hitlerian world. He wrote it to document the crimes against and sufferings of the Jewish people. Golfard was not being modest as an author, for he was assuming a much bigger role as a witness. His main function, as the diary makes evident, was not to indulge in an autobiographical account, but to serve as an interpreter, conveyer, and reporter of events. He deliberately provided the family names of other victims, rescuers, and perpetrators. He memorialized his siblings by naming them, albeit using their personal, diminutive forms. Yet Samuel wrote nothing of his own biography, save for what he experienced during the Holocaust. Maintaining a measure of anonymity was also an act of self-preservation, fearing that the diary might fall into the wrong hands.

Based on Litman's description, we believe that Golfard was born sometime between 1910 and 1912 and came from the town of Radom in Poland.[5] Golfard tells us in his entries that he was the eldest with three younger sisters: Mania, Pola, and Bronia. According to Litman, Golfard was "well-informed, intelligent, and quite perceptive, if not very astute"; he was "seasoned, clever," and rebellious. Golfard "liked to mingle with non-Jews, he was university-educated, well-connected, and a little secretive. A well-spoken, witty cosmopolitan who was part of the emancipated, liberal Jewish intelligentsia, Golfard had a high forehead, receding copper-blond hair, [and a] mustache. He seemed sober, business-like, and witty, but actually inwardly he suffered in deep pain and guilt because his sister had been snatched in the September action of 1942."[6] Litman also placed Golfard within a certain sociopolitical milieu of "emancipated" Jews in interwar Poland. Actually, the word "emancipated" is misleading. Jews (as well as Poles) would not have used this label, since Jews in Poland were officially equal citizens. Assimilated Jews such as Golfard pursued a general education in addition to a traditional Jewish one; they were neither Zionists

---

5. Besides being known for its state munitions factory and leather, metallurgy, and agricultural industries, Radom became the center of an interwar dispute over the election of its chief rabbi. On the "Kestenberg Affair," see Gershon Bacon, "Warsaw-Radom-Vilna: Three Disputes over Rabbinical Posts in Interwar Poland and their Implications for the Change in Jewish Public Discourse," *Jewish History* 13 (March 1999): 103–26.

6. Transcript of Jacob Litman interview, tape #4a.mp3 CD4, 10.58/25.10, June 27, 1982; and Jacob Litman's autobiography, manuscript copy provided by the Litman family, 35 and 50 (1997), United States Holocaust Memorial Museum Archive (USHMMA) Acc. 2008.316, Litman family collection. During the war, German officials used the euphemism *Aktion* to refer to an orchestrated attack against the Jews, such as the destruction of a ghetto and deportation to a killing center. Here references to German action or actions will refer to this anti-Jewish violence.

nor socialists (Bundists).[7] In his hometown of Radom, the Jewish population numbered about twenty-four thousand, or nearly 30 percent of the town's inhabitants. There the close interaction of Poles and Jews occurred in several areas—socially, culturally, and economically. Local commerce, indeed people's livelihoods, regardless of class, religious affiliation, and ethnicity, depended on this interaction, since Jews had successfully established merchants' and artisans' banks, trade unions, welfare organizations, a hospital, a tannery, bakeries, barbershops, and establishments for furriers, goldsmiths, engravers, metal workers, and watchmakers, in addition to engaging in numerous other crafts and trades. Golfard seems to have played a part in bridging the Jewish and Polish intelligentsia. Among the several, mostly Yiddish Jewish newspapers in circulation in Radom was a Polish-language weekly, *Trybuna*, edited by S. Goldfarb; this newspaper was known for its "intelligent reporting" and a "serialized history of the Jews in Radom."[8] The editor was possibly our diarist, but so far no corroborating evidence has been found. Literary and Hebrew Bible (Old Testament) references in Golfard's diary indicate that he had some formal Jewish education; his assimilation into Polish society is further supported by the fact that he wrote his diary in Polish, not Yiddish (or Hebrew), and that his Polish was very good. As he witnessed the total destruction of his fellow Jews, he may have also realized that a diary written in Yiddish or Hebrew might not be widely read after the war.[9]

One can only guess that Golfard's early childhood in Radom was not idyllic, though, had he survived the Holocaust, it would have seemed so by comparison. During his youth, Radom was the site of battles between the Russian and Austro-German armies in World War I and occupied by Austro-German

---

7. Information provided by Sara Bender on July 30, 2007, and printed with her permission. On more religious Jews in prewar Radom, see Ben-Zion Gold, *The Life of Jews in Poland before the Holocaust: A Memoir* (Lincoln: University of Nebraska Press, 2007).

8. Alfred Lipson, ed., *The Book of Radom: The Story of a Jewish Community in Poland Destroyed by the Nazis* (New York: United Radomer Relief of the United States and Canada, 1963), 28. Alina Cała, *Żydowski periodyki i druki okazjonalne w języku polskim: bibliografia* (Warsaw: Biblioteka Narodowa, 2005), 180. Also see Sebastian Piatkowski, "Radom," in *The YIVO Encyclopedia of Jews in Eastern Europe*, ed. Gershon David Hundert (New Haven, CT: Yale University Press, 2008), 2:1512–13; Marta Pawlina-Meducka. *Kultura Żydów województwa kieleckiego (1918–1939)* (Kielce: Kieleckie Towarzystwo Naukowe, 1993), 110.

9. Alexandra Garbarini makes this point about the language choices of Jewish diarists in her book *Numbered Days: Diaries and the Holocaust* (New Haven, CT: Yale University Press, 2006), xii.

military forces. There were many reported instances of public hangings of rabbis, rapes, property theft, and other "outrages" in the region, mostly committed by Russian troops, "Cossacks," and "Polish denouncers."[10] During World War I, as many as fifteen thousand refugees sought shelter in Radom, which had been heavily bombarded and ransacked.

Perhaps Golfard witnessed the dramatic "rebirth" of the Polish republic after the war, the Polish-Ukrainian conflict over Galicia, and the Polish-Soviet struggle over Poland's eastern border. His father may have fought in any one of these wars and instilled in Golfard the Polish patriotism that is evident in the diary. Did Golfard develop his wit and cosmopolitanism in the 1930s as a rebellious youth, arguing for reform in the old order of the *kehillot* (sacred communities), mocking local politicians, and debating international events and ideological movements with his friends in coffeehouses and university seminar rooms? Did he observe the grand reception for Marshal Józef Piłsudski and the parade of ten thousand legionnaires, Polish war veterans, who marched through Radom in August 1930? How did he and his family experience mounting Polish antisemitism in the 1930s, including anti-Jewish riots and murders between December 1935 and March 1936, specifically in the Radom region?[11] We can only speculate about Golfard's youth, education, family background, and what he witnessed prior to World War II.

Golfard's diary was entrusted to his wartime rescuer, a Polish civil servant named Tadeusz Jankiewicz, who mailed it to Jacob Litman sometime before 1974. Like Golfard, Litman was a Polish Jewish refugee (from Warsaw) who landed in the small town of Peremyshliany not long after the outbreak of World War II. But Litman arrived alone, hoping that conditions would be better in

---

10. "Rabbi Serving with German Army Sends Long List of Pogroms and Outrages. Tells of Russians' Murders of Jews," *New York Times*, February 4, 1915, 3. Radom is featured in this report of Russian atrocities, which the *Berliner Tageblatt* also published. According to the governor of Radom, streams of refugees fled from the estimated five hundred destroyed villages in the Radom region, only to find the town in rubble, lacking food and clean water. See "Burnt-Out Poland, Literally a Desert," *New York Times*, May 10, 1915, 11, and "Polish Jews Killed as German Spies," *New York Times*, October 10, 1915, 15.

11. In towns such as Radom, Jews made up a sizable minority but not a cohesive one, contrary to the typical antisemitic accusation at the time that "conspiring" Jews posed a unified threat to Poland's national security. The interwar period was a heyday of antisemitic conspiracy theories, the most famous incited by the fabricated *Protocols of the Elders of Zion*. See Ezra Mendelsohn, *The Jews of East Central Europe between the World Wars* (Bloomington: Indiana University Press, 1983), 38. On riots in Radom, see "Two Jews Killed in Poland Rioting. Scores Hurt in Radom Town, Disorders Going on for Hours Before Police Get Control," *New York Times*, March 10, 1936, 12.

the Soviet-occupied zones of Poland. Because of housing shortages, local Soviet authorities ordered Litman to live with the Jankiewicz family. The friendship Litman had developed with the family would later prove crucial to his survival. Jankiewicz and his wife helped several Jews during the Holocaust, among them Golfard. However, Litman's first encounter with Golfard was not through Jankiewicz but through Dr. Jacob Katz, a respected lawyer and math teacher at the local Jewish middle school. Litman also worked as a teacher there. With the Nazi occupation of the town on July 1, 1941, which brought intensified antisemitic regulations and violence, Litman moved to the home of Dr. Katz to avoid putting the Jankiewicz family at risk. The Germans decreed that those found sheltering Jews would be subject to the death penalty. This was no mere threat: many rescuers and their families were hanged or shot for violating this decree, which the Nazis enforced until the last days of the war. The Katz home became a refuge and meeting place for the Jewish intelligentsia from this town and elsewhere, so it is not surprising that Golfard turned up there; in August 1941, he was introduced to Litman. Since Golfard was about ten to twelve years older, Litman did not regard him as a friend, but later in the war, when they were among the handful of Jews left in town, their relationship deepened, as they both relied on Jankiewicz to survive and decided together to escape to the forests.

These two men, thrown together in the terror storm of the Holocaust, could not have imagined how inextricably linked their biographies would become during and after the war, even as Golfard's life was cut short in 1943. Litman, as the survivor, took on the role of caretaker and guardian of Golfard's testimony. Additionally, he became an accomplished historian of Polish Jewry. In fact, Litman wrote his dissertation on Yitzhak (Ignacy) Schipper, a victim of the Holocaust who ranked in the interwar period with Simon Dubnow as a top scholar of Jewish history. Perhaps when Litman translated and prepared Golfard's diary for publication, he was heeding Schipper's last exhortation before he was killed at Majdanek in 1943:

Everything depends on who transmits our testament to future generations, on who writes the history of this period. History is usually written by the victor. What we know about murdered peoples is only what their murderers vaingloriously cared to say about them. Should our murderers be victorious, should *they* write the history of this war, our destruction will be presented as one of the most beautiful pages of world history, and future generations will pay tribute to them as dauntless crusaders. [. . .] But if *we* write the history of this period of blood and tears—and I firmly believe

we will—who will believe us? Nobody will *want* to believe us, because our
disaster is the disaster of the entire civilized world.[12]

Litman's translation and commentary on Golfard's diary offer a multilay-
ered testimony combining the perspectives of two Holocaust victims.[13] Litman's
work contains an intimate and scholarly knowledge not only of Golfard's
Holocaust history but also of Litman's own biography. Litman's experiences as
a Holocaust victim and his postwar scholarship on Polish Jewry add another
dimension to the diary, in most cases corroborating Golfard's story, but also
refracting it through Litman's own lens.[14] For these reasons, the editors of
this volume chose to utilize mainly Litman's original translation, which has
been checked for accuracy. Excerpts of Litman's postwar testimonies are also
included, since they are integral sources on the history of Golfard and his diary.

In preparing the diary for publication, the editors decided to enhance its
historical value by juxtaposing the text with other, related sources of the time.
Holocaust survivor testimonies from Peremyshliany (Przemyślany), as well as
personal and official accounts by German, Polish, and Ukrainian eyewitnesses
from the wartime and postwar eras, can be compared with Golfard's testimony
and Litman's recollections, thereby deepening and broadening the larger historical context of the diary. The vibrancy of Golfard's writing contrasts with the
mundane calculations of a corresponding Nazi wartime document in which the
commander of the SS and police for the District of Galicia, SS-Gruppenführer
(General) Friedrich (Fritz) Katzmann, itemizes Jewish valuables plundered

12. Yitzhak Schipper (1884–1943) is quoted by his friend who survived, Alexander
Donat. See Donat's *The Holocaust Kingdom* (New York: Holt, Rinehart and Winston, 1963),
211. The quote appears in Annette Wieviorka's concise analysis of Holocaust testimony, *The
Era of the Witness* (Ithaca, NY: Cornell University Press, 2006), 2; and in Samuel D. Kassow,
*Who Will Write Our History? Emanuel Ringelblum, the Warsaw Ghetto, and the Oyneg Shabes
Archive* (Bloomington: Indiana University Press, 2007), 210.

13. On the various approaches for analyzing Holocaust testimony, see "The Humanities
of Testimony," special issue, *Poetics Today: International Journal for Theory and Analysis
of Literature and Communication* 27 (summer 2006); and Lawrence Langer's *Holocaust
Testimonies: The Ruins of Memory* (New Haven, CT: Yale University Press, 1991).

14. In 1968, Litman completed his dissertation manuscript at New York University under
the guidance of Dr. Abraham Katsh. The thesis analyzes the historical works of Yitzhak
Schipper, prolific scholar in the interwar period, who along with Majer Balaban researched
the history of Jews in Poland. Schipper influenced fellow Galician Emmanuel Ringelblum
and other intellectuals and activists in the Warsaw ghetto. He perished in July 1943 at
Majdanek. See Litman's published dissertation, *The Economic Role of Jews in Medieval Poland:
The Contribution of Yitzhak Schipper* (Lanham, MD: University Press of America, 1984);
Kassow, *Who Will Write Our History*, 336, 366.

in the killing actions in and around Peremyshliany. Unlike the more volumi-
nous captured German documents, with their cold, bureaucratic euphemisms,
Golfard's words breathe life into some of the millions of individual victims otherwise reduced in Nazi sources to numbers. And when compared with the typi-
cally filtered recollections of postwar testimonies, Golfard's raw reportage is all
the more compelling. The diary remains the centerpiece of this book. It serves
as a unique window through which we can glimpse the thoughts and struggles
of a man who, according to the executioners of the "Final Solution of the Jewish
question," was not to be regarded as an individual, thinking person—much less
remembered.

ACKNOWLEDGMENTS

I N THEIR nurturing of this publication, the Litman family has been extremely supportive. Sadly, Jacob Litman passed away just as I began to work on the diary and became acquainted with his sons and daughter. I gratefully acknowledge the help and assistance provided by Jacob Litman, Anita Millman, Robert Litman, and Julius Litman, as well as the authorship of the diary by Samuel Golfard and the authorship of the translation by Jacob Litman. Numerous friends, colleagues, and institutions have helped bring this publication to fruition, above all Professors Pamela Nadell and Richard Breitman at American University; Vladimir Melamed, historian from Lviv, Ukraine, now at the Los Angeles Holocaust Museum; Paul Shapiro, director of the Center for Advanced Holocaust Studies, United States Holocaust Memorial Museum (USHMM); Dr. Jürgen Matthäus, director for applied research and series editor at the center; and Jacek Nowakowski, chief of art and artifacts at the museum. Dr. Matthäus and Jan Lambertz, contributing editor for the series, devoted countless hours discussing the book with me and editing its contents. The museum's representative in Warsaw, Alina Skibińska, researched the Golfard/Goldfarb name in Radom and facilitated our communications with the Polish Institute of National Memory. Dr. Melamed provided his expertise as a researcher, interpreter, and translator. Since we aimed to contextualize the diary within the various perspectives of the history (Polish, Ukrainian, Jewish, Russian, and German), this project could not have been completed without the contributions of colleagues fluent in several languages. Magdalena Norton completed a second English translation of the original Polish Golfard diary. Professor Monika Adamczyk-Garbowska at the University of Lublin read the diary and provided her erudite comments about its literary and historical content. Andrzej Anczura also translated Polish letters from Jankiewicz and helped me track down Jankiewicz's granddaughter in Poland. Rochelle Uffman, a Polish Jewish survivor and volunteer at USHMM, translated letters. Felix Starovoitov kindly secured several documents for me from the Central State Archives of Public Organizations of Ukraine, Kiev. Irena Spiech, at the Ukrainian Free University in Munich, corrected the translations of the Ukrainian material. Avi Patt assisted with the Hebrew testimonies from Yad Vashem. Other colleagues at the USHMM were especially generous with their time and resources, especially Martin Dean, Karen Auerbach, Suzy Snyder, Judy Cohen, Michlean Amir, Bill Connelly, Teresa Pollin, Megan Lewis, Aleksandra Borecka, Vadim Altskan, Nadia Ficara, Anna Borejsza-Wysocka, Greg Wilkowski, Leah Wolfson, Peter Black, Jolanta Kraemer, Kathleen Luft, and Ryan Farrell. I would also like to acknowledge the photo and map research contributed by Ray Brandon. I received a faculty-development research grant from Towson University and thank Mary Louise Healy and my department colleagues Professors Robert Rook, Kimberly Katz, Nicole Dombrowski, and Patricia Romero for their support of my work on the diary. Towson students in my Holocaust history course read the diary and offered insightful feedback. Thanks also to Omer Bartov, David Rich, Dalia Ofer, and Tracy Brown. I am grateful to the many survivors who responded to my inquiry letter and spoke with me, in some cases inviting me to their homes for interviews, especially Gisela Gross Gelin, Lynn Bergwerk Weinberger, and Stella Schneider Baum. Staff at the Bundesarchiv and the Forschungsstelle of the University of Stuttgart in Ludwigsburg, including Norbert Kunz and Michael Mallmann, provided valuable documents. The extensive, thoughtful comments on this manuscript provided by John-Paul Himka, an authority on Ukrainian history, and Alexandra Garbarini, a historian of Holocaust diaries, were essential in my preparation of the manuscript for publication.

EDITOR'S NOTE

THE FIRST English translation of the diary from its original Polish was completed by Jacob Litman in 1983. A second translation was completed by Magdalena Norton in 2006 and reviewed by Monika Adamczyk-Garbowska in 2007. The version that follows is mostly Litman's, with some modifications and corrections. The original Polish spellings of place names mentioned by the diarist have been retained. To locate these places within the current borders of Ukraine, readers should refer to the maps and the list of Ukrainian spellings in the Place Names appendix at the end of this volume. The Chronology offers a quick reference for situating the biographies of persons featured in the diary within the time frame of the major events of the World War II era. The Biographies section provides details about persons mentioned in the diary or related to its history.

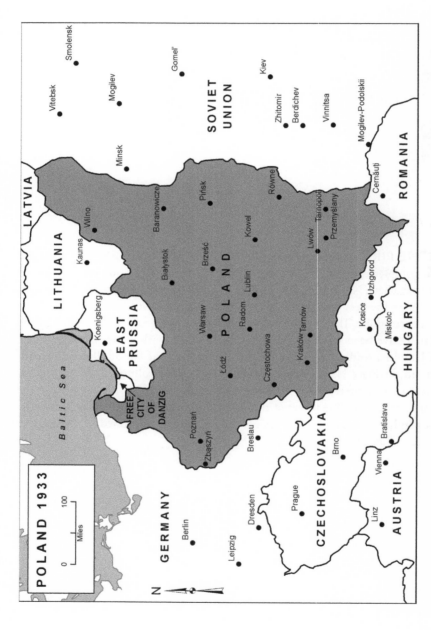

Map 1. Poland 1933 (©USHMM).

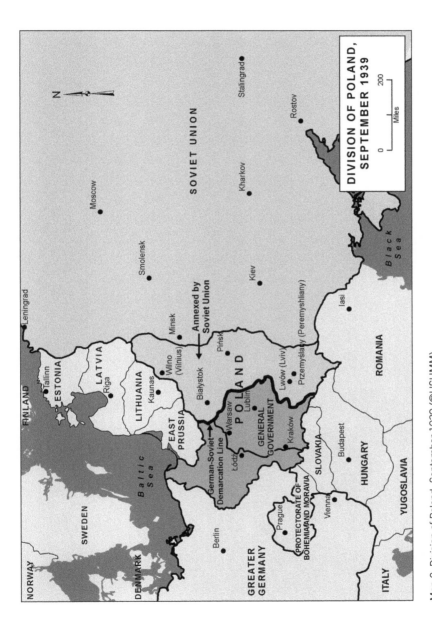

Map 2. Division of Poland, September 1939 (©USHMM).

Map 3. German Expansion in the East, 1942 (©USHMM).

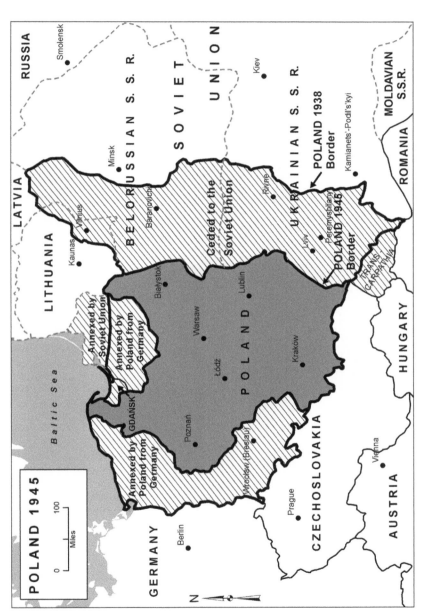

Map 4. Poland 1945 (©USHMM).

INTRODUCTION TO SAMUEL GOLFARD'S DIARY

S AMUEL GOLFARD's diary is a rare remnant of the systematic persecution and mass murder of European Jews carried out by Nazi Germany and its allies between 1933 and 1945. In the Third Reich's attempt to racially reorder Europe, Nazi leaders targeted the mentally and physically disabled, Soviet prisoners of war, Poles, communists, socialists, gays, and others deemed inferior and threatening to German hegemony. At the center of this genocidal plan was the Jewish minority. Prior to the Nazi implementation of the "Final Solution of the Jewish Question," the Jews of Europe had been subjected to various forms of religious, racial, economic, social, and political antisemitism, which became especially widespread and violent in the first half of the twentieth century, the time frame of Golfard's life (ca. 1910–1943).

The fact that two out of every three Jews residing in Nazi-dominated Europe perished in the Holocaust demonstrates that the Nazi machinery of killing in the factory-style gas chambers was, as many have stressed, tragically efficient, bureaucratic, and modern. But this perception of the Nazi genocide, usually focused on the unprecedented horrors of Auschwitz-Birkenau, overlooks nearly half of the Jewish victims who perished not in the killing centers but in the ghettos, at mass shooting sites, and in smaller labor camps in places such as Ukraine. The story of the Holocaust as it occurred in Ukraine is not widely known. With the collapse of the Soviet Union, new information has become available to researchers in the former Soviet archives and the testimonies of survivors and eyewitnesses. Recent research is finding in particular that the number of Jewish victims in Ukraine, the former center of Jewish life in the tsarist empire, is in fact higher than previously

1

estimated. Within the borders of independent Ukraine as it appears today, about 1.5 million Jews died in the Holocaust (roughly 300,000 more than earlier estimates and by far the bulk of Soviet Jewish victims, estimated at about 2 million). The vast majority died at gunpoint.[1]

To this day, scholars and laymen alike struggle to make sense of the genocide of European Jews, to answer questions such as, how could it happen, and why did it happen? There are a number of explanations for its origins, and as recent research has stressed, geography mattered a great deal. All Jews in Nazi-dominated Europe faced the same threat of persecution and extermination, but there were significant regional variations in how individual Jews experienced Nazi occupation. In the case of western Ukraine, the setting of Golfard's diary, the Holocaust combined the history of internal or local developments in Galicia with the external or imperial influence of Soviet and Nazi forces. Ukraine was not an independent country but historically a European frontier to the east, coveted for its rich agricultural resources. From the perspective of the Great Powers and in German geopolitical thinking of the first half of the twentieth century, Ukraine was an ideal space to expand, a utopian "living space" (*Lebensraum*) for colonization where the "Aryan race" would thrive.[2] This perspective translated into a particularly brutal occupation by German soldiers and officials eager to eradicate racially "undesirable" population groups, resettle the territory with ethnic Germans, and enrich themselves.

World War II began with the Nazi invasion of Poland in September 1939, but in Nazi thinking the real test of German superiority and control of Europe

---

1. Historian Aleksandr Kruglov calculated the figure of 1.5 million, drawing mostly from wartime German and underground Ukrainian reports, postwar Russian (Soviet) and German trial testimonies, and survivor accounts. See Aleksandr I. Kruglov, *The Losses Suffered by Ukrainian Jews in 1941–1944* (Kharkov: Tarbut, 2005). Also see Joshua Rubenstein and Ilya Altman, eds., *The Unknown Black Book: The Holocaust in the German-Occupied Soviet Territories* (Bloomington: Indiana University Press, 2007). The importance of the mass shootings was established in Raul Hilberg's foundational work, *The Destruction of the European Jews* (New York: Holmes & Meier, 1985), and highlighted recently in Father Patrick Desbois, *The Holocaust by Bullets: A Priest's Journey to Uncover the Truth Behind the Murder of 1.5 Million Jews* (New York: Palgrave Macmillan, 2008).

2. Ihor Kamenetsky, *Hitler's Occupation of Ukraine: A Study of Totalitarian Imperialism* (Milwaukee, WI: Marquette University Press, 1956); Wendy Lower, *Nazi Empire-Building and the Holocaust in Ukraine* (Chapel Hill: University of North Carolina Press, 2005); Ray Brandon and Wendy Lower, eds., *The Shoah in Ukraine: History, Testimony, Memorialization* (Bloomington: Indiana University Press, 2008). On the broader regional issue, see Alexander V. Prusin, *The Lands Between: Conflict in the East European Borderlands, 1870–1992* (Oxford: Oxford University Press, 2010); Timothy Snyder, *Bloodlands: Europe between Hitler and Stalin* (New York: Basic Books, 2010).

lay farther east, in the lands of the Soviet Union. Operation Barbarossa, the Nazi-led invasion of the Soviet Union launched on June 22, 1941, was supposed to be a "war of annihilation" with the largest military force ever amassed, consisting of more than 3 million Germans, Italians, Hungarians, Slovaks, Romanians, Croatians, and Finns, among other Axis collaborators. Accompanying these regular armed forces were special mobile units of the German Security Police and Sicherheitsdienst (SD), known as *Einsatzgruppen*. Together with the military administration, they were given the task of securing the newly occupied territory through ethnic and political "cleansing." In Ukraine, the small subunits of *Einsatzgruppen* C and D fanned out from military headquarters to the villages, and under orders of the chief of the Security Police and SD, Reinhard Heydrich, these mobile units began arresting and shooting communists, male Jews, and other so-called security and racial threats. In the first six months of the occupation, the *Einsatzgruppen*, Waffen SS troops, and regular German police expanded the massacres by targeting Jewish women and children. Tens of thousands of Jews were killed in mass shootings organized and carried out by combined SS and police forces, military units, and local (indigenous) militia. The largest of these mass shootings occurred outside Kiev in a ravine known as Babi Yar, where (according to a report of *Einsatzgruppe* C sent to Berlin) 33,771 Jewish men, women, and children were murdered on September 29 and 30, 1941.[3]

In a deliberate attempt to involve local populations in Nazi mass-murder operations, Heydrich also encouraged his men in the *Einsatzgruppen* to incite pogroms against all Jews. The pogrom (a Russian word meaning "thunderous beating") was a historically familiar phenomenon of anti-Jewish rioting in Europe (particularly in Ukraine) perpetrated by mobs during times of crisis and often incited by governing authorities. Though these massacres were an important feature of the escalating violence of the Holocaust, they were distinct from the systematic, genocidal mass shootings and gassing of Jews by Nazi occupiers and their collaborators. The largest pogrom during Operation Barbarossa occurred in Lviv

---

3. See Geoffrey P. Megargee, *War of Annihilation: Combat and Genocide on the Eastern Front, 1941* (Lanham, MD: Rowman & Littlefield, 2006); Christopher R. Browning, with contributions by Jürgen Matthäus, *The Origins of the Final Solution: The Evolution of Nazi Jewish Policy, September 1939–March 1942* (Lincoln: University of Nebraska Press, 2007). The *Einsatzgruppe* report on Babi Yar was translated and excerpted in Yitzhak Arad, Shmuel Krakowski, and Shmuel Spector, eds., *The Einsatzgruppen Reports: Selections from the Dispatches of the Nazi Death Squads' Campaign against the Jews in the Occupied Territories of the Soviet Union, July 1941–January 1943* (New York: Holocaust Library, 1989). See Dieter Pohl, "The Murder of Ukraine's Jews under German Military Administration and in the Reich Commissariat Ukraine," in Brandon and Lower, *The Shoah in Ukraine*, 23–76.

(Lwów, Lemberg), where between twenty-five hundred and four thousand Jews were massacred in late June and July 1941. Thousands more died in pogroms in neighboring towns, including, as we shall see below, in and around Peremyshliany. As was the case elsewhere in eastern Europe, much of this anti-Jewish violence was not organized by German or other Axis occupation officials, but was the work of local militias, power-seeking petty officials, and Jew-hating activists. It exploded along the western borderlands of Ukraine, Poland, and the Baltic states in areas that had just experienced the upheaval of Soviet occupation between 1939 and 1941. During the Nazi invasion and occupation that followed, Jews became the immediate targets of homegrown greed, xenophobia, anticommunism, and anti-semitism. Nazi political and racial aims do not provide a complete explanation for the origins and course of the Holocaust because the genocide, while triggered and facilitated by the German occupation, was very much a part of the social, cultural, political, and geographic settings in which it occurred.[4]

Given Ukraine's own checkered history of regionalism, imperial rule, inter-ethnic violence, nationalist factionalism, and economic depression, one can better appreciate how local conditions contributed to the extreme violence of the Holocaust. Centuries of tsarist and Hapsburg governance and colonization had created a land that was ethnically diverse, though the majority peasant class remained Ukrainian. Galicia (eastern Poland during the interwar years) was the cradle of the Ukrainian nationalist movement centered in Lviv, a univer-sity town and historically Polish city.[5] During the partitions of Poland in the

---

4. For more details about the significant local factors that contributed to the violence described in Golfard's diary, see the next section on the themes of the diary and the local history of Peremyshliany. See Elazar Barkin, Elizabeth A. Cole, and Kai Struve, eds., *Shared History, Divided Memory: Jews and Others in Soviet-Occupied Poland, 1939–1941* (Leipzig: Leipziger Universitätsverlag, 2007). Also see Jan T. Gross, *Neighbors: The Destruction of the Jewish Community of Jedwabne Poland* (Princeton, NJ: Princeton University Press, 2000). Hugh Seton-Watson's classic study explores the fate of Jews in light of policies on minorities and the rise of antisemitism in the interwar period: *Eastern Europe between the Wars, 1918–1941* (Cambridge, UK: The University Press, 1945), 288–96. Andrzej Żbikowski has studied local causes; see his work on the 1941 pogroms, "Local Anti-Jewish Pogroms in the Occupied Territories of Eastern Poland, June–July 1941," in *The Holocaust in the Soviet Union: Studies and Sources on the Destruction of the Jews in the Nazi-Occupied Territories, 1941–1945*, ed. Lucjan Dobroszycki and Jeffrey Gurock (New York: M. E. Sharpe, 1993), 173–79; and Joanna Michlic-Coren, "Anti-Jewish Violence in Poland, 1918–1939 and 1945–1947," *Polin* 13 (2000): 34–61.

5. See Kai Struve, *Bauern und Nation in Galizien: Über Zugehörigkeit und soziale Emanzipation im 19. Jahrhundert* (Göttingen: Vandenhoeck & Ruprecht 2005). In the early modern period, it was more "Ukrainian-Galician" than Polish. The city was founded in the mid-thirteenth century by the Rus' prince Danylo of Halych and incorporated into Poland in the late fourteenth century.

late eighteenth century, the Hapsburgs took the city of Lviv and surrounding region, which became an eastern jewel of the Austro-Hungarian Empire in the nineteenth century. Jewish merchants, bourgeois entrepreneurs, and graduates of the schools and universities aligned themselves with the liberal Polish intelligentsia (not the struggling "underclass" of Ukrainian peasants and revolutionaries). When the Russian and Austro-Hungarian empires collapsed at the end of World War I, the Ukrainian bid for independence failed. Dreams of a united Ukrainian People's Republic fell apart, as the regions of Galicia and most of Volhynia ended up in Poland, and the rest of Ukraine became the Ukrainian Socialist Soviet Republic in 1922. Embittered and exiled, Ukrainian patriots of the interwar era found refuge in Berlin, Munich, Prague, and Paris, while others who remained in Galicia were incarcerated as terrorists in Kraków, Warsaw, and Lviv.[6]

During the 1930s, the anti-Jewish, anti-Polish, and anti-Russian stance of the Ukrainian nationalist leadership hardened. The fascist tendencies of the movement flourished. Under the sway of ideologue Dmytro Dontsov, the most influential propagator of the Ukrainian nationalist movement, the Organization of Ukrainian Nationalists (OUN) declared, "The Jews are guilty, horribly guilty, because they were the ones who helped secure Russian rule in Ukraine. [. . .] Only when Russia falls in Ukraine will we be able to order the Jewish question in our country in a way that lies in the interest of the Ukrainian people."[7] These sentiments turned lethal in the summer of 1941 when Nazi leaders launched their campaign against the Soviet Union and endorsed a genocidal "answer" to

6. Franziska Bruder, *"Den ukrainischen Staat erkämpfen oder sterben!" Die Organisation Ukrainischer Nationalisten (OUN) 1929–1948* (Berlin: Metropol, 2007), 51–52, 99–104, 126–27; Alexander Motyl, *The Turn to the Right: The Ideological Origins and Developments of Ukrainian Nationalism, 1919–1929* (New York: Columbia University Press, 1980).

7. Besides such "integral nationalist" propaganda, one event in the interwar period became a crucible for the movement: the trial of Symon Petliura in 1926. This trial forged a link between anti-Soviet and anti-Jewish sentiments among Ukrainian patriots in both the Polish- and Soviet-controlled regions. A national hero and martyr of the Ukrainian nationalist movement, Symon Petliura fought the Bolsheviks, and his units (along with units of the Red and White armies and anarchists) carried out pogroms in eastern Ukraine from 1918 to 1920. He was assassinated by Samuel (Shalom, Sholom) Schwarzbart in Paris in 1926. During his trial, Schwarzbart stated that he was avenging the deaths of Jews—including his own relatives—perpetrated by Ukrainians. Schwarzbart was acquitted by a French court, and Ukrainian supporters of Ukrainian independence viewed his release as a betrayal maneuvered by Russian Jewish interests centered in Moscow and Paris. The Donstov quote and the trial are analyzed in Frank Golczewski's "Shades of Grey: Reflections on Jewish-Ukrainian and German-Ukrainian Relations in Galicia," in Brandon and Lower, *The Shoah in Ukraine*, 121–22; and his *Deutsche und Ukrainer 1918–1939* (Paderborn: Ferdinand Schöningh, 2010).

the "Jewish question." But even earlier, when the Nazis began carving up eastern Europe in 1939 and incited acts of revenge against Poles and "Muscovite-Bolshevik" Jews, they found a receptive audience among Ukrainians, who had struggled against Polish rule in Galicia and Volhynia and shared with most Europeans an ambivalent yet potent perception of Jews as outsiders, an unwanted minority to be tolerated, scorned, and feared.

For Ukrainian patriots, Stalinist-style communism was clearly not an option. The deportations and massacres that accompanied Sovietization in eastern Galicia (1939–1941) were disastrous for tens of thousands of Ukrainians in the noncommunist intelligentsia, especially nationalists and priests but also peasants who resisted collectivization.[8] For many Poles and Ukrainians alike, communism threatened another orthodoxy of historical determinism, that of the "national spirit." Moscow posed the biggest barrier to Ukrainian sovereignty, or so it seemed, and the Jews as a whole came to embody that very obstacle. They were depicted as the main props of Stalin's regime, as members of the detested NKVD (Soviet secret police), even though the Jewish minority in Galicia was persecuted, purged, deported, and killed alongside other ethnic, religious, and political "enemies of the people." In fact, relative to their size in the population, they were disproportionately deported.[9]

Jews did not dominate the leadership or rank-and-file posts of the Soviet administration, but in contrast to pre-Soviet times, when they were barred

---

8. In the initial months of Soviet occupation (October and November 1939), Ukrainians and Jews together persecuted the Poles in Lviv as acts of revenge or to affirm the removal of this centuries-old "ruler." Even the Soviet authorities had "to put an end to these spontaneous anti-Polish activities." Joanna Michlic, "The Soviet Occupation of Poland, 1939–1941, and the Stereotype of the Anti-Polish and Pro-Soviet Jew," *Jewish Social Studies: History, Culture, Society* 13 (spring/summer 2007): 144. On the actual diversity of the Jews in interwar Poland, including Galicia, and the complex dilemmas they faced, see Ben-Cion Pinchuk, *Shtetl Jews under Soviet Rule: Eastern Poland on the Eve of the Holocaust* (Oxford: Basil Blackwell, 1990); and Dov Levin, *The Lesser of Two Evils: Eastern European Jewry under Soviet Rule, 1939–1941* (Philadelphia: Jewish Publication Society, 1995).

9. Though Jews made up 30 percent of those deported by the Soviets who resided in the territory of interwar Poland (including Galicia), they comprised 10 percent of the population. Many of those deported were deemed threatening because they belonged to the "enemy" class of intellectuals, religious leaders, and the bourgeoisie or were refugees from the German-occupied territory of Poland. See Omer Bartov, *Erased: Vanishing Traces of Jewish Galicia in Present-Day Ukraine* (Princeton, NJ: Princeton University Press, 2007), 37–38. Much of Bartov's cogent analysis of the Soviet occupation of Galicia is drawn from data in Jan T. Gross's study *Revolution from Abroad: The Soviet Conquest of Poland's Western Ukraine and Western Belorussia*, exp. ed. (Princeton, NJ: Princeton University Press, 2002).

from the civil service and army, they had suddenly become more visible as government officials. To the ethno-nationalists, the Jews appeared as rootless people who had attached themselves to an alien force, communism. These developments were encapsulated in the derogatory terms *Judeo-Bolshevism* and *Judeo-communism*, which branded all Jews as a race with one detested political ideology. In historian Frank Golczewski's words, "The popular belief that all Bolsheviks were Jews was turned on its head to suggest all Jews were Bolsheviks."[10] Racist and political antisemitism coexisted and, in some cases, inflamed older Catholic and Christian anti-Judaism, such as depictions of Jews as Christ killers or ritual murderers. Polish historian Andrzej Żbikowski observes that "the Jewish population living in Soviet territory became, after 22 June 1941, the victims of two tragedies. The first but the more obscure for the majority of these Jews was the Nazi determination to exterminate the Jewish nation; the other, more proximate, was the violent explosion of the latent hatred and hostility of local communities."[11]

Golfard's diary documents the regional features of the Nazi-led "war against Jews," in his case in eastern Galicia. Various forms of violence contributed to the Holocaust in the borderlands of Poland and Ukraine. The Nazi machinery of destruction, with its thorough, factory-style gassings and systematic mass shootings, combined with attacks by locals against Jews that included mass murder, torture, and widespread plundering. Yet as plausible as the Holocaust might appear from our vantage point, the systematic murder of Jewish men, women, and children was at the time neither predictable nor imaginable to those like Golfard who ended up in its maelstrom.

READING JEWISH DIARIES OF THE HOLOCAUST

When Golfard composed his first entry in January 1943, he entered the stream of a long literary tradition of self-expression and documentation that took the form of a journal or chronicle.[12] During the 1930s and 1940s, the high

---

10. Golczewski, "Shades of Grey," 131.

11. Żbikowski, "Local Anti-Jewish Pogroms," 174.

12. Paul C. Rosenblatt, *Bitter, Bitter Tears: Nineteenth-Century Diarists and Twentieth-Century Grief Theories* (Minneapolis: University of Minnesota Press, 1983); Alexandra Garbarini, *Numbered Days: Diaries and the Holocaust* (New Haven, CT: Yale University Press, 2006); Nechama Tec, "Diaries and Oral History: Some Methodological Considerations," *Religion and the Arts* 4, no. 1 (2000): 87–95; Dominique Schroeder, "Motive-Funktionen-Sprache: Zu Tagebüchern als Quellen der Konzentrationslagerforschung," in *NS-Zwangslager in Westdeutschland, Frankreich und den Niederlanden: Geschichte und Erinnerung*, ed. Janine Doerry et al. (Paderborn: Ferdinand Schöningh, 2007), 93–104.

point of totalitarian terror in Europe, diaries were very popular. Individuals turned increasingly to private writing to vent their anguish, secretly express dangerous thoughts, and ease their conscience.[13] Though politically, culturally, and economically diverse, Jews were among the most educated and literary of Europeans; writing as an act of documentation, memorialization, self-expression, and resistance was a likely response to the catastrophe. Indeed, in the Jewish intellectual circles of interwar Poland where Golfard came of age, social scientists had also learned to keep diaries as a research tool for recording their observations of Yiddish folk culture and history, and this trend continued with the famous Ringelblum Archive in the Warsaw ghetto during the war.[14]

Jewish diary writing during the Holocaust was a form of "bearing witness to [this] tragedy as a means of transcending it."[15] In the history of Yiddish and Hebrew literature, this attempt at transcendence in the face of persecution emerged from a deeply rooted Jewish literary effort to write, as scholar David Roskies put it, "against the apocalypse."[16] As historian Alexandra Garbarini argues and the Golfard diary manifests, during the war assimilated and Orthodox Jews alike often lost their faith in "divine justice" and instead clung to a more secular hope of historical justice.[17] Thus, for Golfard and many others—for example, Emmanuel Ringelblum and Chaim Kaplan—the diary itself epitomized the survival of Jewish history. Ringelblum managed the collection of Jewish writings in the Warsaw ghetto, which were secretly placed in milk cans and buried to preserve and continue a tradition of Jewish history and culture.[18] In the restrictive conditions of ghettos, camps, and hiding places, obtaining paper and pen was a physically and materially challenging endeavor, even a potentially dangerous, defiant act. Ringelblum did not survive the war, although most of his archive did. In a similar vein, Kaplan wrote in his last

---

13. Jochen Hellbeck, *Revolution on My Mind: Writing a Diary under Stalin* (Cambridge, MA: Harvard University Press, 2006).

14. Kassow, *Who Will Write Our History?*

15. Garbarini, *Numbered Days*, 2–3.

16. David G. Roskies, *Against the Apocalypse: Responses to Catastrophe in Modern Jewish Culture* (Cambridge, MA: Harvard University Press, 1984).

17. Alexandra Garbarini, "A Tale of Two Diarists: A Comparative Examination of Experiences in Eastern and Western Europe," in *Ghettos 1939–1945: New Research and Perspectives on Definition, Daily Life, and Survival*, USHMM Symposium Presentations (Washington, DC: Center for Advanced Holocaust Studies, USHMM, 2005), 111.

18. Emmanuel Ringelblum, *Notes from the Warsaw Ghetto: The Journal of Emmanuel Ringelblum* (New York: Schocken Books, 1974); Chaim A. Kaplan, *Scroll of Agony: The Warsaw Diary of Chaim A. Kaplan*, ed. Abraham I. Katsh (Bloomington: Indiana University Press in association with the USHMM, 1999).

diary entry, shortly before he was deported to Treblinka, "If my life ends—what will become of my diary?"[19] Likewise, Golfard composed his entries with an eye to the future and specifically addressed an audience of Jewish survivors as "those who will survive and who might quickly forget what they had lived through not so long ago"; he was not "motivated by a writer's ambition," rather "an unspeakable burden." What was this burden? Did Golfard write because he sought to preserve Jewish history, to make sure that survivors would remember the horrible experiences of the war? Or was his act a "renunciation of humanity," a statement of defeat in a world of utter chaos, loss, and isolation?[20]

Besides documenting important events, diaries such as Golfard's also reveal the extreme emotions that Jews experienced and their debilitating effects. In reading these diaries, securely removed from the horrific conditions of the war, we often impose our own desire for a "happy ending" of survival and return to normalcy. Golfard shares some of Anne Frank's optimism in his last entries; he writes that he does believe in the goodness of people, similar to Frank's famous statement that "in spite of everything I still believe that people are really good at heart." The Anne Frank whom we wish to remember is, in literary scholar Alvin Rosenfeld's assessment, one "who stands as a positive symbol of articulate innocence and transcendent optimism in a world of brutal and ultimately lethal adversity."[21] But the popular obsession with the transcendent misses a very important fact about her diary. Writing while in hiding in Amsterdam, Anne was not yet a full witness to the horror of the Holocaust, to which she would later succumb at Bergen-Belsen. What was remarkable, then, about Golfard's diary was its expression of some hope for mankind after having seen and experienced humanity's most evil behavior.

As an assimilated Polish Jew, Golfard wrote from two literary traditions, which Rosenfeld discerns in his work on Holocaust literature. One is a Christian tradition "celebrating those whose beatific nature lifts them above the ravages of human suffering"; the other is a "Jewish tradition of mourning the victims of unjust and unredeemed suffering—precisely the experience of Jews in Nazi-occupied Europe."[22] Though Golfard seems composed and rational in his

---

19. Entry of August 4, 1942, in Kaplan, *Scroll of Agony*, 400.

20. Amos Goldberg, "If This Is a Man: The Image of Man in Autobiographical and Historical Writing During and After the Holocaust," *Yad Vashem Studies* 33 (2004): 422.

21. Alvin H. Rosenfeld, "Anne Frank and the Future of Holocaust Memory" (Joseph and Rebecca Meyerhoff Annual Lecture, USHMM, Washington, DC, October 14, 2004, published March 2005), 3. Available online at www.ushmm.org/research/center/publications/occasional/2005-04-01/paper.pdf (accessed May 10, 2011).

22. Rosenfeld, "Anne Frank," 14.

description of events, his deliberate literary juxtapositions evince a deep skepticism, anguish, confusion, and fatalism. For example, he writes that each day is permeated with a "mist of blood that invisibly whirls around us [illeg.]. Frantic, I cannot for one moment forget what awaits me. [. . .] The numbers that I record in the firm's inventory book are saturated with my thoughts about the life and death of my nation." Similarly, "Every thought is poisoned by death. When taking a spoon of nourishment in my mouth, I see murdered acquaintances. [. . .] I stare at the sun that does not shine for me and that will soon be replaced by impenetrable darkness" (entries for March 30, 1943). Golfard could hardly escape the violent images that pervaded his mind; and with the deportation of his sister, he saw his own present and future rushing into a black hole. Yet between these dark, heavy passages, Golfard writes of hope, the renewal of spring, and the goodness and charity of others.

Few Jewish testimonies written during and after the war combine—as Golfard's does so succinctly and poetically—graphic, factual reportage with philosophical reflection and moral judgment. Golfard's desperate, fluctuating voice reveals an individual stripped of everything and suspended between life and death. He is haunted by the "stamp of death" that he sees on the gaunt, tortured faces around him; but given the horror that he has witnessed in humankind, he also fears life. Imagine a sane person who suddenly finds himself or herself in a world turned upside down, where destruction and hatred are the order of the day. In such upheaval, Golfard reached for pen and paper to make sense of the chaos that engulfed him, to document the crimes occurring around him, and to vent the shock, anger, and frustration that he felt. The diary is also, tragically, a "suicide" note from someone who did not choose to take his own life, who struggled with his own powerlessness. In the end Golfard believed that while Jews could go to their deaths with self-respect, Jewish heroism was not possible in circumstances of total dominance and mass murder. He did not choose to die, but he attempted to face his probable fate in what he believed was a dignified, defiant manner.

The diarist's quest for restored dignity of the self and the Jewish people, evident in Golfard's testimony, has been aptly described by survivor and distinguished author Aharon Appelfeld: "The journals written during the Holocaust are doubtless the most fiery outcries ever raised by the soul. [. . .] They were a last effort to preserve the self before it was taken. One of the horrors of the Holocaust is the eradication of the self. First you lost your house, your personal belongings, you are pressed into a crowded ghetto, you are separated from your parents. [. . .] The individual is rubbed out. These journals are the final effort to preserve a shred of one's self before it is rubbed out. Naked anonymity was the gateway to death."[23] Today, Golfard's words, as he wished, tear into "wounds already healed." He feared that with the passage of time, the intense rage, sorrow, and suffering that Jews experienced during the Holocaust might be forgotten or suppressed. During the war such emotions, on the one hand, inspired acts of resistance and revenge and, on the other, immobilized Jews who struggled psychologically with trauma and depression and realized that resistance would be futile. After his sister Mania was deported to the Bełżec killing center, Golfard lapsed into a mental state of disorienting grief. In fact, he seems to have started the diary because of this loss and feelings of guilt: "Ought not an honorable man regard himself as contemptible for letting his nearest kin go to her doom all alone? What, then, is one's will to live, if not proof of the height of egotism? The old Slavonic custom of sharing death on the pyre ought to be revived today" (January 26, 1943). The diary helped Golfard cope, but it was not easy for him to write. He felt "subjected to an unspeakable burden by every word; every reminiscence hurts cruelly [. . .]" (January 25, 1943). Putting pen to paper also marked a turning point when he faced a "moment of truth."[24] Golfard realized the Germans' genocidal intentions, his helplessness, and his own likely fate. Hence, he wrote about the darkening sun, and he stopped weeping for his dead relatives. But the fact that he started the diary reveals his instinctive desire to survive, to preserve his sense of self. Golfard's diary helps us break down the monolithic view of the submissive victim into a more nuanced understanding of how those rendered powerless by the dominance of a criminal regime struggle to survive. To be sure, Jewish victims did not choose to be passive in the face of the mass murder of their loved ones and communities. Under such circumstances, most humans will do whatever is necessary to preserve life and the security of home and family by ameliorating the perceived threat, not by aggravating it with more violence. The experience of being victimized, of being subjected to brutality or witnessing it, also evolved with the changing contexts of the war and radicalization of the Nazi onslaught. Golfard's diary reveals what psychologist Ervin Staub observed—that "as the continuum of

---

23. Aharon Appelfeld, "Individualization of the Holocaust," in *Holocaust Chronicles: Individualizing the Holocaust through Diaries and Other Contemporaneous Personal Accounts*, ed. Robert Moses Shapiro (Hoboken, NJ: Ktav, 1999), 4–5.

24. David G. Roskies, "*Landkentenish*: Yiddish Belles Lettres in the Warsaw Ghetto," in Shapiro, *Holocaust Chronicles*, 19–20.

destruction progresses, there is a parallel progression of psychological changes in victims. They give up hope, moving along a continuum of victimization."[25]

The manner of Golfard's mysterious death in June or July 1943, which is of course not described in the diary, hints at how grief, fear, and hope might have turned into rage and defiance.[26] He managed to obtain a pistol, but his intentions remain unclear. He had no experience handling a weapon. During roll call at the labor camp near the Peremyshliany railway station, he pulled the pistol from his pants and tried to shoot the German commandant. He either missed, or the gun did not fire; most likely we will never know, since the few descriptions of the event are not detailed, and the eyewitnesses have died.[27] It is clear, however, that when he revealed his weapon, the camp guards retaliated by shooting Golfard and about fourteen other laborers standing near him.

What does Golfard's final act reveal about Jewish resistance during the Holocaust and the changing perceptions of resistance then and now? At the time, Jews scorned Golfard for his brazen foolishness; they blamed him for having caused the deaths of the other laborers caught in the spray of gunfire. To German and Ukrainian observers, Golfard's act seemed at once to confirm antisemitic canards about the Jewish threat and to distinguish Golfard, who became known as the "one Jew in town who did not go like a sheep to the slaughter." In 2005 Ivan Fuglevych, a Ukrainian barber in wartime Peremyshliany, reflected on the gesture as a singular act of resistance and memorable wartime event:

> Jews considered themselves victims who should not resist their fate. They suffered the atrocities as if given a punishment which was given to them by a higher force. Although there was one man whom I recall sought heroism. He had a gun. He was seeking revenge on Germans. He pointed the gun on the Germans, but the gun did not go off. He died like a hero. The Germans immediately pierced him with bullets. I did not witness this but

---

25. Ervin Staub, *The Roots of Evil: The Origins of Genocide and Other Group Violence* (New York: Cambridge University Press, 1989), 31.

26. The actual date might have been June 28, 1943, when, according to historian Aleksandr I. Kruglov, "a working party in Peremyshlyany (the Lvov region) was annihilated." See his *The Losses Suffered by Ukrainian Jews*, 346.

27. A Ukrainian wartime resident in Peremyshliany who heard about Golfard's bold act stated, "Pistolet ne spraciuvav," meaning that the pistol did not fire, although Golfard pulled the trigger. According to Ivan Fuglevych, Golfard aimed the pistol toward the German, but there was no shot because the pistol was faulty. If this is true, then the irony here is all the more tragic because Golfard put his faith in a weapon that was broken, and he had possibly been taken advantage of in being sold a worthless pistol. Interview with Ivan Fuglevych, his comment about the legacy of Golfard's act today, Peremyshliany, Ukraine, July 24, 2005.

Ivan Fuglevych points out the location of the mass graves of Jewish victims in the Peremyshliany forest (photograph by Wendy Lower, 2005).

I heard about it at the time it happened from clients in the barbershop where I worked. I heard many things at work, but that incident stayed in my memory as an unusual act of revenge and heroism.[28]

Was Golfard's "suicidal act" one of desperation, martyrdom, revenge, or all three? What thoughts might have raced through his mind when he reached for his pistol? We can rely on Golfard's diary to trace his changing state of mind and perceptions of reality, but he does not write about securing the pistol or his own possible escape plans. Moreover, his diary ends at least one month before that fateful morning roll call. One can only guess from Jacob Litman's testimony and German reports at this time that in Golfard's last weeks of life, he witnessed and heard about intensified camp and ghetto liquidations in the region and continued to work on the construction of the local granary or road.[29] Litman speculated that Golfard reached for the gun at the last minute, when he realized that the camp was being liquidated. But Litman also remained puzzled about Golfard's state of mind in these last months of his life. He acknowledged that the diary's last entries read like a suicide note, which surprised him after the war. This was a side of Golfard that he had not grasped at the time. On the

---

28. Interview with Ivan Fuglevych, his comment about the legacy of Golfard's act today, Peremyshliany, Ukraine, July 24, 2005 (statement translated by Vladimir Melamed). Fuglevych testified about the crimes against Jews in his hometown of Peremyshliany to Polish investigators in 1974. See "Protokół przesuchania świadka, August 19, 1974, Sędzia sądu wojewódzkiego we Wrocławiu," in Bundesarchiv Ludwigsburg (BAL) 162/389 (208 AR-Z 38/98), 22–23. On Fuglevych, see "Biographies."

29. On the final days before Golfard's death as Litman witnessed them, see "Part III: Related Documents," documents 8 and 9. On the German actions of 1943, see Dieter Pohl, *Nationalsozialistische Judenverfolgung in Ostgalizien 1941–1944: Organisation und Durchführung eines staatlichen Massenverbrechens* (Munich: Oldenbourg, 1997), 246–62.

contrary, Litman had looked up to Golfard, entrusted him with their escape plan, and relied on him to be the stronger one.

Above all, Golfard's diary entries embody what many victims experienced: an internal rupture so severe that it poses serious challenges to students and scholars as well as laypersons who wish to understand, let alone judge "the response" of "the victims." Diary writing is an act of self-preservation; yet, Golfard's entire narrative is about witnessing death and anticipating his own death. In scholar Amos Goldberg's view, each diary forces us to confront an individual in his or her "naked vulnerability," to witness "human frailty and fallibility": not to affirm the "triumph of the human spirit," but perhaps to gain a glimpse into man's conscious and unconscious struggle with death.[30] As is evident in Golfard's diary, this struggle could take the form of a final choice between suicide or futile resistance, but most Jews in the Holocaust were helpless to make even this choice or were denied this decisive power over their own fates.[31] How could a person suffering the loss of loved ones, experiencing the upheaval of war, and witnessing the brutal massacre of children, a person who was half-starved, subjected to humiliation, tortured, and treated, as Golfard wrote, "like a stray dog," be expected to act rationally, let alone heroically? Is not our search for heroism under such conditions more a reflection of our own hopes and fears and therefore a hindrance to a deeper understanding of this human crisis and its inherent contradictions, irrationality, and horror? Golfard rejected any romantic notions of heroism, reflecting in his diary on January 31, 1943, that "fear for one's life erased all noble sentiments and precluded any acts of heroism. Only one kind of heroism existed in the face of death—the heroism of people walking to the gallows without a word of complaint. When I consider it, the thought occurs to me that this heroism has been dictated, possibly, by the fear of physical torment before the angel of death descends to deliver one from hell."

THE GOLFARD DIARY AS A SOURCE OF HOLOCAUST HISTORY IN POLAND AND UKRAINE

Golfard's diary gives us a snapshot of the mass murder in settings where perpetrators confronted their victims face to face and the indigenous population

---

30. Goldberg, "If This Is a Man," 397, 402, 406–9, 420–23. Amos Goldberg, "Holocaust Diaries as 'Life Stories,'" *Search and Research Lectures and Papers* (Yad Vashem, International Institute for Holocaust Research) 5 (2004): 14–15.

31. Alexandra Zapruder, *Salvaged Pages: Young Writer's Diaries of the Holocaust* (New Haven, CT: Yale University Press, 2002), 9; Goldberg, "If This Is a Man," 400–6.

assaulted, robbed, or in rarer instances helped Jewish neighbors and refugees. Of the more than 500,000 Jews killed in Galicia, more than 300,000 died by bullets; they were shot in local meadows, forests, and the streets of small towns. After the first wave of killings in the spring of 1942, more Jews understood that they were fighting for their lives. When the German SS police, and Ukrainian auxiliaries surrounded the ghettos, conducted raids for deportations to Bełżec, or simply ordered the Jews to appear with their luggage at a gathering point in the summer and fall of 1942, Jews resisted. In towns such as Chortkiv, Horodenka, Drohobych, and Boryslav, hundreds of Jews did not quietly assemble and march to the trucks or railway cars but tried to flee. The "hunt for Jews" and wild shootings became ever more brutal. German officials wrote about the so-called excesses, including the fact that bodies of dead Jews littered the streets for days; they noted that more bullets were needed for the final ghetto liquidations and deportations to Bełżec in September and December 1942.[32] The Nazi terror in Poland and Ukraine was not secret but very much in the open for all to see and hear. Golfard meticulously chronicled the pogroms, shootings, beatings, public acts of humiliation, deportations, and ghetto liquidations in his region of eastern Galicia. Although brief, Golfard's prescient, compact testimony hits upon almost every contentious theme that has driven research on the Holocaust: collaboration, resistance, perpetrator motivation, bystander inaction, and rescue.

With the benefit of hindsight, readers can place Golfard's diary within a broader chronology of the "Final Solution" policy as it unfolded in Nazi-occupied Poland and Ukraine. For decades scholars have focused on the series of decisions that brought about the mass murder, placing varying emphasis on the top leaders (the "center"), such as Heinrich Himmler and Adolf Hitler, and their enthusiastic minions in the field (the "periphery"). The result has been a focus on the stages leading to the decision to commit genocide and a search for German evidence to reconstruct the policy's implementation in painstaking detail. Less has been published about the victims' changing perception of the genocide as it occurred openly in places such as Ukraine, and little in-depth work has been done on the latter phases outside the killing centers. Golfard's diary helps to fill this void.

Already in 1941, as Golfard recounted, thousands had been killed in pogroms that swept through the region during the Nazi invasion. The largest and best-known occurred in Lviv, but the pogroms were proportionally as devastating to smaller towns such as nearby Zolochiv and Peremyshliany, where

---

32. Pohl, *Nationalsozialistische Judenverfolgung in Ostgalizien*, 223–42.

between 5 and 10 percent of the population was immediately wiped out, among them the local Jewish intelligentsia, which might have later organized a more effective resistance. From late summer 1942 until the summer of 1943, the main time frame of Golfard's diary, almost the entire Jewish population of eastern Galicia was destroyed. In this frenzied period of mass murder operations, thousands of German SS and police officials, as well as civil professionals such as engineers, railway timetable keepers, accountants, chemists, supply requisition clerks, drivers, and so on, were mobilized to coordinate, and in some manner contribute their "expertise" or labor to, the "Final Solution." With local auxiliaries and collaborators, they waged a multipronged assault that included deportations to the gas chambers of Bełżec, ghetto liquidations, forced labor, and mass shootings. Golfard's diary shows how these combined Nazi anti-Jewish policies, actions, and methods struck Peremyshliany and its neighboring towns and villages.

In their sinister quest for a "Final Solution of the Jewish Question," Nazi leaders pursued various measures to isolate, pauperize, and reduce the population of Jews. Among these was the Nazi establishment of ghettos and exploitation of Jewish labor. In the Galicia District of the Generalgouvernement, ghettoization began formally in December 1941, though prior to this, labor demands, curfews, marking of Jewish homes with the Star of David, and residence restrictions had effectively paralyzed the population in de facto ghettos. Between 1939 and 1941, most Polish Jews (as many as 3 million) were forced to live in designated quarters, behind walls and barbed wire, under guard, crammed into buildings and shacks with little sanitation and meager food supplies. Disease was rampant, and as many as five hundred thousand Jews died in the ghettos of Poland between 1940 and 1945. Like the segregationist laws and pogroms, the appearance of ghettos was not something new in the history of European anti-Judaism; however, the manner in which such age-old practices and institutions contributed to a systematic, modern campaign of genocide was unprecedented. Golfard's diary reveals both the fleeting existence of these ghettos as they came to facilitate the Nazis' more radical policy of immediate extermination and the false hope that Jews attached to the ghettos, which they saw as a possible refuge with some historical basis. The behavior and expectations of many Germans, Ukrainians, and other non-Jews were also informed by their perception of Europe's history of anti-Jewish rituals and practices as traditional, and therefore acceptable.

By the summer of 1942, the most influential figure managing the genocidal operations of the Third Reich was Reich Leader of the SS and Chief of the German Police Heinrich Himmler. With Bełżec and the other gassing facilities at Sobibór and Treblinka ready to receive larger numbers of victims, Himmler ordered his subordinates in Poland and Ukraine to destroy all remaining ghettos, retaining only the most essential Jewish laborers. He set a deadline of December 31, 1942.[33] For Galicia's Jewish population, this meant renewed and more aggressive deportations to Bełżec, the site where fifteen thousand Jews (the elderly, orphaned, ill, disabled, and other so-called useless eaters) from Lviv had already perished in March 1942.

In his diary, Golfard refers to the local talk of Bełżec, which he puts in the wrong grammatical case—perhaps a simple writing error but also an indication that this place, prior to the war, was not well-known. Located about fifty miles northwest of Lviv, Bełżec was one of three major killing centers established as part of "Aktion Reinhard." Named after the chief of the Security Police and SD who managed the mobile killing operations of the *Einsatzgruppen*, Reinhard Heydrich, this *"Aktion"* concentrated on the total annihilation of 3 million Polish Jews in stationary killing centers. The application of poison gas and features of the killing process in these centers, such as the fake showers, had already been tested out on the mentally and incurably ill in Germany. The leading medical, technical, SS, and police personnel who developed these methods, most prominent among them Dr. Victor Brack and Christian Wirth, were assigned to "Aktion Reinhard" in Poland. They constructed the first stationary killing center at Bełżec, designated mainly for the murder of the Jews of Galicia.[34]

Located on the railway line that ran from Lviv to Lublin, Bełżec was constructed in late 1941 and early 1942; the first gassings occurred in mid-March 1942 in wooden barracks that could be sealed for gassing about 150 people at a time. Later in 1942, a concrete building was erected with six gas chambers, in which as many as fifteen hundred persons were gassed at one time. A small staff of German SS and policemen resided at the camp, overseeing a much larger

---

33. "Order by Himmler on July 19, 1942, for the Completion of the 'Final Solution' in the Government-General," in *Documents on the Holocaust: Selected Sources on the Destruction of the Jews of Germany and Austria, Poland, and the Soviet Union*, ed. Yitzhak Arad, Israel Gutman, and Abraham Margaliot, 8th ed. (Lincoln: University of Nebraska Press, 1999), 275. While stationed at his Ukrainian headquarters near Zhytomyr, Himmler told his senior SS men during the last week of July 1942 that the territory of Ukraine must be cleared for future German settlement, all Jewish communities be destroyed, and the Ukrainian population brought to a "minimum." See statements of one SS officer present, Paul Albert Scheer, who was interrogated by Soviet investigators on December 29, 1945, USHMMA RG 06.025*02 Kiev. Also see Lower, *Nazi Empire-Building*, 8 and 212n10.

34. Henry Friedlander, *The Origins of Nazi Genocide: From Euthanasia to the Final Solution* (Chapel Hill: University of North Carolina Press, 1995).

auxiliary crew (about 120) consisting of Soviet prisoners of war and specially trained Ukrainian and Polish guards. In the summer and fall of 1942, when Golfard's sister was deported, trainloads of forty to sixty railcars containing as many as one hundred people per car arrived at Bełżec. According to German documentation, more than 434,500 Jews died at Bełżec between March and December 1942.[35]

Golfard heard that Jews sent to Bełżec were killed on an electrified bridge. This rumor about electrocution was also recorded by a Polish diarist who lived near Bełżec.[36] Both were wrong about the method of killing but correct that deportation there meant certain death. The rumor probably confused the electrified bridge with the camp's closed path (known as "the tube") that led from the railway and reception area to the gas chamber. Jewish men, women, and children who had been told that they were going to take showers at this "transit camp" were forced to run naked through the "tube" and into the chamber. After sealing the chamber door, the guards started a stationary engine that pumped carbon monoxide into the chamber through pipes in the floor. Golfard's surmising that electrocution was the killing method suggests a local awareness of the industrial aspects of Nazi mass-murder methods, an awareness that something terrible and unprecedented was happening to the Jews that was difficult to reconstruct in all its technical detail. There were few survivors to substantiate the sketchy reports and rumors.

When Golfard's sister Mania was deported to Bełżec in the late summer of 1942, she was among about forty thousand from Lviv who fell victim to this accelerated, more intensified SS and police campaigns of murder. After the August deportations, the ghetto in Lviv was sealed, and refugees who sought security in the remaining smaller ghettos soon realized that these Jewish "havens" had become traps. The ghettos were transformed into labor camps

---

35. The 434,508 figure originated in a recently discovered German telegram sent from SS officer Hermann Höfle in January 1943. British intelligence intercepted and decrypted the telegram but did not grasp the significance of its content during the war. See Peter Witte and Stephen Tyas, "A New Document on the Deportation and Murder of Jews during 'Einsatz Reinhardt' 1942," *Holocaust and Genocide Studies* 15, no. 3 (2001): 468–86. Saul Friedländer, *Nazi Germany and the Jews: The Years of Extermination, 1939–1945* (New York: HarperCollins, 2007), 283–84, 356–59, 399–400. Browning, *The Origins of the Final Solution*, 419–20. For the history of Bełżec and its links to the "T-4" euthanasia program, see Friedlander, *The Origins of Nazi Genocide*, and Saul Friedländer, *Kurt Gerstein: The Ambiguity of Good* (New York: Alfred A. Knopf, 1969).

36. Diary of Zygmunt Klukowski, *Dziennik z lat okupacji Zamojszczyzny 1939–1944* [*Diary from the Years of Occupation Around Zamosc, 1939–44*] (Lublin: Lubelska Spółdzielnia Wydawnicza, 1958), 251–54, cited in Raul Hilberg, *Sources of Holocaust Research: An Analysis* (Chicago: Ivan R. Dee, 2001), 162.

through a process of selection, and their populations aggressively reduced through raids and killing sweeps, often led by auxiliary police and local thugs. By the beginning of 1943, most of the Jewish population of Galicia was gone, save for laborers and those in hiding.

For Jews facing the dreaded "selection" and their own murder, a labor assignment meant possible survival within the German structure of rule. Golfard managed to escape the deportations in this phase because of his status as a male laborer, specifically as "a garbage collector with no pay but with a tin badge on his chest to prove his special status."[37] The German occupiers' exploitation of Jewish laborers had a historical basis as recent as World War I, and often the terms *slave* and *slave laborer* have been used in descriptions of the Nazi policy. Of course, European enslavement of Africans offered the Nazis an economic and racial model of persecution. However, there are important ideological and policy differences. German leaders, including the SS and police leader (SSPF) for the Galicia District, Fritz Katzmann, who controlled the use of Jewish labor there, considered the use of Jewish "specialists" a short-term, stopgap measure. Non-Jews were trained to replace them. In Nazi thinking, Jewish laborers were expendable and they had limited to no value as a commodity within a state whose expressed aim was to annihilate them.[38]

In Ukraine, as many as twenty-five thousand Jews perished in or near the work sites connected to the construction of a large roadway (supply line) named Thoroughfare IV (Durchgangsstrasse IV) that ran from Galicia toward the Black Sea. Golfard's work at the Jaktorów camp and Litman's in the nearby quarry contributed to one stretch of this major project. Yet, as Golfard wrote his last entries in 1943 and recorded the destruction of the labor camps, he realized that his privileged status as a laborer would no longer ensure his survival. The relative quiet of the first part of 1943, which afforded him the chance to write his diary, soon changed to a renewed German campaign of killing, this time with the aim of a final razing of the remains of ghettos and labor camps. Jews who miraculously escaped these last German mass-murder raids in Galicia fled to the forest, often falling victim to hostile Poles, Ukrainians, ethnic Germans (*Volksdeutsche*), Russians, and others who denounced Jews, robbed them, assaulted them, and turned them over to the German authorities.

---

37. Jacob Litman, introduction to *Golfard's Testimony* (1983), 7, USHMMA Acc. 2008.316, Litman family collection.

38. Wolf Gruner, *Jewish Forced Labor under the Nazis: Economic Needs and Racial Aims, 1938–1945* (New York: Cambridge University Press in association with USHMM, 2006).

Faced with threats of death for aiding Jews and feeling powerless against Nazi rulers, most non-Jews in Poland and Ukraine remained outwardly indifferent to the plight of the Jewish minority. Yet, a significant number collaborated: they openly promoted the antisemitic Nazi agenda and exploited the policy to enrich themselves, achieve political aims, or exact personal "revenge." From the first days of German occupation to the last, expressions and acts of local antisemitism abounded. Whereas earlier explanations for the Holocaust focused almost exclusively on the perpetrators as Germans who supported Hitler's regime, recent attention has shifted to the role of hundreds of thousands of non-German auxiliary police, guards, and neighbors who were more than passive bystanders. The fact is that the German administration could not have expropriated, deported, ghettoized, enslaved, and ultimately killed millions of Jews without the active participation of local populations residing across Nazi-occupied Europe, especially in the killing fields and death camps of eastern Europe. Golfard's testimony affirms the sadism and greed of auxiliary police and collaborators, among them Ukrainians and ethnic Germans.

Golfard's diary also casts light on the courageous individuals who aided and rescued Jews, in his case the local Ukrainian priest, Father Omelian Kovch, and Polish civil servant Tadeusz Jankiewicz. Father Kovch is among 2,185 Ukrainians formally recognized as a rescuer by the Israeli national Holocaust memorial and research center, Yad Vashem, and Jankiewicz is among more than six thousand such Poles.[39] Nevertheless, Golfard's sympathetic presentation of Poles in eastern Galicia was based on his personal experience of having been aided by the Pole Jankiewicz. His portrait of Jankiewicz's decency and care contrasts with the image of pogromists found in *Neighbors*, an important study of Polish collaboration by Jan Gross.[40] While pogroms were widespread in Golfard's region, most perpetrators in eastern Galicia belonged not to the Polish minority but to the Ukrainian majority. The topic of Ukrainian collaboration is complex. In fact, the entire discussion of collaboration is changing because the post-Soviet political climate and archival access allow for more research and

39. See testimony on behalf of Kovch in Vladimir Melamed, "Organized and Unsolicited Collaboration in the Holocaust: The Multifaceted Ukrainian Context," *East European Jewish Affairs* 37 (August 2007): 223. Though Golfard does not mention the rescue efforts of Ukrainians near Peremyshliany, Kliment Sheptytskyi (brother of Metropolitan Andrei Sheptytskyi) sheltered Jews at the Univ monastery. See David Kahane, *Lvov Ghetto Diary* (Amherst: University of Massachusetts Press, 1990), 122.

40. Gross's book was heavily criticized by many Polish historians because it showed how Poles in Jedwabne brutally killed the town's Jewish population without German instigation and opened up debate on Jewish-Polish relations and Polish antisemitism. See Joanna Michlic and Antony Polonsky, eds., *The Neighbors Respond: The Controversy over the Jedwabne Massacre in Poland* (Princeton, NJ: Princeton University Press, 2003).

open debate on this topic. However, most of the research and critical analysis is occurring outside of Ukraine itself. As in Soviet times but for different, nationalistic reasons, the history of collaboration is generally suppressed or considered taboo in Ukraine. Nation builders in the parliament and education ministry are more focused on identifying Ukrainian heroes, not villains, and the Holocaust as a topic is marginalized in the revised history textbooks.[41] In wartime and postwar German accounts, one often reads that "the more gruesome tasks were given to the local population." But what exactly were these tasks? Since 2004 Father Patrick Desbois and his research team (supported by Yahad-In Unum) have begun to define them. They have identified more than six hundred mass graves in Ukraine and collected interviews with Ukrainian eyewitnesses, including some who participated in the genocide. This new data is adding specificity to the definition of collaboration, not to make a blanket condemnation, but rather to provide a fuller picture of the division of labor necessary for the perpetrators and their helpers to commit mass murder. At recently uncovered mass-murder sites, including in areas mentioned by Golfard, regional German officials requisitioned local women, youth, and any available men to assist them in a variety of roles: as pit diggers; as "Jew carriers" providing carts for the elderly; as "corpse carriers" picking up the dead off the street; as "packers" walking over the bodies to press them down into the mass graves; as collectors of hemp, which was placed in the pits to burn human remains; as clothing sorters; as menders (women who sewed tattered clothing that was distributed to ethnic Germans); and as cooks who fed "the shooters" during long shifts.[42] Aside from the ethnic German and Ukrainian policemen, most local helpers did not volunteer for this work, though, to be sure, some participants appeared at the scenes to assist because of greed, antisemitism, and other motives.

The involvement of Ukrainians in general must be understood within the framework of Nazi realpolitik, whereby Ukrainian nationalists were allies in the war against "Judeo-Bolshevism," and Poles and Slavs in general were an "inferior" population to be fully exploited. Indeed, German attitudes and policies toward Ukrainians were often ambivalent. Ukrainians' future as Slavic "*Untermenschen*" was certainly not bright; during the war, more than 4 million Ukrainians died, and more than 2 million were enslaved by their Nazi

---

41. On these textbook developments and the theme of competitive victimization, see Johan Dietsch, *Making Sense of Suffering: Holocaust and Holodomor in Ukrainian Historical Culture* (Lund: Lund University, 2006).

42. For Father Desbois's work, see *The Mass Shooting of Jews in Ukraine, 1941–1944: The Holocaust by Bullets* (exhibition catalog, Mémorial de la Shoah and the association Yahad-In Unum, Paris, France, May 20–November 30, 2007). Also see "A Priest Methodically Reveals Ukrainian Jews' Fate," *New York Times*, October 6, 2007.

overseers.[43] The lack of Ukrainian statehood meant that there was no official leadership, no government-in-exile, no Quisling or Vichy government that represented a "national" or collective policy of Ukrainians. Advocates of a Ukrainian state who coalesced around the OUN were themselves divided into two factions, though both were anticommunist and had formal dealings with the Third Reich. In fact, armed units of Ukrainians, which had been trained by the German military and worked with Nazi intelligence services prior to 1941, participated in Operation Barbarossa.[44]

Radical Ukrainian nationalists promoted a fascist, monoethnic, territorial concept of statehood, a Ukraine for Ukrainians only. Leaders in one faction of the OUN declared Ukraine's independence in Lviv on June 30, 1941, which the Nazis quickly suppressed. The Germans welcomed Ukrainian help in the fight against "Judeo-Bolshevism," but Hitler would not tolerate a sharing of political power with Slavic "*Untermenschen*." Meanwhile, OUN task forces fanned out across the region, infiltrated local militias, and initiated pogroms as a form of revenge politics against "Jewish Moscow" and to cleanse "their" territory of Jews. During the so-called Petliura Days in the summer of 1941, thousands of Jews in Lviv were massacred in an orgy of violence that the German occupiers, local thugs, and nationalist radicals organized and promoted.[45] In the Generalgouvernement, Ukrainians fared relatively well, especially when compared to their treatment under earlier Polish and Soviet rule, at least in the realm of cultural and religious activities. Even in the area of forced labor, Ukrainians in Galicia and the Generalgouvernement faced milder policies and practices than Ukrainians living in neighboring zones of the Reich Commissariat Ukraine.[46]

---

43. Paul R. Magocsi, *A History of Ukraine: The Land and Its Peoples* (Toronto: University of Toronto Press, 1996), 638.

44. Bruder, *"Den ukrainischen Staat erkämpfen oder sterben,"* 113–75.

45. The phrase "Petliura Days" was rumored during the war to denote these pogroms in Lviv. More research is needed to establish precisely who perpetrated the violence. However, it is clear that as part of the preparations for the Nazi occupation, the OUN trained Ukrainians for police duties, and during the invasion, the OUN was instrumental in the formation of the militia in Galicia and other parts of western Ukraine. After the war the phrase continued to be a lightning rod in the often polemical exchanges among Soviets, Ukrainians, and Jews concerning culpability for the massacres.

46. This was epitomized by Himmler's concession in early 1943 to allow Ukrainians to form a military force, a Waffen SS division for which the Germans received an overwhelming eighty thousand volunteers (in one month) for eighteen thousand positions, recounted in Golczewski' "Shades of Grey," 134–37. For the subdivision of Ukraine as parts of the Generalgouvernement (led by Hans Frank in Kraków) and the Reich Commissariat Ukraine (a region formally subordinated to the Reich minister for the occupied eastern territories, Alfred Rosenberg, in Berlin), see Maps 2 and 3, pp. xxvii–xxviii.

As the largest population under Nazi rule, Ukrainians outnumbered other non-Germans in the auxiliary police forces that brutalized Jews. They also appear more frequently in survivor testimonies as "the worst" among the camp guards. Several thousand Ukrainians were drafted (many from the horrible conditions of the POW camps) to be trained as guards in the Trawniki camp near Lublin. More than one hundred thousand Ukrainians served in the local police forces and as firemen in Ukraine, in both stationary and mobile units, in the city and the countryside. Hundreds of thousands more were recruited and placed into formations in the military and SS.[47] They were most visible in the rural gendarme units, where they had considerable leeway and power. Since Germans did not have the manpower, language, and local knowledge of the terrain and population, and their occupation depended on large security forces, they relied heavily on the use of local able-bodied men who were initially sympathetic to German rule.[48] Thus, indigenous policemen and guards had more contact with the Jews than the Germans did during the first assaults and in the subsequent registration, ghettoization, and deportations. Later in the war, as the Red Army advanced westward, Ukrainian support of German rule over an impending Soviet reoccupation was strongest in Galicia, particularly in collaborationist forces, as well as in the Ukrainian Insurgent Army (UPA).[49] One mobile police unit, the 205th Schutzmannschaft Battalion, was formed from guard units in Lviv and deployed in April or early May 1943 around Galicia for special actions.[50] Detailed documentation of its activities is lacking, but its

---

47. Dieter Pohl, "Ukrainische Hilfskräfte beim Mord an den Juden," in *Die Täter der Shoah: Fanatische Nationalisten oder ganz normale Deutsche?* ed. Gerhard Paul (Göttingen: Wallstein, 2002), 205–7.

48. Martin Dean, *Collaboration in the Holocaust: Crimes of the Local Police in Belorussia and Ukraine, 1941–1944* (New York: St. Martin's Press, 2000).

49. Golfard did not live to witness the next phase of extreme violence in Galicia between the Poles and Ukrainians or the return of the Red Army, with its own destructive SMERSH units. An estimated five hundred thousand Ukrainians were deported from Western Ukraine between 1944 and 1949, and ninety thousand Ukrainians were killed, while the estimated number of Poles killed runs from ten to one hundred thousand. See Shimon Redlich, *Together and Apart in Brzezany: Poles, Jews, and Ukrainians, 1919–1945* (Bloomington: Indiana University Press, 2002), 144–47; and Jeffrey Burds, "AGENTURA: Soviet Informants' Networks and the Ukrainian Underground in Galicia, 1944–1948," *East European Politics and Societies* no. 11 (winter 1997): 89–130.

50. Golczewski, "Shades of Grey," 140; Pohl, *Nationalsozialistische Judenverfolgung in Ostgalizien,* 93.

deployment coincided with the final liquidations of camps and ghettos so vividly and horrifically described by Golfard.[51]

Golfard condemned Ukrainian involvement in the mass murder of Jews as a national trait of "hypocrisy and cruelty," explaining that it developed "as a result of their political situation, always uncertain," and as a response to centuries of hardship as "the tenant peasant" was used by the Poles "as an instrument of economic and political oppression." He believed that national differences were really a smokescreen for the base problem of "class discrimination." In trying to make sense of the cruelty of Ukrainians, Golfard could not avoid being judgmental, but he was careful to interpret such sadistic and collaborative behavior as a function of external factors, such as political weakness and economic oppression. Golfard's judgment of his fellow Jews was harsher.

In order to deceive, exploit, and ultimately annihilate their victims, Germans relied on the help of Jewish functionaries. Nazi officials established *Judenräte*, or Jewish Councils, to implement local anti-Jewish measures and manage daily life in the ghettos. Given the councils' role, they have been the subject of much debate and controversy. Qualifying earlier statements by other scholars,[52] Isaiah Trunk's classic history of the Jewish Councils in Nazi-occupied Europe (which Litman cites in his introduction) argues that Jewish participation in the deportations as council members "had no substantial influence—one way or the other—on the final outcome of the Holocaust in Eastern Europe." To his great credit, Trunk produced the only European survey of the councils and paid close attention to regional variations, warning strongly against making any generalizations, despite his own conclusion. Trunk also established that the composition of the Jewish Councils changed as the Germans periodically

---

51. According to historian Aleksandr I. Kruglov, in July 1943 the commander of the UPA, Roman Shukhevych, ordered that "Jews roaming about forests trying to save their lives are to be killed by shooting them at the backs of their heads and declared to have been executed by the Germans." Kruglov's source for this order has not been corroborated and should be further investigated. However, such an order seems more than possible, given the historical circumstances and the position and approach of the UPA in the summer of 1943. See Kruglov, *The Losses Suffered by Ukrainian Jews*, 348. Shukhevych was posthumously granted Ukraine's highest honor, the title "Hero of Ukraine," in 2007.

52. Isaiah Trunk, *Judenrat: The Jewish Councils in Eastern Europe under Nazi Occupation* (Lincoln: University of Nebraska Press, 1996), xlvii. In a different vein, Holocaust scholar Raul Hilberg argued in 1961 that "the Jewish leadership both saved and destroyed its people. . . [. . .] Some leaders broke under this power; others became intoxicated with it." Raul Hilberg, *The Destruction of European Jews* (New York: Holmes and Meier, 1985), 1:218. Hannah Arendt, *Eichmann in Jerusalem: A Report on the Banality of Evil* (New York: Viking, 1963). Also discussed in Doris L. Bergen, *War & Genocide: A Concise History of the Holocaust* (Lanham, MD: Rowman & Littlefield, 2009), 116.

killed the council members and installed replacements. Over time, with mounting German assaults, the need for stronger leadership within Jewish communities increased; however, after the summer of 1942, the "social-moral niveau" of the councils in Poland was lower, corruption increased, and some members exploited their power to the detriment of the communities they were supposed to serve. Aside from Trunk and more recent work by Dan Michman, Sara Bender, and Gustavo Corni, postwar examinations of the Jewish Councils have been mired in moral judgments and have not progressed in terms of in-depth research on the individual council members and the local settings in which they operated.[53]

There were significant regional variations in the composition and conduct of the councils. Usually the most educated and respected members of the local Jewish communities were the first targets of mass murder, for in Nazi thinking they posed the greatest threat of resistance. Germans approved or appointed the Jewish Council leaders and preferred people who could be easily coerced into imposing the worst measures against the Jews. Some who could not, such as the leader of the Warsaw ghetto, Adam Czerniaków, committed suicide. Those who could be co-opted were often not locals and consequently lacked strong ties to the local community. All faced the impossible task of trying to preserve Jewish life, an aim antithetical to the Nazi policy of genocide, and most wrongly assumed that the Germans would take a rational approach by retaining Jewish laborers. Golfard also warned his readers against passing judgment on Jewish victims; at the same time, he could hardly contain his resentment of the *Judenrat* in Peremyshliany and his disgust for the Jewish police. He could not forgive the Germans for the death of his sister, but he was more deeply troubled by the capacity for evil he saw in all men, especially the betrayal by his fellow Jews. Golfard's view reflects ghetto society (not administration) and its prevailing tendency to stress Jewish "abuses," while the Germans are hardly in the picture.

Another common perception among victims that is found in Golfard's diary is a bifurcated view of reality dividing the hell of the genocide in Nazi-dominated Europe from the civilized "outside world." Golfard's entries contain a surprising number of references to global events, including Allied reactions

---

53. Dan Michman, *Holocaust Historiography: A Jewish Perspective: Conceptualizations, Terminology, Approaches and Fundamental Issues* (London: Vallentine Mitchell, 2002); Dan Michman, "Reevaluating the Emergence, Function and Form of the Jewish Councils Phenomenon," and Sara Bender, "The Bialystok and Kielce Ghettos: A Comparative Study," in USHMM Symposium Presentations, *Ghettos 1939–1945*; Gustavo Corni, *Hitler's Ghettos: Voices from a Beleaguered Society, 1939–1944* (London: Arnold, 2002).

to the Holocaust as it unfolded. Though remote, Peremyshliany was not cut off from the various channels of rumor and the latest news reports from the front and abroad. Besides illegal BBC broadcasts, one of the main sources of information was the underground press, and in this region it came from Polish partisans in the national and communist movements. The Polish Council to Aid Jews (Żegota) and the Home Army (Armia Krajowa, or AK) associated with the Polish government-in-exile in London probably circulated information about a speech given in London by Polish premier Gen. Władysław Sikorski, which Golfard refers to in his diary. In late October 1942, Sikorski protested the treatment of Jews, declaring, "I warn the German torturers that they will not escape retribution for all the crimes they have committed," but to no avail. Joining Sikorski at this protest meeting was the archbishop of Canterbury, who explained that the average Briton did not grasp what the Jews in Europe were suffering: it is "difficult for him to feel the horror appropriate to the facts."[54]

Through the pages of Golfard's diary, we can glimpse how a Jew marked for annihilation viewed the outside world and its failure to affect the course of the Holocaust.[55] By expressing his "contempt for the world's cowardice and heartlessness," he spoke for other Jews who were just as outraged that the Allies did not intervene to stop the Holocaust. Perhaps Golfard assumed that the Allies should have known better or were morally superior and prepared to act. His view of a post-Holocaust world was not one of reconciliation, but one plagued by vengeance and haunted by the landscape of mass graves. In his diary he wrote on April 11, 1943, "The tombs and graves of people murdered in martyrdom are ever increasing all over the country. Every village and town, every forest abounds with graves looming from a distance as a historical lesson and a warning. Once the living witnesses are gone, then those graves will speak volumes. They will accuse the whole world ~~and more~~, with an eloquence a hundredfold mightier, of having committed or having failed to act against the cruelest of crimes."

---

54. See news coverage of the speech in "Canterbury Asks Vengeance Curb," *New York Times*, October 30, 1942, 2; and in the *Aufbau* article reprinted as document 6 in Part III of this volume. Compare Richard Breitman, *Official Secrets: What the Nazis Planned, What the British and Americans Knew* (New York: Hill & Wang, 1988); and Laurel Leff, *Buried by The Times: The Holocaust and America's Most Important Newspaper* (New York: Cambridge University Press, 2005).

55. Tim Cole, "Writing 'Bystanders' into Holocaust History in More Active Ways: 'Non-Jewish' Engagement with Ghettoisation, Hungary 1944," *Holocaust Studies: A Journal of Culture and History* 11 (summer 2005): 57, 59; Hilberg, *Perpetrators, Victims, Bystanders*.

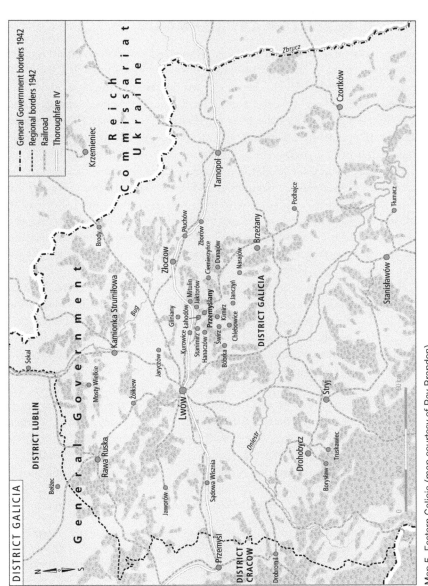

DISTRICT GALICIA

DISTRICT LUBLIN

General Government

Reich Commissariat Ukraine

DISTRICT CRACOW

DISTRICT GALICIA

N

Krzemieniec

Zbrucz

Czortków

Tarnopol

Podhajce

Płuchów

Brody

Złoczów

Zborów

Ciemierzyńce

Dunajów

Brzeżany

Hłumacz

Stanisławów

Narajów

Mitulin

Kamionka Strumiłowa

Bug

Przemyślany

Jaktorów

Janczyn

Sokal

Jaryczów

Gliniany

Kurowice Łahodów

Staninmirz

Kimirz

Świrz

Hanaczów

Chlebowice

Bóbrka

Mosty Wielkie

Żółkiew

Lwów

Rawa Ruska

Bełżec

Dniestr

Stryj

Jaworów

Sądowa Wisznia

Drohobycz

Truskawiec

Borysław

Drohobroml

Przemyśl

0   20   40   60 km

Map 5. Eastern Galicia (map courtesy of Ray Brandon).

THE LOCAL SETTING OF GOLFARD'S DIARY: PEREMYSHLIANY (UKRAINIAN), PRZEMYŚLANY (POLISH), PEREMYSHLANY (GERMAN)

Golfard and his sister were among the two thousand Jewish youth from Radom and the two to three hundred thousand Jewish refugees who fled German-occupied Poland in late 1939. Their flight was the result of the Nazi-Soviet Pact of August 1939 whereby Hitler and Stalin divided up Poland among themselves. In the first weeks of the Nazi blitzkrieg of September 1939, German military and police forces initiated pogroms and mass shootings against Jewish rabbis, Polish priests, government officials, teachers, and other members of the intelligentsia.[56] The wave of German violence triggered a mass exodus to the east into the Soviet zone of occupation. Many Jewish refugees came to Lviv, the capital of eastern Galicia (now western Ukraine), but found they had to continue eastward to the next villages because Lviv suffered drastic food and firewood shortages in the winter of 1939–1940. One of the towns that absorbed these refugees was Peremyshliany, located twenty-seven miles southeast of Lviv, which is the setting of Golfard's diary.[57]

Peremyshliany is set off from the main road at a local juncture. Nestled among forested hills and rolling farmlands, the town is situated in the historical borderland of four major empires: the Polish-Lithuanian, Austro-Hungarian, Russian, and Soviet-German (1939–1941). In medieval times it was controlled by Ruthenian (Ukrainian) princes and eventually absorbed into the Polish-Lithuanian Commonwealth. Settlement and trade regulations (such as the Magdeburg Laws) together with the feudal system created a social structure for perpetuating ethnic and economic hierarchies. The Polish aristocracy, largely of the Roman Catholic faith, established agricultural estates worked by Ukrainian peasants, who were first Christian Orthodox and later mostly Greek Catholic (Uniate) believers. Jews in a variety of trades and professions established their own communities in the region where Hasidism took root.[58]

---

56. Alexander B. Rossino, *Hitler Strikes Poland: Blitzkrieg, Ideology, and Atrocity* (Lawrence: University of Kansas, 2003).

57. Norman Davies, *God's Playground: A History of Poland*, vol. 2: *1795 to the Present* (New York: Columbia University Press, 1982); Timothy Snyder, *Sketches from a Secret War: A Polish Artist's Mission to Liberate Ukraine* (New Haven, CT: Yale University Press, 2005); Keith Sword, *Deportation and Exile: Poles in the Soviet Union, 1939–48* (New York: St. Martin's Press, 1994); Gross, *Revolution from Abroad*.

58. Teresa Andlauer, *Die jüdische Bevölkerung im Modernisierungsprozess Galiziens (1867–1914)* (Berlin: Peter Lang, 2001).

Jewish school groups in Przemyślany/Peremyshliany, 1920s (USHMMPA WS# 65317 and 65318, courtesy of Sidney and Phyllis Leinwand).

Religious differences appeared in the town's architecture of ornate churches and synagogues. The wealthier ruling class of Polish Catholics built a Dominican monastery in a late sixteenth-century baroque style. A century later, the town's prominent Roman Catholic church opened its doors. A more modest Ukrainian Orthodox church still exists on the town's main street but has been overshadowed by the towering white and gold new Ukrainian church that stands on the hill at the town's entrance. The two synagogues in Peremyshliany were both ransacked and razed in the first weeks of the Nazi occupation. Today on the grounds of the former main synagogue one finds no trace of the Jewish history there. Instead, an oversized bronze statue of the Ukrainian Cossack Bohdan Khmel'nyts'kyi wielding a mace stands on a stone plinth.

The mostly peaceful coexistence of these distinct cultures and classes usually had more to do with the need for order, which was based in the traditional estate system defined by social class and family background, than with a mutual understanding and respect for each other's differences. Tolerance as we know it was not part of the local vocabulary; rather, Peremyshliany was a small provincial town like any other at the time, characterized by mutual suspicion and rumor. Daily interaction among Jews, Ukrainians, Poles, and ethnic Germans in and around Peremyshliany was usually a matter of necessity because of commercial and professional interests. In 1920, about 30 percent of the doctors in Galicia and 58 percent of the lawyers were Jewish.[59] Most civil servants were Poles. Ukrainians brought their produce to the shopkeepers in Peremyshliany to the Honig family, Jacob Litman's in-laws, who owned the general store not far from the synagogue.

Pressure to modernize economically and politically, and major crises, such as bad harvests, the spread of plague, and war, could tear apart the tenuous social fabric of eastern Galician towns. This was the case in the mid-seventeenth century, when waves of pogroms swept the region, incited by the uprising of the Ukrainian revolutionary Bohdan Khmel'nyts'kyi, hetman of the Cossack army, whose followers associated the Jews with the Polish "occupiers" of Ukraine. Three centuries later, the memory of Khmel'nyts'kyi's campaigns resonated in the Ukrainian-Polish-Jewish violence in the German-occupied forests and villages of eastern Galicia.[60] Golfard refers to the hetman in his diary and to the iconographic Ukrainian peasant rebel struggling against oppressive overlords. Golfard believes that this rebellion forms a backdrop to the "innate traits" of

---

59. Andlauer, *Die jüdische Bevölkerung*, 341.

60. Alfred J. Rieber, "Civil Wars in the Soviet Union," *Kritika* 4 (2003): 129–62; John-Paul Himka, "War Criminality: A Blank Spot in the Collective Memory of the Ukrainian Diaspora," *Spaces of Identity* 5 (2005): 9–24.

Ukrainians. Khmel'nyts'kyi is a telling example of the complicated, triangular history of Jewish-Polish-Ukrainian relations. To this day, Jews perceive him as an antisemitic villain and liken him to Haman and Hitler; Ukrainians revere him as a savior of oppressed Ukrainian peasantry and national hero; Poles view him disparagingly as a rather ambivalent figure, a frustrated nobleman and misguided rebel. Though these depictions are simplistic, they should not be underestimated, for such common perceptions of a contentious past influenced behavior during crisis and wartime.[61]

With the first partition of Poland in 1772, Peremyshliany fell within the borders of the Austro-Hungarian Empire, and German colonists arrived. Farming and small, related industries such as beekeeping remained the town's economic mainstays; there were no factories or major industries to speak of, despite the establishment of a railway link to Lviv. About 75 percent of the population belonged to the peasantry and barely eked out an existence, making the region one of the poorest in Europe (though in many respects it was no more "backward" than other parts of eastern and southeastern Europe).[62]

With the disintegration of the Austro-Hungarian Empire at the end of World War I, the borderland of Galicia became the center of territorial disputes and nationalist clashes between Ukrainians and Poles. In the Ukrainian-Polish War of November 1918 to July 1919, Galician Ukrainians struggled to retain a West Ukrainian People's Republic. As part of this contest for control over the region, Polish leaders laid claim to the city of Lviv in November 1918; they inaugurated their rule with a pogrom.[63] When the Poles returned as the victors over Bolshevism in 1920, they symbolically staged another pogrom, which took the form mainly of property destruction and limited violence. These anti-Jewish riots in Galicia were not nearly as widespread as those in eastern Ukraine

---

61. The fractured history and ethnicized memory of this figure is explored in nine articles analyzing Jewish, Ukrainian, and Polish perspectives in *Jewish History* 17 (2003). Among the volume's contributors are Kenneth Stow, Adam Teller, Shaul Stamper, Frank Sysyn, Zenon Kohut, Natalia Yakovenko, and Gershon Bacon.

62. Andlauer, *Die jüdische Bevölkerung*. Life expectancy in these parts at this time fell below thirty years. "Przemyslany," *The Encyclopedia of Jewish Life Before and During the Holocaust*, ed. Shmuel Spector (Jerusalem: Yad Vashem, 2001), 2:1035–36; "Peremyshliany," *Encyclopaedia Judaica* (Jerusalem: Keter Publishing, 1971), 13:277; "Peremyshliany," *Encyclopedia of Ukraine*, ed. Danylo Husar Struk (Toronto: University of Toronto Press, 1993), 3:845–46.

63. William W. Hagen, "The Moral Economy of Ethnic Violence: The Pogrom in Lwów, November 1918," *Geschichte und Gesellschaft* 31 (2005): 203–26. Alexander V. Prusin, *Nationalizing a Borderland: War, Ethnicity, and Anti-Jewish Violence in East Galicia, 1914–1920* (Tuscaloosa: University of Alabama Press, 2005), 75–91, 107–9.

at this time, where supporters and adversaries of the Bolsheviks, anarchists, and Ukrainian nationalists were engaged in a bloody civil war that included systematic assaults against Jewish men, women, and children. By contrast, in western Ukraine the fledgling Ukrainian state maintained relative order over Galicia, and warfare was mostly limited to the battlefront. In fact, Jewish-Ukrainian relations seemed relatively amicable. A Jewish military unit of one thousand men joined the Ukrainian war against the Poles, and in June 1919 the Ukrainian Galician Army was victorious in a battle near Peremyshliany. Nevertheless, Poland won the war through its superior military forces.[64] The Polish minority maintained a tight grip over the region in the face of a growing Ukrainian nationalist movement. In the 1930s, Polonization campaigns directed from Warsaw resulted in the suppression of Ukrainian political parties and leaders and a radicalization of the Ukrainian nationalist movement. Ukrainian-Polish tensions mounted as more Poles colonized eastern Galicia, leading many Ukrainians to take action by ransacking estates; according to historian Orest Subtelny, as many as twenty-two hundred acts of sabotage were registered in the summer of 1930 alone. The Polish response was so extreme that a special committee of the League of Nations investigated the brutalities of the Poles against the Ukrainian minority, concluding that the Ukrainians had in effect brought such suffering upon themselves by initiating sabotage that provoked the Poles. These findings did not ameliorate the situation.[65] On the contrary, in 1938 about thirty thousand Ukrainians were arrested in Poland, mostly in eastern Galicia, for "violating" the security of the Polish state. Ukrainian politicians and intellectuals were crammed into prisons, subjected to quick trials, and mostly given three-year sentences. Some were sentenced to death. A systematic resettlement policy of the Polish government brought Polish farmers to the region, much to the ire of the dislocated Ukrainians whose property—down to the last cow—had been confiscated by the state.[66] This anti-minority "Poland

---

64. Western Galicia fell securely within the borders of the new Polish state. With the Soviet Russian retreat, the Poles occupied eastern Galicia, an annexation not internationally recognized until 1923. Andrzej Chojnowski, "Ukrainian-Polish War in Galicia, 1918–19," *Encyclopedia of Ukraine*, ed. Danylo Husar Struk (Toronto: University of Toronto Press, 1993), 5:457–58. Available at www.encyclopediaofukraine.com (accessed December 21, 2010). Magosci, *History of Ukraine*, 393–94.

65. Orest Subtelny, *Ukraine: A History*, 3rd ed. (Toronto: University of Toronto Press, 2000), 430.

66. For detailed reports on these anti-Ukrainian Polish measures, see the records of the German consul in Lemberg, 1938–1939, U.S. National Archives and Records Administration (NARA), RG 242, DW files, box 24, folder 20A.

for Poles first" approach of the new nationalist Polish government also put the Jews at a disadvantage, who in the same period were subject to university quotas, school closures, pauperization, and occasional violence. The rise of Zionism offered Jews an escape from European antisemitism, but it was not very popular in this provincial setting and mainly served to increase local tensions and accusations of disloyalty to the Polish state. In Peremyshliany, the Jewish community elected a Zionist as president of its local council in 1933, and demonstrations of antisemitism followed. The *bet ha-midrash* (Jewish house of study or high school) was bombed in 1935. The increase of Polish-led antisemitism, coupled with Nazi and Soviet threats and incursions on the region's borders, fueled interethnic tensions and anti-Jewish sentiment that later exploded during the war.[67]

PEREMYSHLIANY BEFORE THE NAZI OCCUPATION

The population of Peremyshliany and its surrounding villages was 70 to 80 percent Ukrainian, with sizable Jewish and Polish minorities as well as smaller Russian and German populations. Among western Ukrainians (known in the Austro-Hungarian Empire as Ruthenians, or "Little Russians," that is, as eastern Slavs distinct from Poles), the economic differences were not as great as the political ones would become. After its acquisition of Galicia in 1772, Vienna had recognized Ruthenians as a distinct nationality in the Hapsburg Empire and allowed for the growth of all Ruthenian cultural "enlightenment" societies (known as the *Prosvita*), newspapers, political parties, and schools. Spread largely through networks of Greek Catholic priests, nuns, and monks, the Ukrainian national idea took root in Galicia and fostered the region's reputation as a Ukrainian piedmont.[68] The Ukrainians in eastern Galicia were among the most spiritual (they were ardent followers of the Greek Catholic Church), nationally conscious, and economically strong in the rural cooperatives. But outside of the seminary and church hierarchy, the Ruthenians often lacked the power of public office obtainable with university degrees. And Ruthenian

---

67. Shimon Redlich's work on nearby Brzeżany explained similar tensions in the Jewish-Polish-Ukrainian triangle. See Redlich, *Together and Apart in Brzezany*.

68. Paul Robert Magosci, "Galicia: A European Land," Jerzy Motylewicz, "Ethnic Communities in the Towns of the Polish Ukrainian Borderland in the Sixteenth, Seventeenth, and Eighteenth Centuries," and John-Paul Himka, "Confessional Relations in Galicia," in *Galicia: A Multicultured Land*, ed. Christopher Hann and Paul Robert Magosci (Toronto: University of Toronto Press, 2005).

autonomy was made all the more unlikely vis-à-vis the Polonizing efforts of the Polish elite, especially after 1867.[69]

The timing of the first Jewish settlements in Galicia is not certain, perhaps occurring as early as the tenth century, when traveling Jewish merchants founded workshops along the trade routes. But these were not permanent settlements. In retrospect, the medieval period seems to have been a golden age for Jewish life in the region, which came to a violent end with the waves of pogroms in the mid-seventeenth century, sparked by the Cossacks' war against Poles and Jews and led by Khmel'nyts'kyi. Galicia was the cradle of the Hasidic movement, and Peremyshliany itself was the hometown of Menakhem Mendel (1728–1772), one of the disciples and followers of the founder of Hasidism.[70] At the time, the shtetl contained about seven hundred Jews. Not until the nineteenth century, with the spirit of emancipation spreading from the French Revolution, did Jews enjoy more mobility and opportunity in the Hapsburg Empire. Like most in east central Europe, the Jews of Galicia struggled with the uneven fits and starts of a largely state-directed campaign of industrialization. As a class of small shopkeepers, craftsmen, and traders, many lost their livelihoods and chose to emigrate from the region. As many as 350,000 Jews left Galicia between 1880 and 1914.[71]

Even with the emigration wave, Jews still made up more than half the population of Peremyshliany in the 1920s and 1930s. Those who remained and gained access to universities in Lviv, Vienna, Kraków, and Warsaw became the local lawyers, dentists, doctors, and teachers. A shrinking number of these university-educated Jews adopted Yiddish as their mother tongue, owing to

---

69. John-Paul Himka, *Galician Villagers and the Ukraine National Movement in the Nineteenth Century* (New York: St. Martin's, 1988); John-Paul Himka, *Religion and Nationality in Western Ukraine: The Greek Catholic Church and the Ruthenian National Movement in Galicia, 1867–1900* (Montreal: McGill-Queen's University Press, 1999). In his doctoral dissertation on Yitzhak Schipper, Jacob Litman provided a brief history of Schipper's Tarnów at the turn of the twentieth century, highlighting Jewish life in eastern Galicia, especially the rise of the Jewish socialist and Zionist movements and Polish laws concerning the Jews. See Litman's *The Economic Role of Jews in Medieval Poland: The Contribution of Yitzhak Schipper* (Lanham, MD: University Press of America, 1984), 1–39.

70. On the history of Hasidism (Chassidism), see Simon Dubnow's classic works, *History of the Jewish People* (1929) and *History of Hassidism* (1888). A brief but revealing account of the influence of Hasidism on a small town near Peremyshliany is presented in Leon Weliczker Wells, *The Janowska Road* (Washington, DC: USHMM, 1999), 21–26; cf. Raphael Mahler, *Hasidism and the Jewish Enlightenment: Their Confrontation in Galicia and Poland in the First Half of the Nineteenth Century* (Philadelphia: Jewish Publication Society of America, 1985).

71. Pohl, *Nationalsozialistische Judenverfolgung in Ostgalizien*, 23.

increasing assimilationist and secular trends, as well as a heavy Polonization push. The interwar generation chose Polish. In Peremyshliany, Jews, Poles, Ukrainians, and ethnic Germans attended the Polish *gimnazjum* (high school) on today's Halytska Street (the main street in town). At the same time, the increase in Polish spurred a local effort to preserve Yiddish and Jewish folk music. In the interwar period, Peremyshliany was probably best known in Galicia and other parts of Poland as a center for klezmer bands that played at events around the region. In fact, most Jews held fast to their regional identity as *Galitsiyaner.* Jacob Litman recalled that Peremyshliany

> was blessed with a number of talented musicians. In fact there was a family of well-known klezmers. [. . .] Two households of barbers, the Vogel family and the Kleinman family—were probably appreciated more for their musicality than their daily trade. [. . .] Peremyshlany was by no means an industrial place. With the exception of a small flour mill and an equally small sawmill, there was no industry to speak of. Craftsmanship carried out at home was also very limited because before the war most resident Poles were employed as governing functionaries or in local municipal services. The Jewish population was mostly involved in petty commerce or as middlemen between town and countryside, that is, as brokers in the exchange of goods and products with the peasantry in the surrounding villages.[72]

Whereas Jews, Russians, and Poles resided in the town's center, in the surrounding farming villages the population was mostly Ukrainian, with some patches of German settlement. This ethnic distribution stemmed largely from the social engineering of Polish and Austrian rulers, who used migration incentives to increase the farming and trade in Galicia. These ethnic groups retained separate cultural and religious traditions, but they interacted in everyday activities of commerce, governance, and schooling. A Polish directory of leading figures in the town of Peremyshliany reveals that in 1934, nearly half the town council was Polish; the other half was Jewish. The mayor was Polish, the secretary Ukrainian. There were two banks in town, one directed by a Pole and the other by a Jew named Klemens. The leading industries were a power plant and a meat-processing factory. Poles, who had been encouraged to move into the region in the 1930s, attained the leadership positions in the government; besides the mayorship, they also controlled the city court. Most doctors in town

---

72. Jacob Litman, *Autobiography* (unpublished manuscript, 1997), 26, 28.

were Jewish, but the director of the hospital was Polish.[73] Given their percentage of the general population, Ukrainians were starkly underrepresented; there was one Ukrainian lawyer, one official working in the post office, one midwife, and one serving as a treasurer in the local government. Lucy Gross grew up in Peremyshliany in the 1930s and recalled the ethnic and cultural differences, as well as the small-town interaction:

> Peremyshlany, a small dot on the map [. . .] it was picturesque and clean. It was inhabited by Poles, Ukrainians and Jews, each of them had their families, their work, religions and their own customs. Everyone felt comfortable in our town knowing no other as no one ventured further than nearby Lviv. At the end of the main street, on a hill, there was a hospital, and further was a wood, and it was a wood of great beauty.
>
> Peremyshlany was a district town and naturally, apart from the magnificent district authorities building, it also had its own coeducational gymnasium, which was the envy of all the neighboring towns as it had prestigious teachers and tutors. Next to the Roman Catholic church there were two elementary schools: one school for boys and one for girls.
>
> The schools were attended by all of the children irrespective of their religion. Located in the middle of the town, in the main street, was our beautiful synagogue, and the Ukrainian Orthodox church stood opposite. All three national groups had their own community centers: the Poles had their *Sokół*, the Ukrainians had their community center, and the Jews had their Tarbut, whose construction had never been fully completed due to a lack of funds.[74] All self-respecting Jewish families would send their children to Tarbut to attend Hebrew lessons despite an intensifying anti-

---

73. See the directory of Peremyshliany officials and businesses, *Schematyzm woj. yarnopolskiego* (1934): "Przemyślany," 20. Also see Rosa Lehmann, *Symbiosis and Ambivalence: Poles and Jews in a Small Galician Town* (New York: Berghahn, 2001). The fate of the Polish ruling elite in neighboring Volhynia, where a similar triangle of Poles, Jews, and Ukrainians existed, is masterfully presented in Snyder, *Sketches from a Secret War*.

74. One of the oldest youth organizations in Poland, the Sokół was a traditonal sports movement that proved important in cultivating nationalism. It originated in the Czech lands during the late nineteenth century and took hold across Europe. The movement promoted fitness, healthy living, and traditional moral values, but propagated nationalistic, patriotic ideas as well. Nazi and Soviet authorities later banned the organization. Tarbut (Hebrew, "culture" or "civilization") consisted of a network of Hebrew-language, secular, Zionist educational institutions for Jewish youth in interwar eastern Europe, and emerged primarily in the former Pale of Settlement.

semitism. Jews were increasingly striking roots into everything Polish, yet they did not want to forget or obscure their origins.[75]

Though, as Gross writes, it seemed as if modern, secular forces were "obscuring their origins," the dominant political movements that transformed Peremyshliany during World War II were primarily concerned with determining its inhabitants' class, race, and nationality. Moreover, as Golfard points out in his diary, local efforts at "national self-determination" in the 1930s and 1940s were suppressed, exploited, and ultimately exacerbated by Soviet and Nazi empire builders. As a result of the Hitler-Stalin Pact, the Red Army occupied the town in the fall of 1939 and it became part of the Ukrainian Soviet Socialist Republic. Rapid Sovietization, in the form of state confiscation of private industry and property, along with deportations of "enemies of the people," began in 1940. The Poles bore the immediate brunt of this. In the neighboring region of Volhynia, an estimated one in seven Poles was arrested, executed, or transferred east into crammed, unheated cattle cars; in total, close to four hundred thousand Polish citizens were deported from the territories occupied by the Red Army in 1939.[76] But the Soviet rulers who arrived from Moscow and other parts of Soviet Ukraine were not in town long enough to implement full-scale collectivization and Sovietization. If there were any economic advantages to the Soviet modernizing experiment, they were not felt in Peremyshliany between 1939 and 1941. The town remained economically behind and became even more unstable than before. Two main streets were partially paved. The back-streets were dirt roads, often with wooden planks leading to single-story homes that lacked indoor plumbing. The pauperization and deportation of the Polish elite in 1940–1941 opened up opportunities for Jews and Ukrainians, but the ostensible conspicuousness of Jews in the Soviet system put that minority in an even more vulnerable position.

THE GERMAN OCCUPATION OF PEREMYSHLIANY, 1941–1944

During World War II, the Jewish population in Peremyshliany fluctuated dramatically. It doubled between 1939 and 1941; an unknown number then left

75. Lucy Gross [Raubvogel] (b. April 18, 1926), typed memoir with corrections and notations, written just after liberation in Germany and then in Israel (approximately 1946–1950). Polish original translated into English by Magdalena Norton. I am grateful to Gisela Gross Gelin for allowing me to copy the original Hebrew-language manuscript.

76. Gross, *Revolution from Abroad*, 193–94.

during the Soviet evacuation in late June 1941. By the war's end, however, the Jewish population in town had been reduced to about five families, according to one survivor. And even these few survivors (along with the remaining Poles) were eventually forced or pressured to leave.[77] The estimated three thousand Jews who were in Peremyshliany when the Wehrmacht first arrived on July 1, 1941, were mostly murdered, and with the Soviet deportations and forced emigration of Poles, the World War II era effectively marked the end of centuries of Jewish and Polish life in eastern Galicia and of the multiethnic society that had enriched this otherwise poor region.

The genocide of the Jews began three days after the German army arrived. All Jewish men aged fourteen to sixty-five were forced to appear for registration and work assignments. Abetted by a local mob and Ukrainian militiamen, the Germans decimated the leadership of the Jewish community. Survivor Jacob Litman recounted these events as well as his first encounter with Golfard:

> On Tuesday, July 1, 1941, German troops advanced upon Peremyshliany. There were still many Jewish refugees in that place. Escapees from Hitler's onslaught and occupation of Poland in September 1939, they had come to this town which, by the Hitler-Stalin Non-aggression Pact, had been apportioned to the Ukrainian Republic of the Soviet Union.
>
> Now, almost two years later, with Stalin betrayed by Hitler, the Red Army beating a chaotic retreat, and the strike forces of the German Security Police operating on the heels of the advancing German troops, the remaining and frightened Jewish community here did not expect additional Jewish refugees. However, that was not to be the case. Rural Jews in the vicinity, afraid to stay in their villages among the Ukrainian peasantry, began moving to town to live among relatives and friends. There were also new outsiders who, for one reason or another, turned up in Peremyshliany. Among them was Samuel Golfard and his sister, Mania.

77. Rubin Pizem (b. 1933) returned to Peremyshliany after the war. Soviet and Ukrainian authorities forcibly or under great pressure sent the Jews in Galicia and Volhynia to Poland. Pizem went in 1957; that is, the Soviets and Ukrainians completed what the Germans had started, reducing the Jewish population in Peremyshliany to zero. Author's interview with Pizem, March 30, 2006. I am grateful to Anita Litman Millman for referring me to Mr. Pizem. See Timothy Snyder, "'To Resolve the Ukrainian Question Once and for All': The Ethnic Cleansing of Ukrainians in Poland, 1943–1947," *Journal of Cold War Studies* 1 (spring 1999): 86–120; and "The Causes of Ukrainian-Polish Ethnic Cleansing 1943," *Past and Present*, no. 179 (2003): 197–234. The population of Peremyshliany in 1943 was estimated in two German wartime sources as 4,453 and 5,000 (i.e., half the prewar population). Karl Baedeker, *Das Generalgouvernement: Reisehandbuch* (Leipzig: K. Baedeker, 1943).

I learned later that these two refugees had begun their flight from the German invaders at the very outset of the war, leaving their home city of Radom in Central Poland and eventually finding refuge in the southern part of Volhynia, where they got jobs and shelter from the newly established local Soviet authorities. But this refuge lasted only until June 22, 1941. [. . .]

The Lviv region, including Peremyshliany, was at first passed over by the Germans in their swift drive eastward, and this area remained in Russian hands for ten days after the initial Nazi onslaught. However, by the time Golfard and his sister arrived, it was too late. They were trapped in Peremyshliany. I had no idea that our paths would fatefully cross more than once. [. . .]

At that time I was still living in the modest but comfortable one-family house of Thaddeus [Tadeusz] Jankiewicz, his wife Helena, and ten-year-old daughter Danuta. As the new, and quite youthful, teacher appointed to the newly organized Jewish Junior High School in Peremyshliany, I was assigned living quarters in this Polish household by the local Soviet authorities not long after I came to town, in December of 1939, following weeks of being a lonely, hungry, and roving fugitive from Warsaw.

I was comfortably accommodated in a separate, furnished, cozy room, and despite initial feelings of misgiving and distrust, I became before long more than a lodger. Mrs. Jankiewicz, reared in the bustling homestead of her father, a prosperous farmer of Czech descent, excelled in the art of good home cooking and agreed to add board to my room at a reasonable price despite the existing shortages and the restraints imposed by the Soviet economic order. As the days passed, my standing in the house came quite close to that of being a member of the family. We grew to respect and like one another and, whenever necessary, did things for one another. The treacherous and unexpected German invasion put a sudden end to what may be described, in relative terms, as a refugee's fortunate lot both at home and at work. My Christian landlords realized that I had become an inexpedient liability, as a man with neither job nor money, and a Jew at that, but they asked me to remain, insisting that I stay home, out of people's sight, during the first impetuous weeks of German and Ukrainian atrocities in town. Feeling beholden as well as distressed, I ventured out one Sunday morning while the Jankiewicz family was in church. I thought to "pay my way" by going to town and queuing up for a bread ration. No sooner had I taken my place in line than two Ukrainian militiamen approached and carried me off to their station on the concocted charge of having participated in the murder of the three Trofimayak brothers. These were Ukrainian nationalists whom the Soviet security police killed in cold blood just before the German invasion.[78]

According to an OUN sympathizer who was Jewish and survived the war in Peremyshliany under a false identity, four brothers were killed by the Soviets during the evacuation of 1941.[79] As part of its evacuation plan, NKVD (Soviet secret police) forces raided prisons and massacred inmates. Soviet authorities did not have the time or transportation resources to bring the prisoners with them; nor did they want these persons to be liberated by the Germans and join Hitler's forces in the fight against Bolshevism. Many of the prisoners were local intelligentsia, including priests, nationalists, and so-called class enemies, or "bourgeois nationalists," as well as peasant resisters to collectivization. Across the region of Galicia, as well as in Volhynia, Podolia, and parts of Zhytomyr (for instance, in Lviv, Drohobych, Złoczów, Boryslav, Stryj, Luts'k, and Radomyshyl), tens of thousands of prisoners in dozens of prisons were brutally killed, or deported eastward and then killed (in the prisons of Lviv alone, four thousand were murdered).[80] Grenades were thrown into cells and victims' body parts dumped into the prison courtyards. In Peremyshliany, "victims' noses, ears, and fingers were cut off and their eyes put out."[81] Scholar Jan Gross estimates that in Peremyshliany about forty to seventy prisoners found themselves crammed into a cell designed to hold fourteen inmates and received no care, save for the charity of locals.[82]

---

78. Jacob Litman, introduction to *Golfard's Testimony* (1983), 4.

79. See testimony of Faina L., 1998, Peremyshliany, Ukraine, interview code 45446, USC Shoah Foundation Institute for Visual History and Education.

80. The discovery of these atrocities and the ensuing reprisals and pogroms were also a key feature of the discussion about crimes of the German army, since German soldiers as well as SS, police, local Ukrainian militia, and townspeople participated in the pogroms. For related events near Peremyshliany, see Bernd Boll, "Zloczow, Juli 1941: Die Wehrmacht und der Beginn des Holocaust in Galizien," *Zeitschrift für Geschichtswissenschaft* 50 (2002): 899–917. Oleh Romaniv and Inna Fedushchak, *Zakhidnoukrains'ka trahediia 1941* (Lviv and New York: Naukove tovarystvo im. T. Shevchenka, 2002), 56, 109–41, 155–65, 346.

81. See Gross, *Revolution from Abroad*, 181.

82. Gross, *Revolution from Abroad*, 154. According to Litman, *Autobiography*, 40, "Ukrainian nationalists" were shot in the basement of the NKVD during the Soviet evacuation. These murders ignited local reprisals in the form of pogroms incited by the Nazi occupiers. On the anti-Jewish assaults in the borderlands of eastern Galicia, see Żbikowski, "Local Anti-Jewish Pogroms," 173–79; and Per Anders Rudling, "Bogdan Musial and the Question of Jewish Responsibility for the Pogroms in Lviv in the Summer of 1941," *East European Jewish Affairs* 35 (June 2005): 69–89. On the role of Ukrainian nationalists (the OUN), see Franziska Bruder, *"Den ukrainischen Staat erkämpfen oder sterben,"* 130–32, 134–39, 145–52.

These ghastly discoveries ignited outrage among locals, who lashed out with "reprisal" actions against the Jews. Jacob Litman and Gisela Gross (later Gisela Gross Gelin) found themselves the target of such attacks in July 1941. During the first days of the German occupation, Jews and other suspected communists were held in two prisons in town (one in the basement of the courthouse, the other in the basement of the police headquarters). According to Litman, the one at the police headquarters had two cells, one jammed with about forty Jews, the other holding a few Ukrainian communist suspects. To prove themselves loyal to the German and Ukrainian fight against "Judeo-Bolshevism," the suspected Ukrainian communists were ordered to beat the Jews each day. Litman knew one of the three Ukrainian prisoners turned torturer; he was a high school student and former leader of the Komsomol.[83] He wrapped Litman in a blanket and bludgeoned him with wooden planks, striking Litman first in the mouth to keep him quiet. These daily beatings occurred each morning and night for three or four weeks. Gisela Gross was also tortured in a cell in this prison. Ukrainian guards stomped on her as she lay on a floor covered with broken glass. When they were finished, they threw her out the prison window. A Ukrainian priest found her bloody body on the sidewalk and brought her home.[84] Jacob Litman was released from jail; he was, in his words, "acquitted of the charges."

The first pogrom occurred in town on July 4, 1941. The Belzer rebbe (the head of a historic Hasidic dynasty), Aharon Rokeach (of Belz), who was also a refugee in Peremyshliany, barely escaped the massacre. However, his son was thrown into the burning synagogue.[85] Jewish homes were destroyed and plun-

---

83. Komsomol, the Communist Union of Youth, was the main youth organization in the Soviet Union and prepared future members of the Communist Party.

84. See Litman, *Autobiography*, 23–31. Another survivor identified the Ukrainian police chief as a man named Boiko. But this man, who had a leading role in the prison, also helped a Jewish family by warning them about an impending action. Gross believes that the Ukrainian priest was Father Kovch. See interview with Gisela Gross Gelin, November 3, 2005, notes in the possession of the author. Also see Yetta L. interview, 1999, Margate, New Jersey, interview code 50384, tape 3, segments 76–77, USC Shoah Foundation Institute for Visual History and Education.

85. The son's name was Moishe. The Belzer rebbe was hidden with a Polish family, then given a disguise and taken out of town by Hungarian counterintelligence officers. See video testimony of Basia K., 1997, Brooklyn, interview code 6510, tape 1, segment 4; Israel L., 1995, Brooklyn, interview code 8358, tape 2, segment 33; and Ida K., 1996, West Orange, New Jersey, interview code 20097, tape 1, segments 18–20, all USC Shoah Foundation Institute for Visual History and Education. Yosef Israel, *Rescuing the Rebbe of Belz: Belzer Chassidus: History, Rescue and Rebirth* (Brooklyn, NY: Mesorah Publications, 2005). The burning of the synagogue and murder of the son of the rebbe is also recounted by survivor Kalman Katz in his *Memories of War*, 17.

In July 1941, Jacob Litman and Gisela Gross were held in this Przemyślany/Peremyshliany prison's basement cells and subjected to daily beatings by Ukrainian policemen. The banner draped across the building announces that the building is for rent or sale (photograph by Nadia Ficara, 2010).

dered. Women were also brutalized by Ukrainians who vented their anti-Soviet rage against the Jewish population. As a young woman, Lucy Gross (Gisela's sister) witnessed the atrocities of the first weeks of the Nazi occupation:

> Our large synagogue and all of its annexes were burnt. The flames were rising up high, parched window frames and benches on which our grandfathers, fathers and brothers used to sit now crackled. Fire turned into an awesome element. A throng of peasants gathered around the fire with their sacks ready to plunder; a mass of devoted Christians, their children and the Germans who recorded this overwhelming sight on film. The wind carried sparks from one building to another, the fire crackled and soared into the sky mercilessly, and the bones of the first victims crunched. An enthused mob of shrieking peasants, just like locusts, pounced on everything that belonged to the Jews. They plundered, stole, and in some incredible ecstasy they destroyed within minutes what had sometimes survived the generations.[86]

86. Lucy Gross, memoir manuscript (English translation).

Lucy Gross at fifteen in the Przemyślany/
Peremyshliany ghetto, 1942 (USHMMPA
WS# 67636, courtesy of Gisela Gross
Gelin).

Pogroms had become part of the cycle of popular violence that often
accompanied wars, revolutions, and other major crises. Ukrainians and Poles
responded in a quasi-ritualistic manner once rumors spread that an anti-Jewish
action was imminent.[87] Peasants arrived from the countryside ready to plunder. Militia "vigilantes" formed to pursue Jews in their homes and harass them
on the streets. Jews understood their vulnerability, although not its genocidal
proportions. More than a singular episode, the anti-Jewish violence of the summer of 1941 marked both a culminating moment as well as a historic break.
The German organization and implementation of mass shootings (and later
gas chambers) constituted state-sponsored programs of genocide, distinct
from the popular pogrom-like violence perpetrated by the local non-Jews in
Peremyshliany in the summer of 1941. At the time the pogroms might have

---

87. Philip Friedman, "Ukrainian-Jewish Relations During the Nazi Occupation,"
in *Roads to Extinction: Essays on the Holocaust*, ed. Ada June Friedman (New York: Jewish
Publication Society of America, 1980), 176–208. Kai Struve, "Ritual und Gewalt—Die
Pogrome des Sommers 1941," in *Synchrone Welten: Zeiträume jüdischer Geschichte*, ed. Dan
Diner (Göttingen: Vandenhoeck & Ruprecht, 2005), 225–50.

seemed episodic and historically familiar; in retrospect they contributed to the much larger Nazi campaign of a "Final Solution."

The German military administration in Peremyshliany was short-lived but effective. Before handing over power in August 1941 to the civil administration of imperial-style governors—Hans Frank's Generalgouvernement—the military occupiers ordered the establishment of a Jewish Council. The council included leading figures in the local community as well as Jewish refugees, who were forced to carry out German demands against the Jewish population, such as the registration of the population and collection of exorbitant sums of money and valuables. The Jews were stripped of all civil rights and freedoms and subjected to forced labor assignments. The first mass shooting of 450 to 500 Jewish men occurred on November 5, 1941, at the edge of town in the Brzezina (birch tree) Forest. A German Security Police detachment organized and carried out this shooting. Male heads of households were ordered to report for forced labor assignments at the Polish high school (St. Hedwig's Gymnasium) at the center of town. They were told to bring shovels. In the school, German policemen set up registration tables and asked each Jewish man to fill out a form. From there, they were led to the parking area behind the school. The men were made to run a gauntlet of local German gendarmes who beat them and confiscated their possessions. Some were taken by truck; others were forced to march to the forest. There, they had to dig a pit and, in small groups, were shot at close range while kneeling at the pit's edge.[88] At least one young man survived. He crawled out

---

88. This first action is described by former German policemen, Holocaust survivors, a Polish rescuer, and a Ukrainian eyewitness from the town. There are slight discrepancies about the ages of the victims, varying from fourteen to sixty-five years old, and one testimony dates the massacre in October and describes the gathering point as a Yiddish school, not the Polish gymnasium. See video testimony by Basia K., 1997, Brooklyn, interview code 6510, tape 1, segment 4; Israel L., 1995, Brooklyn, interview code 8358, tape 2, segments 30–32; Esther L., 1995, Brooklyn, interview code 8357, tape 2, segment 35; Ida K., 1996, West Orange, New Jersey, interview code 20097, tape 1, segments 28–30; Lynn W., 2001, Delray Beach, Florida, interview code 51773, tape 1, segment 12; Michal S., 1997, Warsaw, interview code 38053, tape 2, segment 46; Regina P., 1995, Miami Beach, interview code 9289, tape 1, segments 28–29; Jacob L., 1995, Union, New Jersey, interview code 3179, tape 3, segment 87, all USC Shoah Foundation Institute. The few published sources on the town confirm that the massacre occurred but offer slight variations as to its size and date. See *Pinkas ha-kehilot: Encyclopedia of Jewish Communities, Poland, Eastern Galicia*, ed. Danuta Dabrowska, Avraham Wein, and Aahron Weiss (Jerusalem: Yad Vashem, 1980), 2:442; Katz, *Memories of War* (this memoir contains some historical errors). "Przemslany" in *The Encyclopedia of Jewish Life Before and During the Holocaust*, ed. Shmuel Spector (Jerusalem: Yad Vashem, 2001), 2:1035–36; and "Peremyshliany," *Encyclopedia Judaica*, 13:277.

of the grave, found refuge with Lucy Gross's family, and informed them of the mass murder. Golfard also wrote of the one survivor who revealed what happened in the woods that day. The boy had been shot in the face but made his way home "dripping with blood."[89]

A few months later, in early 1942, the German district captain, Hans Mann, posted an order in town that a Jewish "residential district," or ghetto, would be formed.[90] The area consisted of about five or six streets with multiple entry points and unclear boundaries. It covered more than a quarter of the downtown area behind the main street. Multiple families had to live in single rooms in dilapidated housing. Poor sanitation led to the outbreak of diseases, and starvation-level rations also kept the Jews in the ghetto in a weakened state. No Jews were allowed outside the ghetto without permission. Ukrainians, Poles, and other locals who were caught helping Jews found outside the ghetto could be subjected to the death penalty. The ghetto was sealed not with a wall but rather with barbed wire fencing. Ukrainian

---

89. Gisela Gross Gelin testimony, November 2006. Lucy Gross manuscript, 13, translated by Magdalena Norton and described by Golfard in his entry dated January 26, 1943. Lucy and her sister Gisela survived the occupation. Lucy posed as a non-Jew and was deported to work in Magdeburg, Germany, during the war, while Gisela fled to the forest.

90. On German administrative maps, Peremyshliany was part of the Kreishauptmannschaft Złoczów (Zolochiv), a subdistrict (*Bezirk*) of Galicia. The Peremyshliany administrative province covered roughly 360 square miles; in 1941, it contained 89,900 inhabitants, of whom 62 percent were Ukrainian, 26 percent were Polish, and 11 percent were Jewish. The district of Galicia fell within the borders of Nazi-occupied Poland designated the Generalgouvernement, with its capital in Kraków. Hans Mann, the district captain in Złoczów, was replaced by Dr. Otto Wendt in early 1943. Peremyshliany had a *Landkommissar* (present in this office were Fritz Weiss and Herr Suhrbier from Mecklenburg), a Ukrainian police office, a German criminal police (Kripo) office, and a German gendarme office, but not its own SS and police headquarters. Killing actions against Jews were planned in Złoczów and Lviv, and units were brought in (usually by truck) to carry out these actions with the help of the local Ukrainian and German forces in the Kripo and gendarmerie. On the administrative structure, see the records of the Galicia District from the former Lviv Oblast Archive, USHMMA, Acc. 1995.A.1086, reels 7 and 8. A Jewish woman who worked in the local German administrative office secured papers to take on a Ukrainian identity. Several Ukrainians in the office knew this but did not betray her. See testimony of Faina (Anna Gavrylivna) Liakher (b. 1917), who was a sympathizer in the Ukrainian nationalist movement (the OUN); 1998 interview, Peremyshliany, Ukraine, interview code 45446, USC Shoah Foundation Institute for Visual History and Education.

and German police patrolled the areas just outside the periphery.[91] German "resettlement" transports continued to bring more Jews into the ghetto from surrounding villages. Some Jews who had found hiding places with Polish neighbors were forced to leave their shelters and came to the ghetto. The impact of ghetto life on Jewish behavior was noted by Litman: "It became increasingly difficult for the frightened, deprived, and starving Jews in the ghetto of Peremyshlany to hold on to their human qualities. Under savage conditions, man's animal instincts for survival overshadow everything. Such instincts came to 'regulate' ghetto life. The number of ghetto inmates, too, was dwindling. Only those who thought themselves to be productively occupied could still entertain some hopeful illusions, and only such illusions could serve as an antidote to the evil rife around the ghetto's inhabitants."[92]

To "empty" the overcrowded ghetto, German police and civil authorities periodically planned a killing action. In May 1942, 100 to 150 Jews were shot. Many of these victims had been taken from the Jewish hospital. Meanwhile, Jewish laborers were routinely pulled out of the ghetto, brought to the nearby labor camps of Kurowice and Jaktorów, and assigned to quarries and other related road construction work. Golfard's diary is the most detailed account available on victim experiences in the Jaktorów camp. His time there was one of "two woeful blows" that struck Golfard. Litman explained:

> While still an outsider with no kin or solid connections in town, [Golfard] was captured and carried off, in one of the first raids, to the forced labor camp in Jaktorów by the Jewish Ordungsdienst (police) of the local Judenrat (Jewish Council) which was often intimidated by the German SS-men to deliver quotas of laborers. Very few, indeed, could break loose

91. The precise date of the ghetto's establishment is not consistent in the sources, though all agree that it occurred in the first half of 1942 and the ghetto's existence was short; about three to four months passed before the onset of regular killing actions. See video testimonies of Ida K., 1996, West Orange, New Jersey, interview code 20097; Mayer K., 1997, Palm Beach, Florida, interview code 26616; Michal S., 1997, Warsaw, interview code 38053; Yetta L., 1999, Margate, New Jersey, interview code 50384; and Regina P., 1995, Miami Beach, interview code 9289, all USC Shoah Foundation Institute for Visual History and Education; Aleksandr Kruglov, "Przemyślany," in *The United States Holocaust Memorial Museum Encyclopedia of Camps and Ghettos, 1933–1945*, vol. 2: *Ghettos in German-Occupied Eastern Europe*, ed. Martin Dean (Bloomington: Indiana University Press in association with the USHMM, 2011), 817–19. According to Kruglov, the ghetto was liquidated on May 22, 1943; two thousand Jews were shot, and fifty were placed in a labor unit. See Kruglov, *The Losses Suffered by Ukrainian Jews*, 342.

92. Jacob Litman, introduction to *Golfard's Testimony* (1983), 6.

from the clutches of the Jaktorów camp and the notorious sadism of its SS commandant [Paul] Fox.[93] People of greater means and better connections were seldom able to extricate their relatives and loved ones. Nonetheless, Golfard was set free after two weeks. Apparently, his sister [Mania] was relentless in her efforts and pleas before the Jewish council, and one of its leading members, begged and pressured by certain sympathetic individuals, succeeded in getting Golfard released. Less than a year later, his sister herself was caught and sent off forever to some unknown place, which even then was rumored to be the extermination camp at Bełżec. That tragic loss gnawed away at Golfard and may have set in a gradual weakening in his will to live.[94]

The first deportations of Jews from Peremyshliany to the gassing facility of Bełżec began in the late summer of 1942. In August and September, nearly two-thirds of the town's ghetto population was deported. These operations involved the combined efforts of the German civil administration in the local gendarmerie and Security Police forces from the neighboring headquarters in Zolochiv (Złoczów). They, in turn, relied upon Ukrainian policemen and Jewish Council members to assist with the implementation. Golfard's sister Mania was among those rounded up from the "open" ghetto and taken to the basement of a building on the main street. This basement served as a prison, or "collection point," for Jews awaiting deportation. Jewish Council members, who were required to fill a certain quota of deportees, compiled a list of names of those arrested. In vain Golfard tried to persuade the council to remove his sister's name from the list, which would have resulted in her release from the basement. To his horror, Mania was forced onto a truck and taken to Zolochiv, where the railcars departed to Bełżec. Reeling from this traumatic loss and alone in a town he could hardly call home, Golfard started his diary.

93. For more on Paul Fox, see Biographies.
94. Litman, introduction to *Golfard's Testimony*, 6.

PART II

SAMUEL GOLFARD'S DIARY, JANUARY TO APRIL 1943[1]

JANUARY 25, 1943

I am not composing these words for myself. They are intended for those who will survive and who might quickly forget what they had lived through not so long ago. Let these words refresh in their memory the moments of horror, the bloody scenes that took place before their eyes, the black night of savagery. Let it [open?] wounds already healed.[2]

In embarking upon this notebook, I am not motivated by a writer's ambition. I am subjected to an unspeakable burden by every word; every reminiscence hurts cruelly; contemplating present-day events fills me with despair. I realize that these words will not alleviate my own suffering, but since I do not want to spare others, it is fair to have no regard for myself.

Outside the window there is a shroud of sparkling snow. A dazzling whiteness strikes the eyes. Total stillness reigns, but in my heart a storm is raging. I

---

1. USHMMA Acc. 2008.316, Litman family collection. This translation from Polish comprises the full text of the diary, including deletions by Golfard (indicated by crossed out words) other than small orthographic corrections. Stylistic peculiarities and illegible passages in Polish are flagged in the following translation with brackets.

2. Golfard may be paraphrasing "One must rip open the wounds of Poland lest they heal over with scabs of baseness," which comes from Stefan Żeromski's drama *Sułkowski* (1910). Żeromski's oft-quoted literary work touches upon ethical and historical issues that appeal to the "collective conscience." Golfard may not have read or seen this particular drama, but he had probably heard this quote in some form. Żeromski's statement remains a point of reference or a topic for essays in Polish schools today.

see beloved faces with a mute reproach in their eyes. The image of thousands of murdered—children, boys, and girls—appears before me. Among them I see the tormented face of my dearest sister. With her hand in the sling, she sat cowering in the square among hundreds of other victims. I did not manage to give her a sign. She noticed me briefly, she looked startled and frightened as I was being brutally driven away and was denied the chance to exchange another glance with her.

What did she think of me? Did she know that I ran to save her? In vain. I distinguished her screams among the cries of others, swollen with despair, and coming from the truck as I, dazed and unaware of what was really going on, desperately begged for help. I reacted with a fierce shriek, which did not seem to come from my mouth. And the cry of my little sister amid that of others faded away into the darkness. But I still hear it. What did she think about on the way! Perhaps the pain in her hand, recently operated on, dulled her fear for her life. Did she know that she was on her way to Złoczów to die a horrible, tortuous death? Could she believe this until the very last moment? My dearest Maniusia [Mania]! Forgive your brother for leaving you on your own, that he did not share your fate. Perhaps if you were with me, it would have been easier for you to die. Mania, I was paralyzed with despair. Even now I am shaken by sobs at the thought that terror robbed me of my will, the will to die together with you.

You had enough time to draw up the balance sheet of your young life. They seized you, leaving your brother in a camp from which there was seemingly no way out, your beloved parents having apparently been murdered in faraway R., your siblings seized and most probably put to death as well.[3] And with all that the terrible pain in your finger.

What had your life been? Full of devotion to our parents, to me. Your patience and angelic goodness did not make life easier for you. After a day's hard labor you walked barefoot many kilometers to the camp in Jaktorów,

---

3. Golfard often used initials for places, groups of peoples, and individuals, in some cases to perhaps protect them, but in most other cases as a form of shorthand. The "R." refers to Radom, located in central Poland, about sixty miles south of Warsaw (and 190 miles northwest of Przemyślany/Peremyshliany). In 1939 the city was inhabited by twenty-five thousand Jews, about one-third of the total population. There were two ghettos in Radom during the German occupation, which were formed by April 1941. Hundreds of Jews were deported from Radom to Auschwitz in early 1942; the rest were sent to Treblinka as of the summer of 1942. Many Jews escaped to the surrounding forest and joined the resistance, including the Polish uprising in Warsaw in August 1944. Jacek Andrzej Młynarczyk, *Judenmord in Zentralpolen: Der Distrikt Radom im Generalgouvernement 1939–1945* (Darmstadt: Wissenschaftliche Buchgesellschaft, 2007); Robert Rozett and Shmuel Spector, eds., *Encyclopedia of the Holocaust* (Jerusalem: Yad Vashem, 2000), 371.

bringing me greetings from the world of the living with a forced timid smile, ~~for me,~~ [illeg.] ~~which~~ [illeg.]. You witnessed how they beat me and tormented me. You lived through hell before you could see me at home. And you underwent all this alone, surrounded by indifference and hostility. When you were no more, people told me that during my stay in the camp you regarded even those who wished me well as foes. You thought that no one should laugh, eat, or walk while your brother suffered.[4]

When they snatched you away from me, you wore a brown silk blouse, the gray jacket that I myself had bought for your birthday before the war, and on your feet—summer clogs. Oh, how cold you must have been.

I must stop writing now. My hand is trembling, and sobs are ripping through my chest. Before me I see only you and the gray pavement. My ears are filled with the sound of your cry for life fading in the misty night.

JANUARY 26, 1943[5]

I began writing with reminiscences about my little sister. ~~I was avoiding~~ This happened against my will. I wished to give an impersonal testimony of objective truth

---

4. The Jaktorów camp was established at the site of a former estate with small production facilities known as Gruszka. It was set up shortly after the Germans arrived in September 1941 and liquidated in July 1943. Multiple postwar testimonies from Jewish survivors and Polish and Ukrainian eyewitnesses confirm that the camp commandants, Paul Fox and Josef Grzimek (for more on both, see "Biographies"), abused and killed prisoners who labored in the nearby sandpit. The exact number of deaths at the camp is unknown, but the camp housed three to five hundred Jewish laborers, some as young as fourteen years old. When it was liquidated in July 1943, 320–350 prisoners were shot, while some 80 Jewish prisoners managed to flee to the forest on the night before the liquidation. After demonstrating his sadism in Jaktorów, Grzimek was assigned to "purify the ghetto" in Lviv. See Philip Friedman, "The Destruction of the Jews of Lwów," in *Roads to Extinction*, 286–87. Pohl, *Nationalsozialistische Judenverfolgung in Ostgalizien*, 170, 341. Crimes of the German and Ukrainian police, including names of Jewish victims, are detailed in the indictment of Ernst Epple u.a., Bundesarchiv Ludwigsburg (BAL) 162/19230 (Sammelakte no. 181) (208 AR-Z 294/59). Also see testimony of survivor Henry C., 1996, Warsaw, interview code 14823; Mark T., 2001, Chicago, interview code 51758, segments 153–155; Martin S., 1996, Brooklyn, interview code 18607, segments 94–95, all USC Shoah Foundation Institute for Visual History and Education.

5. It seems that Samek wrote intermittently on single days; when he returned to his diary to take up another topic or continue his stream of thought, he wrote the date again, hence the multiple appearances of "January 26" for several entries. It is possible that Samek began writing in October 1942 in another book that is missing. Jacob Litman stated in his autobiography that Samek wrote his diary from October 1942 until May 1943. See Litman, *Autobiography*, 49–50.

and render a dry description of facts. Our reality needs no lyrical phrases. Our life is colored by the truest human blood, which just recently stained the snow-covered pavement. One must write with blood, is [illeg.] ~~Yet Difficult~~. It is now less valued than ink. The chivalrous German people, these modern cannibals and murderers of children, are always ready to deliver it in sufficient quantities.

But I must return to my sister. As long as I do not free myself from the choking pain, I shall not be able to transmit the whole cruel truth of this day to those who will survive. ~~They are deluding themselves They are claiming that~~ I do not hope to relieve my suffering with memories. The thought that I am writing about her as nonexistent frightens me. I catch myself in the act, and my heart is numb from fear.

I probably lost my dear parents. I hardly remember them. They do not appear in my dreams. The frailty of my feelings for them dismays me. I lost them when they were far away from me. I did not see the seal of death on their faces. I have lost my most beloved Bronia, the youngest child, whom I doted on from the day she was born. I have lost my sixteen-year-old sister Pola, whom I nursed in her illness. The thought of losing any one of them would have ordinarily driven me, their only son and brother, to despair. But now I go on living. A while ago I was laughing heartily with my guests, although I collected myself from time to time, and the laughter died on my lips. Why am I alive? Ought not an honorable man regard himself as contemptible for letting his nearest kin go to her doom all alone? What, then, is one's will to live, if not proof of the height of egotism? The old Slavonic custom of sharing death on the pyre ought to be revived today.

JANUARY 26

~~I want to I wish to wri[te] I am going back to even[ts]~~ The small town of P.[6] lived through so much up to this day! On November 5, 1941, the registration of the town's Jewish population took place. Sensing misfortune but fearing that if they disobeyed their families would be murdered, only 300 people reported at the place of assembly. Threats to that effect were disseminated by the traitors of the Jewish people. For the most part, invalids of World War I with medals for merit and bravery reported, as well as some young men employed in German enterprises. These people, driven to the town square, were first

---

6. Przemyślany/Peremyshliany. Hereafter, the town's name will be included, though in the original only a reference to *P.* was used. See the Place Names list at the end of this volume for the Polish and Ukrainian spellings of places mentioned in the diary.

whipped and then, with shovels in their hands, led in groups to the woods. What happened there was veiled in secrecy until one young man in the group returned. According to his report, the report of a boy who literally rose from his grave, the massacre was carried out in this way: the men, having dug out a large grave, were led individually to its edge and shot in the temple. Then, one after the other, they were kicked into the grave. The boy who miraculously survived was shot in the face but not mortally, kicked into the grave, and covered with other corpses. After the massacre ended, at nighttime, he returned home dripping with blood. Three women also met with their deaths in the grave, for they had gone into the woods despite the ban and were shot there by the same murderers.

A few days after the massacre, I arrived in town from the countryside. I talked to the wives and fathers of the murdered. No one wanted to believe that all had perished. They were willing to believe that it happened to the invalids, the old men, but nobody dared believe that all had perished at the hand of such insane criminals. Today nobody doubts it anymore.

At this point I must retrace my steps somewhat and proceed chronologically. Immediately after Przemyślany was invaded by the Germans, large-scale pillaging took place, combined with burning of the synagogue and Jewish homes, in which the U.[7] participated. People were thrown into the flames alive. The son of the Rebbe of Bełz, thrown by the Ukrainians into the flames of the burning synagogue, died a martyr's death.[8]

We looked for the reasons for these insane crimes. One could not believe that people were being murdered simply because they belonged to a certain nation, so in June [1941] everything was imputed to Karl Sołdaleski [the identity of this person could not be established]. Again in November it was established that the local Ukrainians brought a denunciation to the German authorities against the Jews, who allegedly were guilty of the death of several Ukrainians. At a mine-clearing operation, as a result of carelessness, an explosion took place in which several laborers perished. The blame was pinned on the Jews who hired these laborers. The truth is that in both cases, during the invasion in June and at the time of the penal expedition in November, the G.[9] had been the killers, and the Ukrainians had been their assistants.

---

7. *U.* refers to Ukrainians. Hereafter, the reference will be "Ukrainians."

8. The Belzer rebbe was head of a historic Hasidic dynasty. He had sought refuge in Przemyślany from Nazi-occupied Poland and barely escaped this massacre.

9. *G.* refers to Germans. Hereafter, the reference will be "Germans."

JANUARY 26

Before I proceed with the current bloody chronicle, I must finish the account of past events.

In August 1942 the wave of so-called "actions" began. Even now I cannot mention this word without a shudder, although every one of us had become accustomed to the sound of this dreadful term and familiar with its bloody purport. But then we still had our illusions.

The "action" in Przemyślany was preceded by grim news of the killings in the vicinity of Złoczów, Bóbrka[,] [Chronil?]. The wealthy and a few desperate young people took refuge in the country. They were a minute percentage of the population. One morning alarming news about an "action" in Złoczów was spread, in the evening, about 5 o'clock, as an exodus from the town began, a German unit descended on the town, blocked the roads, and began the "actions." Soon over 700 people found themselves in the square. At the time, I was returning from work at camp. I began looking for my sister and found her, at last, among the many on the square. The Jewish militia drove me away. I could not see her again. I ran to the Jud. [*Judenrat*, Jewish Council] to seek a way of rescuing her from the square.[10] I was told that it was impossible. Later on I learned that some people were rescued for vast amounts of money, for gold and diamonds, but I could offer nothing.

Dazed, I ran to speak to a German who was quartered in the same house in which we lived and who somehow seemed to us to be friendly. He was drunk and scared. He promised to save us, but it turned out to be an empty promise.

I kept vigil at the office of the Jewish Council, but without any hope of saving her. Suddenly I heard a terrible scream from a truck passing by. It turned out to be the first "transport" loaded, and in it was my dearest Mania.

As if through a fog I heard what happened, then everything quieted down. I lay down in the doorway of my quarters, half dozing and stunned. My head was burning, my temples were buzzing. I felt I was being trampled upon. I was indifferent to everything.

---

10. Two brothers bearing the family name Kahane, allegedly unsavory characters from out of town, headed the Jewish police (militia). The Jewish Council was established in July 1941 under the leadership of Dr. Rotfeld, who was killed and replaced with David Mendel. Another member of the *Judenrat* was named Judah Lichtenberg. Dr. Yehuda Kahane at Tel Aviv University provided information on the *Judenrat* and translated from Hebrew related information found in *Pinkas ha-kehilot: Poland, Eastern Galicia*, vol. 2. Phone interviews with Gisela Gross Gelin, October 14, 2005; and Rubin Pizem, March 30, 2006. According to a wartime eyewitness, Ivan Fuglevych, the *Judenrat* was located on the main street at Halyts'ka Street 44 and a prominent lawyer named Zimmerman was also a member. Fuglevych interviews conducted by Wendy Lower, 2005, 2010; Katz, *Memories of War*, 20.

The dawn brought me to my feet. I ran out to the square with a dying hope in my heart. I was told that only one part of the people was taken away and that the rest were in the basement, destined for the next transport. I began calling out for Mania. The reply was the sobbing of hundreds of people. Mania was not among them.[11]

I did not move away from the basement. I saw how people were being exchanged. Old people were brought in, orphaned and wretched children, and those swollen from hunger were snatched off the streets. All these were designated "junk."[12] In exchange for them, older wealthy people were pulled out. Some girls were rescued out of pity, but mostly for money. The next day the remaining "contingent" was loaded. Not a single person was missing from the quota. The Jewish Council received praise from . . .[13] The murderers were treated to a splendid feast, which was paid for in the form of a tax collected from the J. [Jews].

With this "action" the Jewish militia participated actively for the first time, breaking into hiding places, seizing children, young people, women, and old men in the streets. ~~Not everyone~~ For thousands of złoty and for dollars they saved certain people. In this respect they were not better or worse than many Germans, who for a bottle of vodka or a can of sardines spared one's life. They [Jewish militia] were just somewhat cheaper.

JANUARY 26, 1942[14]

~~Horrifying. The days that followed, never The days that followed were a true nightmare.~~ After the "action" I lay on my straw sack in my room for several days delirious with fever. No one spoke to me. The landlord who occupied the next two rooms returned from his shelter and began to keep house again as if nothing had happened. He came one day and demanded that the shattered windowpane in my room be replaced. At first I did not wish to see anyone. I felt hatred toward anyone who remained alive. I could not look at young girls without experiencing pain ~~people's scabs~~ or at emaciated old men who had been spared and whose remaining days were few anyway. My sister was constantly in my thoughts. Her unfinished cigarette lay on the windowsill. I was afraid to throw it away, and looking in its direction caused me almost physical

---

11. The Germans installed machine guns around the perimeter of the market square and facing the basement collection spot, effectively preventing escapes.

12. This word could also be translated as "scrapped," meaning that these designated persons were tossed aside like garbage.

13. Golfard left out the names of those who praised the council.

14. The year is incorrect in the original; the entry appears within the sequential days of January 1943.

pain. Lately Mania did not allow herself to smoke a whole cigarette. She would always leave a stub for the next day.

I could not forgive myself for living, for eating.

A friend pulled me out of the room. He proposed that I share his living quarters with him. I went to live with him, taking mementos of my sister. He began bringing me back to life, suggested joint rescue plans, demanding that I become active. Although I did not like him and reacted to all his ideas with antagonism, my renewed contact with life must be credited to him.

I turned from loneliness to the other extreme. Making the rounds of homes all day long, I eagerly sought the company of people. I could not be alone for a minute. And I lulled myself to sleep by contriving rescue plans. I do this to this day because only the fear for my own life can still the grief for the loss of my sister.

JANUARY 27

~~We are looking for~~ We nurture the memory of our nearest ones with the utmost care. We do not want to ever part with the merest trifles left by them. We feel a lifelong gratitude to those who witnessed the last moments of our nearest kin, those who can convey to us what they sensed and said. My sister's things remained with me for a short time. They were soon stolen. All I have left of hers is a sweater, which I wear, and a small student ID picture of her with which I will never part.

How did she behave in her final moments? Perhaps she died on the way, before falling into the hands of the executioners? This supposition, however terrible, brings me a certain comfort. For I do not dare to think that she reached the place of execution, whether Bełżec or anywhere else.[15] We have been told that people are being put to death there on a suspension bridge charged with electricity, and then the victims are thrown into the abyss.[16] Those who have not experienced the hell following the loss of their dearest ones delight in relating these details overheard somewhere. I myself have witnessed a conversation between a peasant and a salesman in a cooperative who praised the soap in bulk. The peasant rejected his offer with aversion, stating, "This is soap from

---

15. In the original, the word Belzec (Bełżec) is not presented in the correct grammatical form, suggesting that it was largely unfamiliar or only known through hearsay.

16. Ivan Fuglevych recalled the same rumor of electrocution at Bełżec discussed in the barbershop: interview with author, October 8, 2010. Electrocution was also mentioned in an official government report, "The Mass Extermination of Jews in German Occupied Poland," Republic of Poland Ministry of Foreign Affairs Report to the United Nations, December 10, 1942, reprinted in Andrzej Kunert, ed., *Polacy-Żydzi, 1939–1945: wybór źródeł* (Warsaw: Oficyna Wydawnicza Rytm, 2006).

murdered Jews." Perhaps in that B. there is a soap factory, made from human flesh—people say various things. Until recently I experienced heart contractions every time the B. word [Bełżec] was mentioned. Today I write about it, and the pen does not fall from my hand.[17]

JANUARY 27

A month after that "action," the next one took place, at the same time as the one in Złoczów. Złoczów fell short of its quota by about 200 victims, and Przemyślany was supposed to provide them. I was then in the country, among friendly people. My good friend Dr. G., together with his wife and child, was taken away.[18] To the last day, he studied English with the enthusiasm of a youth while his wife and child suffered utter destitution and misery. They were caught in the woods by one of their best friends, G. [Grinblot or Grunblat], who—it must be admitted—was accompanied by the militia. After the victims had been taken away, the uneasiness did not subside. In view of the small number of deportees led to slaughter, those who remained alive feared a repetition. Had 2,000 been taken away instead of 200, they would have undoubtedly felt safer.

---

17. The word "Bełżec" was added by pencil in different handwriting, most likely by Jacob Litman. Remains of Holocaust victims were used in experiments and processed for other applications. For example, human hair was used to produce felt slippers for the German navy, as well as insulation materials. Human fat was tested as another by-product, but Chief of the SS and of the German Police Heinrich Himmler disapproved of its use as soap. Despite Himmler's disapproval, the "soap" rumor became the most commonly cited example of the horrific scientism and criminality of the Nazi genocide. Bełżec was one of three gassing facilities specially constructed as of October 1941 in occupied Poland with the sole purpose of exterminating Jews. The Jews in wartime Ukraine who were murdered in stationary facilities (not mobile gas vans) were mostly deported from eastern Galicia to Bełżec as of March 1942. Jews from Przemyślany began arriving there in the late summer of 1942. When Bełżec was shut down at the end of 1942, at least 434,000 Jews had been killed there. Witte and Tyas, "A New Document," 468–86; Yitzhak Arad, *Belzec, Sobibor, Treblinka: The Operation Reinhard Death Camps* (Bloomington: Indiana University Press, 1987); Dariusz Libionka, ed., *Akcja Reinhardt. Zagłada Żydów w Generalnym Gubernatorstwie* (Warsaw: Instytut Pamięci Narodowej, 2004); Bogdan Musial, ed., *"Aktion Reinhardt": Der Völkermord an den Juden im Generalgouvernement 1941–1944* (Osnabrück: Fibre, 2004).

18. Dr. Arthur Gabel was a respected lawyer in town. Survivor Stella Schneider Baum remembered that Dr. Gabel and Dr. Katz visited her home; they were friendly with her father, Frederick Schneider, who was a well-known dentist in town. Telephone interview, August 24, 2005, Fort Lee, New Jersey. Another survivor from the town, Gisela Gross, worked with Dr. Gabel in his law office. When the Soviets occupied the region in 1939, they shut down her Jewish school. Instead of attending another school, Gisela went to work for Dr. Gabel. Interview with Gisela Gross Gelin, October 14, 2005, Baltimore.

The Jewish militia also played a prominent part in the "action." After the completed "job," the Jewish Council gave the "heroes" a party paid for by the families of the murdered.

JANUARY 27

And so, again 2 months of "peace" passed, interrupted by Job-like reports of mass killings in Warsaw, Kraków, Stanisławów, Lwów, until the ghetto was formed.[19] It was preceded by the resettlement of Jews from the countryside into the towns. The number of Jewish militiamen parading with their rubber truncheons was increased fivefold. The trapped Jews of the vicinity paid fantastic sums to the Jewish C[ouncil] and the militia for living quarters, knowing that they were getting shelter for a few days only. "We are paying slaughter fees," they said with tears in their eyes. At last, all were crammed into narrow, dirty huts, into spat-upon holes. After the ghetto had been sealed, an SS commander named Ludwig arrived from Lwów on an inspection tour. He surveyed the fenced-in ghetto with satisfaction, saluted the Jewish militiamen guarding the exit, and then drove away. Two days later a slaughter took place in which 2,400 people perished, 600 of whom were killed on the spot in the ghetto.[20]

I spent the night preceding the slaughter outside the ghetto at the home of a friendly Ukrainian, Mr. H.[21] Shots woke us up in the morning. My host, who only

19. "Job-like" refers to the biblical story of Job, whose faith in God was tested through a series of painful losses and ordeals. References to Job's suffering were common among both Polish and Jewish writers (religious and secular) at the time.

20. Herr Ludwig was identified as head of the Gestapo in the SD office in Złoczów in the testimony of survivor Salomon Altman (Haifa, 1959) and former deputy district captain in Złoczów Gerhard von Jordan; see BAL 162/19244 (II ar Nr. 1422/1966). The exact date of the ghetto formation varies in the testimony between May and October 1942. Litman dates it in early spring 1942, "when the snow began to melt"; see Jacob Litman, *Autobiography*, 41. But other towns in the area formed ghettos in the first half of 1942; see Pohl, *Nationalsozialistische Judenverfolgung in Ostgalizien*, 157, 158, 258. The Przemyślany ghetto was relatively "open" in the sense that its perimeter was defined by certain streets forming a Jewish district; no wall was erected, but in parts barbed wire fencing marked off the area. Police patrolled its perimeter. See video testimony of Ida K., 1996, West Orange, New Jersey, interview code 20097, tape 1, segment 33, USC Shoah Foundation Institute for Visual History and Education. To prepare for its final liquidation, Higher SS and Police Leader for the Generalgouvernement (HSSPF) Friedrich-Wilhelm Krüger ordered that Jewish ghettos in Poland, including the Przemyślany ghetto, be completely sealed by December 1, 1942. At this time, there were about three thousand Jews living there, among them Samuel Golfard. German polices forces arrived from Złoczów on the night of December 4 and surrounded the ghetto. Nearly all of its inhabitants were sent to Bełżec on December 5, 1942.

21. Here and elsewhere in the diary, Golfard uses first initials, presumably to conceal the full names and identities of those who might be endangered, should his diary fall into German hands during the war.

recently assured me that in case of peril I may always count on him, firmly showed me the door. I did not protest. I left, wading in knee-deep snow until I reached a cave on the so-called tragic, "livid stone."[22] There I remained for half a day. Very few people escaped from the ghetto. Toward evening I started on my way back, but a glare in the sky made me turn around. The ghetto stood in flames.

JANUARY 28

The course of this "action" was quite different. To be sure, it was preceded by seemingly absurd rumors about a Jewish police unit called a "Rollbrigade,"[23] whose task was to purge several towns of Jews, among them Jaworów and Sądowa Wisznia. No one, however, believed that such a band existed, though it was seen at work in Przemyślany. At its head stood a certain Golliger, a bandit from Lwów who used to be a flour merchant. He commanded a band of 80 people who carried out the worst slaughters together with G.[24]

---

22. The original text is partially illegible, but Golfard uses the word "livid" to describe the rocky face of the cave, referring to its bruised, ashen hues.

23. A special commando of Jewish police was sent out from Lviv to Bóbrka and Jaworów in April 1943 to assist with the ghetto liquidations; see Pohl, *Nationalsozialistische Judenverfolgung in Ostgalizien*, 254, citing Isaiah Trunk, *Judenrat*, 514. The German term that Samek used, *Rollbrigade*, was not very common in the language and terminology of the Nazi occupation apparatus. Perhaps he confused it with *Totenbrigade* (death brigade). It seems to refer to a mobile unit with a specific task, in this case nonstationary Jewish police forces deployed in the area to assist with ghetto liquidations. It is also similar to the term *Rollkommando*, such as the Rollkommando Hamann, a unit of Lithuanian auxiliaries that assisted one German killing unit (*Einsatzkommando* 3) in mass shootings. For Rollkommando Hamann, see Knut Stang, "Kollaboration und Völkermord: Das Rollkommando Hamann und die Vernichtung der litauischen Juden," in *Die Gestapo im zweiten Weltkrieg: "Heimatfront und besetztes Europa,"* ed. Gerhard Paul and Klaus-Michael Mallmann (Darmstadt: Primus, 2000), 464–80.

24. *G.* could refer to Gestapo or again to Golliger, which seems more likely. The Golliger family had many branches in Galicia, and one was indeed in the flour business in Lviv; some resided in Przemyślany itself. Most of the family, however, was deported to gassing centers such as Bełżec or died in the camps and ghettos of the region. See Alexander Beider, ed., *A Dictionary of Jewish Surnames from Galicia* (Bergenfeld: Avotaynu Publishers, 2004), 229. As Jacob Litman writes in his assessment of the "Golliger gang," "there is no evidence of its actual existence." Litman believes that the gang was a German invention "designed to intensify fear among Jews." Descendants in Israel and the United States who were contacted about Golfard's claim stated that they had no knowledge of this gang or their family members' involvement in the Jewish police. In the town of Przemyślany, there were about ten stationary Jewish policemen supporting the Jewish Council and "keeping order" in the ghetto for the Germans. At least one Jewish policeman named Kleinmann survived the war, according to Ivan Fuglevych; interview with Vladimir Melamed, July 25, 2005.

I returned to the ghetto the next day at dawn, after spending the night in the woods, and found a ghastly sight. Corpses with broken skulls and black faces stiffened by the frost covered the marketplace. Next to each corpse, a bloodstain reddened the snow. Not far from the burnt-down buildings there were charred corpses of women. In front of my eyes someone choking with tears was carrying a suffocated child.

I walked through the ghetto holding back my sobbing. From all sides came a wailing that penetrated the marrow of one's bones. Children who escaped were coming back to find that their parents or siblings had been murdered. Survivors who had jumped the train were wandering about with a lost look in their eyes. I saw an old woman of 75 who had jumped from the running train. The faces of all who escaped from the train looked like faces of knocked-out boxers: their heads broken by the fall, black blotches instead of eyes, cut lips, sooty noses, blackened ears. Those survivors came from Brzeżany, Narajewo, and other towns. Human shreds, they left all their most valuable possessions in the train.[25]

Near my place, a father bewailed the loss of his two children, an 18-year-old son, who had been dragged out from a hiding place and shot on the spot, and a 16-year-old daughter. He was talking deliriously, half-conscious. He had been in town only 3 days with his 2 children. Now, left alone, he and his wife stood in front of the house recounting their tragedy to every passerby. He told me in confidence that he had strangled someone's 2-year-old baby in their hiding place, fearing that its crying would betray them. "God's punishment came upon me," he kept saying. When I saw him 2 days later, he was very sick with typhus fever. In his delirious state, he kept mentioning the name of a child, and his fingers would stiffen. My attention was turned to a corpse of a young boy of 14–16 years. He was lying with his face in the snow near a mass of coagulated blood. He had run into the street when his shelter had been discovered. Realizing that there was nowhere for him to hide, he dropped next to another corpse and buried his face in the snow. He lay there, seemingly saved, till 2 o'clock. At that time a Gestapo man passed by. The lack of blood at the boy's side seemed suspicious to him. He turned over the boy with a kick and began lashing his face with a rubber truncheon until the unfortunate youngster blinked his eyes, not having uttered even a yelp of pain. A bullet in the head put a final end to the martyr's young life. Infants who had been left home were shot mercilessly. Whoever refused to go to the assembly place was shot on the spot. The Gestapo men carried out the killing while the Jewish militiamen of the

---

25. For a detailed history of the Holocaust in Brzeżany, see Redlich, *Together and Apart in Brzezany*.

Golliger gang and the locals routed the hiding places with an exceptional eagerness, looting at every opportunity and taking money for allegedly saving lives.[26]

The removal of corpses along with stripping bodies of their garments and money lasted more than a week. The Jewish militia lacked no volunteers to carry out this job.

It is difficult to describe the Dantean scenes that took place during the slaughter. But they pale in significance when compared with the horror of those who, having been loaded like cattle, traveled to the place of execution fully aware of the inevitable. People who escaped from the train related that many old Jews, having collectively recited their last prayers, awaited the end quite calmly. They submitted to God's will and refused to jump. I know a lady who, having been brought to the train station together with her daughter, managed to redeem the latter with a stupendous sum of money and, when put on the train herself, swallowed a prepared dose of cyanic acid. She put an end to her life in a manner envied by all others, for not everybody, few indeed, could afford such an easy death. Before the "action" the price of a dose of poison was exorbitant.

A number of people came back from the freight cars, which they had broken open. Many, however, perished during their escape from bullets of the Gestapo men present, who traveled along in adjoining cars. The escapees came back seriously ill, virtually incapable of the slightest effort. Children, pushed out through tiny freight car windows by mothers who themselves could not escape, wandered around helplessly. Beaten, tormented, the unfortunates returned. Despite these tragedies, in comparison to which Job's tragedy seems trifling, there was everywhere a will to exist, to endure against all odds. I recall some people telling me that what made them jump from the train was the lack of air and the terror of suffocating in a crammed car. During the summertime "actions," people in the cars tore off their clothes and underwear. Some of them escaped completely naked. Many a railcar reached the unknown place of execution with only corpses left aboard.

On the day following the terrible "slaughter," one of the local German gendarmes named Dorn came to the office of the Jewish C[ouncil].[27] By mistake he went into private quarters and there found three train escapees and 2 old

---

26. According to testimony collected in the Stuttgart case, SS officer Karl Wöbke was sent from Lwów to lead a ghetto massacre in Peremyshliany in December 1942, and in the December "action" he was seen shooting a Jewish boy, whom he left on the ghetto street. See the indictment, March 10, 1965, case 12 J S 1464/61, pp. 53–54 (USHMMA, RG 17.003M, reel 98).

27. The reputation of this brutal gendarme who caroused with the locals was corroborated by survivor Gisela Gross Gelin: interviews of October 14, 2005, and November 3, 2005, Baltimore.

men from a well-known family in Przemyślany. Where were you yesterday—he yelled, killing all of them with 5 shots. Then he calmly proceeded to the Jewish C[ouncil] to issue an order. I saw him recently at the home of a certain lady to whom he came to get vodka. She simpered at him, she drank with him happily. My foot will never again step into her house.

JANUARY 29

And a period of calm came again. In the face of all these calamities, my own pain subsided. I forgot about my sister for a few days. People slowly returned to life. Not too long afterwards, while the blood still stained the pavement, I witnessed a fierce argument over a few wooden planks that a poor old man pulled from someone's fence to heat his hovel, perhaps for the first time. Brawls started over stolen things, people accusing one another of robbery. Children bustle again in the ghetto streets with matches and candles for sale. Cakes are being baked again. It is impossible to satisfy the demand. The price of everything went down. People allow themselves extravagances. They do not make provisions for the winter. The militia is drinking with stolen money. A fever has taken hold of everyone.

But this too came to a stop. Two weeks without an "action" sufficed for people to delude themselves again that a remnant will be saved. Rumors spread that killings had been called off as of January 15 because the Allies intervened on behalf of the Jews through diplomatic channels. The Germans gave assurances that whoever lives to see the year 1943 will survive the war, since a completely new course, a sort of amnesty, is to ensue.

JANUARY 29

Over 6 months have passed since the loss of my sister.[28] Until now nothing could soothe my pain. I am able to laugh with people. They even consider my disposition as cheerful. But when I am alone, I am often seized by spasms. I constantly see my sister on the gray pavement at the assembly place. Her screaming still rings in my ears.

I received a communication from my [other] sister in Radom. She sent me a package with clothing. I considered her lost together with the others. I accepted this seemingly very happy communication with a dismal indifference. There was no thrill of joy in my heart, though I love my light-haired Belutka

---

28. This statement is puzzling. Golfard refers to his sister's departure in the context of a wave of deportations that began in August 1942, but "over six months" prior to the dating of this January entry would mean that her deportation occurred in July 1942.

very much. Of all my sisters she is the only one who is alive, ~~When she was~~ but who knows for how long. I realized then that genuine joy had abandoned me forever. ~~comes back from~~

I am afraid of what will be after the war, when I shall be allowed to spend the balance of my life, in peace. I dread it just as I dread the loneliness today. The fear of life pushes aside the hardest sufferings. But I know that they rule over me entirely. And maybe this is why good news from the front and predictions of our speedy victory do not make me happy.

The reports are better again and again as the German bulletins become desperate. Their garrison at Stalingrad—they say—is defending itself "convulsively."

JANUARY 30

And again, "action." It began in Lwów. Not long ago the ghetto delivered a "quota" of 5,000 people. Every day dozens of people disappear. Jewish workers are going to work under escort. The end of Lwów is near, someone told me who stayed there several days. Even the lovely cemetery of Lwów, with its monuments of renowned scholars, artists, and Polish patriots, has not been spared. Artistic marble reaching back several centuries and historic statues are shattered by Jewish martyrs in camps and made into gravel to be put under German wheels lubricated with the blood of subjugated peoples.

An eyewitness related what happened in Jaryczów Nowy. Its ghetto had been surrounded under the pretext that typhus fever prevailed there. The well of the ghetto dried up. People paid 20 złoty for a pail of water from the outside. No wonder typhus fever broke out. Owing to a denunciation by the local physicist and the bailiff, a mass pogrom was organized, and the entire Jewish population slaughtered. Corpses are still laying there on the streets. Such a terror fell upon the town that nobody dared to loot.[29]

JANUARY 30

I am constantly writing about the martyrdom of the Jews. ~~I cannot~~ [illeg.] ~~about~~ But I know that not only we are suffering. In the camps the flower of the Polish nation is perishing. Millions of Poles in Germany do the work of hard labor convicts. Tens of thousands have perished in camps. Suffering hunger and disease, the whole nation gives itself with blood for the "contribution." Children

---

29. The massacre of two thousand Jews shot in Jaryczów Nowy on January 15, 1943, is mentioned in Pohl, *Nationalsozialistische Judenverfolgung in Ostgalizien*, 249.

are torn away from their mothers. Fourteen-year-old girls carry out the hardest jobs as farmhands on German farmsteads. The [Polish] nation in bondage is carrying a heavy yoke. But not for a moment does the nation lose hope that freedom and the fatherland will be restored. Such hope has been taken away from the Jews, and this is why their fate is so tragic, why it is so difficult to last through every death-branded day. They envy the Poles and rightfully so. Moreover, they bear a grudge against the Poles for not being fellow sufferers in misery and brothers in misfortune. They forget that the Polish nation is defenseless. Reports arrived from the province of Lublin about the murder of [Polish] peasants who refused to be resettled. There are more gloomy and bloody reports from the Zamość area.[30] I talked with a fine Polish woman about the murder of elderly Polish men in Lwów. ~~Life of someone old~~ Heartbroken as she was, she had to accept it and return to her daily business. She shared the same anguish for the Jewish victims. The thing of greatest consequence is that there is general passivity dictated by weakness. No one can save his neighbor. Everyone's life is threatened. And if in a moment of great danger somebody is in a position to save the life of someone else, he cannot do so while being in ghastly fear for his own life. However, there are even such people who, endangering their own lives, hide and save Jews. And the Jew today is, after all, lower than a stray dog.

~~I was sorry~~ Perhaps there also are those who in the face of the massacres think, not without a certain satisfaction, that the Germans render a service to Poland by clearing it of Jews. I believe there are few such people. I heard that at the time of the last "action," which took place in sight of the population, very respectable Poles, and undoubtedly great patriots, were playing chess with utter indifference. But even if that were true, I would not blame them. Two days after the "action," when the corpses were still lying on the streets, I was wooing a

---

30. According to Heinrich Himmler, Zamość and nearby Lublin, Poland, were central areas for carrying out a master plan of colonization. The region was designated a major settlement area for Reich and ethnic Germans (*Volksdeutsche*) and would be renamed Himmlerstadt. To "Germanize" the area, SS, police, and civil administrators deported 110,000 Poles (including 30,000 children) and tens of thousands of Jews. Resettled ethnic Germans were placed on the vacated farms. To facilitate this program, agencies of the SS police utilized concentration camps, ghettos, and killing centers in the area (among the best-known are the Lublin ghetto, Majdanek, and Auschwitz), which were used to "dispose of" the unwanted Jews and Poles and enforce a system of forced labor. See Richard C. Lukas and Norman Davies, *Forgotten Holocaust: The Poles under German Occupation, 1939–1944*, 2nd ed. (London: Hippocrene Books, 2001); and Elizabeth White, "Majdanek: Cornerstone of Himmler's SS Empire in the East," *Simon Wiesenthal Center Annual* 7 (1993): 3–21; Helena Kubica, *The Extermination at KL Auschwitz of Poles Evicted from the Zamość Region in the Years 1942–1943* (Oświęcim: Auschwitz-Birkenau State Museum, 2006).

woman with whom I had gotten acquainted and who, having lost her parents and siblings, was left alone. The bourgeois Jews were refusing a little warm food to small orphans. Black marketeers kept profiting from the fall of food prices. Money speculators kept purchasing currency. Bakers were again baking pastry. Everybody's pain was personal and related only to the loss of very dear ones. An "action" in another town casts fear on local Jews only if it also threatens them. The national tragedy is overshadowed by personal dramas.

The out-and-out fact is that in the present situation the Jews cannot count on anybody. Their fate is sealed.

JANUARY 30

Yesterday they were seizing people to be taken to the camp [*lager*] in Kurowice. About 100 were captured, but 34 were actually sent. It hardly made any impression on the population, with time got used to [it]. Prior to the "actions" everybody was shocked by the roundups. Today names of new camp inmates are not even mentioned. These are new nameless martyrs.

Jaktorów camp, 1942–1943. This rare photograph of the camp where Golfard was a prisoner shows the camp watchtower and long stables where Jews were housed (USHMMPA WS# 61154, courtesy of the Institute of National Memory, Poland). Compare this wartime photograph with the ones on page 73.

SS and police chief Heinrich Himmler during an inspection tour of the labor camps in Galicia, August 1942.[31] Pictured in the photograph are Heinrich Himmler (see x by his feet), Friedrich Warzok (on his left), and in the last row on the far left Friedrich Katzmann. Katzmann's original German caption for this photograph was "The SS men were delighted when in 1942 the Reichsführer [Himmler] personally visited some camps along the main supply route [*Rollbahn*]." The photograph was included in Katzman's report (see pp. 101–106) (USHMMPA WS# 82795, courtesy of the Institute of National Memory, Poland).

There are two camps in the close vicinity of Przemyślany [P.], in Kurowice and in Jaktorów.[32] A little farther there is one in Lacki and another in Mitulin.

---

31. His trip included stops in at least two Jewish labor camps, Jaktorów and Lackie. Peter Witte et al., eds., *Der Dienstkalender Heinrich Himmlers 1941/42* (Hamburg: Christians, 1999), 522n75.

32. Kurowice and Jaktorów were part of a series of labor camps assigned to road construction in the area. The German plan was to complete a new highway or major thoroughfare that would stretch eastward from Lviv to Rostov-on-Don (the foothills of the Caucasus Mountains). The camps were managed by SS and police and private firms that held contracts for the road construction. The chief of the labor camp administration for the district of Złoczów (including Przemyślany) was Friedrich Warzok. By early 1942, thirteen of the fifteen labor camps in the region that had been set up were dedicated to road construction. The camps of Jaktorów, Kurowice, Złoczów, and Lacki had the highest mortality rates. The commandant of Kurowice was Ernst Epple, a name that still evokes horror among the locals, who recount how he left victims hanging from trees across from their local church. Fritz

These camps have already consumed thousands of victims, but they are not yet sated with human blood. Of all these camps, I know Jaktorów the best, and in the literal meaning, as torture. I was kept there only two weeks and each day was true hell.

The camp is located in former farmstead buildings. It takes up a large tract surrounded by a wall. The huge farmyard is divided with barbed wire. On one side there is a wide one-story building, the headquarters of the camp commandant and the Ukrainian militia; on the other side, the barracks consisting of three camp halls. Nearby, a kitchen, small infirmary, and a disinfection building.

We were then over 300 of us from Gliniany, Przemyślany, Jaworów, Dunajew, Sądowa Wisznia, and remnants from Stanisławów. Only a few remained from Stanisławów; they survived by working in the kitchen. When they were brought from Stanisławów, the camp commandant shot 150 of them at the first screening, the rest perished gradually, with only 5–6 remaining. A similar tragedy took place in Sądowa Wisznia, from which all men capable of working were taken. When I arrived, only 12 of the original 116 remained. The same fate was shared by the men from Jaworów. A common grave in the nearby woods is their tomb.

If there is someone of the Jaktorów martyrs still alive, he will remember the bloody Sunday in August. It was a day free from work. Following the morning roll call, a cleaning of clothes and underwear was ordered. The day was sunny. Everyone began cleaning and dusting their clothes. Suddenly the commandant

---

Katzmann, who referred to Kurowice as a "model camp," was also alarmed by the potential repercussions of Epple's behavior. An underground flyer of the Soviet communist resistance publicized Epple's behavior, calling on locals to resist the Germans (see document 4 in part III of this volume). Epple was transferred to the front with a Waffen SS unit in 1943; his replacement was Karl Kempka. Kempka was known for his drunkenness and wild shooting into the barracks. He personally shot the camp elder, Rothenberg, and his family when Kurowice was liquidated in July–August 1943. The number of Jews at the Kurowice labor camp was three to four hundred, of whom about 10 percent were women. German camp personnel numbered about five, supported by a few dozen Ukrainian guards. Testimonies of former prisoners Moses Gruengarten, August 25, 1947; Zosia Gruder, December 31, 1947; and Samuel Mueller, January 22, 1953, in the investigation of Karl Kempke, Landesgericht Vienna, Vg 80 Vr 292/52 (USHMMA RG 17.003M, reel 98). Crimes of the German and Ukrainian police, including names of Jewish victims, are detailed in the indictment of Epple, BAL 162/19230 (Sammelakte no. 181); the survivor testimony is available in BAL 162/2096 fol. 1 (208 AR-Z 294/59), Staatsanwaltschaft Stuttgart, 12 (10) Js 1460/61. Author's interviews with Kurowice eyewitnesses (translated by Vladimir Melamed), July 24, 2005, Kurowice, Ukraine. See Pohl, *Nationalsozialistische Judenverfolgung in Ostgalizien*, 170, 324, 341. On the liquidation of Kurowice and Jaktorów, see Eliyahu Yones, *Smoke in the Sand: The Jews of Lvov in the War Years, 1939–1944* (New York: Gefen, 2004), 207–9.

appeared. He was in a terrible mood that day. He wore his pajamas, the attire in which he often appeared in the yard in the company of his mistress. Everybody knew that he had been angry since early morning. He woke at five a.m. and, noticing inmates in the yard already pumping water at the well, he fell into a rage and savagely beat our foreman, an engineer from Lwów named Dreksler. The water was pumped every day in the morning from half past four to 6 o'clock for the bathroom of the commandant and the militia. The inmates on duty had to get up at 4:00 in the morning.

That day the commandant disliked that clothes were being cleaned. Having bloodily beaten up the engineer and the group leaders a second time, he ordered another assembly. We were lined up in two rows facing one another, and passing the clothing to one another, we kept dusting them off. This continued for two hours while we were thrashed terribly. Our hands weakened, but apparently the senior SS officers, who just then arrived to inspect the camp, found the sight very much to their taste.

Cleaning straw from the yard [square] followed. With backs bent, 300 inmates picked up the tiniest shred of straw from the ground. Whoever tried to straighten up felt the blows of rubber clubs on his body. This truly Sisyphean labor lasted a full hour.[33]

~~After lunch consisting of soup~~ For lunch, as every day, there was soup made of cabbage leaves without a single potato.

At 4 o'clock, the execution of the so-called simulants began.[34] Our engineer had announced this two days ago. He delivered a bombastic speech and pointed to 8 tottering men, calling them simulants who would be receiving their well-deserved punishment. He spoke ironically of them as "the flower of the nation," "the future of society," and so on, and described their death on the gallows to them: "You will turn like buffoons on a string!" He boasted that it was he who built the barracks and the latrine for the inmates and had now erected the gallows. He announced that, by the order of the commandant, the simulants would now stand in the yard two days and two nights without food and would, on the third day, be executed. And so it happened.

---

33. This refers to the legendary Greek king of Corinth, Sisyphus, who in his afterlife was cursed with the task of rolling a boulder up a hill, only to watch it escape him and roll down again. Here Golfard is stressing that this grueling cleaning of the yard was maddening and pointless.

34. The term "simulant" in this context was a German accusation of fraudulence, of pretending to be sick to avoid work, similar to "malingerer" or "slacker." In fact, camp conditions were so unhealthy that most were physically unable to work or in a weakened state and had to "pretend" to be fit.

I knew the "simulants" personally. They all had feet swollen from hunger and exhaustion. Their bodies—nothing but skin, and on their faces—not a trace of blood. They begged from other inmates and collected bread crumbs from the table. They threw themselves greedily on cucumber peelings and looked with envy upon people eating. Death was written on their faces. They were mostly lonely and poor men without relatives who could help. They were carried back to camp after work. At work they kept fainting. Their number was ever increasing. The other inmates did not like them, did not pity or help them, but spurned and beat them. If it were not for a few sensitive and compassionate people, they would have perished long ago. The camp condemned them to death before it was bound to happen. The physician, a Jew, willy-nilly confirmed they were "simulants," thus carrying out the will of the commandant. He could not keep them in the infirmary because no more than six to eight people could be there. Nor could the infirmary cure them. They were already unfit for work. Such people were called "simulants" destined for torturous deaths.

After two days of starving under a clear sky, the final act of execution took place. All inmates formed a quadrangle facing the gallows. The condemned stood leaning against it. The commandant's assistant, a baby-faced degenerate, arrived. Heinsel from Jaworów, a hangman Jew with a dull butcher's mug, came forward. More candidates, all of them group leaders, volunteered. Among them, one from Stanisławów with a limping foot, which the Germans had shot through in an "action" in Przemyślany, where he had worked as a male nurse in the hospital for contagious diseases. The condemned walked one after another to their death, to their final deliverance from suffering. The execution lasted twenty minutes until the physician declared the function as having been completed. But we were in attendance at this for 100 minutes. The commandant's assistant amused himself with the hanging victims, he kicked them and gazed at their faces imprinted with torture. One of the martyrs from Świrz (sent to camp in a most pitiful state by the Jewish councilman Rajchman, who used to be a film editor and journalist in Warsaw) was able in his last moment of life to lift his arms toward heaven and murmur the prayer said after a death.[35] As for

---

35. The Rajchman family in Warsaw (another branch was in Łódź) was well-known: one member had founded the philharmonic orchestra; another (Ludwik Rajchman) was a diplomat who played an important role at the United Nations after the war. It is possible that the person in charge of the *Judenrat* was indeed related to them; however, most members of the Rajchman family around Warsaw were deported to Treblinka. The fate of the *Judenrat* elder mentioned here is unknown. Golfard does not use the term *kaddish* here, the Jewish prayer recited to mark a death; it is possible he heard a prayer affirming the man's faith instead.

the others, their fingers stiffened convulsively, their shoulders trembled, the eyes bulged out of their sockets, and the feet straightened in deadly spasms. After that, the lifeless bodies of martyrs swung around [*sic*] the rope. They had gone to their deaths without fear, stepping by themselves on the stool and throwing the loop around their necks. There was little for the hangmen to do.

That day a father died ~~the son at the last moment~~ while his son stood in line and had to witness everything in silence. He begged that his father be spared. But they allowed him only to take his father's jacket and cap. Then the inmates in line had to bury the corpses. I saw how one of them, with a prayer on his lips, removed the corpses from the gallows and then volunteered to bury them. During the execution many fainted, and some remained unconscious for a long while.[36]

Following the conclusion of the action, we headed for the kitchen, stood in line for coffee, and as usual quarrels broke out about places in line.

I was on fire. I went to my bunk and lay there with my eyes open until dawn.

JANUARY 30

I spent two weeks in that camp [Jaktorów]. But beyond that which I have described above, the very first day of my camp experience also imprinted itself upon my memory. At 6 o'clock we marched from camp to work at the border of Kurowice, about nine kilometers. Marching out was accompanied by singing. Some rascal put together idiotic words praising the rule of the camp, the kitchen, etc., to the tune of a popular song. Whoever did not sing was looked upon unfavorably by the group leaders. There were also other songs of generally vulgar content sung for the enjoyment of the Ukrainian militia. (One time, we returned to camp with a song on our lips and marched by a corpse hanging on the gallows.)

The first day began with pushing wheelbarrows full of gravel. The German foreman lay his eyes on me. As I was pushing my wheelbarrow, he beat me over my back and shaven skull at the slightest pretext. It was forbidden to look

---

36. Both this particular incident and the earlier description of the commandant's obsession with cleanliness and abusive behavior are consistent with the testimonies presented in the investigation and trial of former commandants Grzimek and Fox. See records of the Lviv trial ("Lemberg Prozess") in Stuttgart in 1968 and video interviews conducted by the USC Shoah Foundation. One survivor, Leon S. (b. 1915), was in the camp with Golfard. See his interview, 1996, La Canada, California, interview code 21004, USC Shoah Foundation Institute for Visual History and Education.

back or to let go of the wheelbarrow, for then he could kill on the spot. The only way out was to speed up one's step while fainting and numb hands hardly held up the fully loaded wheelbarrow. He kept beating me with a branch until noon, save for short intervals, and then chose other victims for himself. While lashing, he laughed like a happy child at play. Many other Germans behaved in this same peculiar fashion. Apparently, maltreating people provided a sadistic delight and relieved their naturally criminal inclinations.

A few days later I was reported by a Ukrainian militiaman together with six other men. I was working earnestly that day, piling up rocks, and did not dare lift my head to rest in the infernal heat. Nevertheless, he put me down, undoubtedly to extort a pair of pants or a pullover from me. But I could not promise or provide him with anything. At the evening assembly, after a day of terrible labor, I received, in front of the assembled camp, 25 blows. I was forced to lie down. Two hangmen who always assisted at executions held my head and feet, and two militiamen beat me with cudgels. I did not feel anything at the outset, only blunt blows. I did not realize that I was screaming. It seemed to me that the cries did not emanate from my mouth, for I had decided not to utter a sound. But the inmates told me that I had screamed frightfully. I slept on my stomach six nights in a row. I writhed during the nights re-experiencing palpably but silently the blows of the cudgel.

A few days later they hanged my companion at work, a likable boy from Chlebowice, because he fainted on the job from lack of food. In spite of his previous twelve-month stay in camp at Kurowice, he had not lost the sensitivity of a human being. He helped me at work, and I reciprocated as well as I could. He had been sent to camp a second time by Mr. Rajchman from Świrz. Not long after that, Rajchman deported a dental technician to the camp in whose house he had found hospitality. Now he is sleeping in his host's bed.

JANUARY 31

Not only was every day like a day spent in hell. At nighttime, too, the weary inmates were not allowed to rest. When lying on our boards dozing or half asleep, the militia with the assistant to Foks [Fox], the camp commander, often descended upon us like dogs to check the cleanliness of our feet.[37] Everyone had to show his feet, and if they did not pass the test of cleanliness, our feet received terrible blows. Moreover, the "delinquent" was compelled to get off the boards in his underwear and walk through the courtyard, under the blows of

---

37. For more on Paul Fox, see Biographies.

militiamen arranged in a cordon of two rows, to the so-called bathroom. The most careful washing was to no avail. Back on the boards the feet were wiped with wet towels, but if one's feet were cracked from working and walking barefoot, one was exposed to beatings every time. I was spared this suffering. My feet were as white as my hands because I always walked in shoes.

At times we were awakened by fights in which inmates themselves administered their justice to thieves. Acts of stealing increased beyond measure. The very first day when I got my quarter of a bread loaf, it was snatched from under my nose while I sat down to drink the coffee. I do not blame the thieves from the camp. For most of them it was a way of saving their lives for another day, another week. Moreover, those who had more would not share it with the needy. Some bourgeois lordlings, who would not eat the camp soup, sold it rather than give it to the beggars. If one collapsed near death, no one would move to help with a sip of milk. Inmates' hearts hardened and the most obdurate, stripped of any human tenderness or generosity, were some young, well-fed, healthy boys. But there were a few 14-year-old children among us who were wasting away in front of our eyes.

A general bestiality became dominant. I was struck by the fact that older people in their fifties used the most vulgar language. I brought this to the attention of an elderly inmate while walking in line with him to work. He reminded me of my father, and I wondered whether my father could be like that. He told me, weeping plaintively, that since his stay in camp, he had ceased to be himself, descending every day lower and lower because one could not endure being here otherwise.

Jaktorów was a camp for Jews. There were no Poles here, as in the Lacki camp. I got to know the very lowest depths of life here, the Jewish and human psyche [illeg.]. I saw with my own eyes what man may become. I became convinced that there is no and has never been any racial solidarity among Jews. Instead, here in [the] camp a solidarity of the rich and a solidarity of the poor existed, a solidarity of the sated and a solidarity of the hungry. But in the midst of great misfortune one actually remained alone; fear for one's life erased all noble sentiments and precluded any acts of heroism. Only one kind of heroism existed in the face of death—the heroism of people walking to the gallows without a word of complaint. When I consider it, the thought occurs to me that this heroism has been dictated, possibly, by the fear of physical torment before the angel of death descends to deliver one from hell.

JANUARY 31

~~Today mine~~ Yesterday, 10 years have passed since ~~rule of the regime~~ Hitler's regime seized power. An address by Hitler was expected, but only Goebbels and

In this recent photo of Jaktorów, the balconies mark where the camp commandant had his quarters. From there, Golfard wrote, German camp commandant Paul Fox shot at prisoners in the courtyard below (photograph by Wendy Lower, 2010).

The wartime buildings of the Jaktorów camp remain largely intact, and the site is now used as a state asylum for the mentally ill (photograph by Wendy Lower, 2010).

Goering spoke. We do not know yet exactly what they said.[38] The situation on the front already seems to be quite difficult for the Germans. Apparently, the Casablanca Conference demanded Hitler's and Mussolini's capitulation.[39] I do not attach any great weight to this declaration. The determining events are on the eastern front. The seriousness of the situation is reflected in the German bulletins, which speak about the heroic but hopeless German battles at Stalingrad, about being outnumbered eight or ten times by the Soviets on the Leningrad front, about a planned disengagement from the enemy in the Caucasus, about the massive offensive west of Voronezh. It seems that the African stunt has been in process of liquidation.[40]

Today no one doubts any longer that the Germans will be defeated, not even the Ukrainians and the *Volksdeutsche* [local ethnic Germans], nor even the Germans themselves. When in June of 1941 German officers took leave of one another saying "see you in the Kremlin," there were many among them near despair. There were even some who already foresaw their end at that time. I talked then with a German chauffeur of the Dunkirk group who, repairing to the front, sincerely wished for a defeat and the consequent fall of the regime. He was a German patriot in the best sense of that word.

Ten years [have] passed with this regime in power. During that time the nation of philosophers turned into a nation of murderers who killed defenseless women and children. Slaughter and plunder became the philosophy of their life.

~~On behalf~~ A few million defenseless Jews, millions of harassed workers, millions of soldiers killed in European and African battles—on land, on the sea,

---

38. For the speeches by Reich Minister for Public Enlightenment and Propaganda Dr. Joseph Goebbels (1897–1945) and Reich Marshal Hermann Goering (1893–1946) on January 31, 1943, see document 3 in part III of this volume.

39. During the Casablanca Conference (January 14–24, 1943), the western Allies demanded the unconditional surrender of the Axis powers, agreed to assist the Soviet Union with supplies and decided to open up a southern front by invading Italy. Benito Mussolini (1883–1945) was the leader of the Italian fascist movement, and from 1922 to 1943 the prime minister and dictator of Italy, Nazi Germany's close ally. After Italy's secession from the Axis in the summer of 1943, the Germans kept him in power as head of a fascist rump state (Republic of Saló) until April 1945, when he was captured and executed by Italian resistance fighters.

40. Golfard uses irony here to indicate that the Germans' campaign in Africa was winding up (they were losing). German forces were pushed out of El Alamein and then Tripoli between October 1942 and February 1943. On the major battles in the east and important turning points in the war, such as the battle for Stalingrad in the winter of 1942–1943, see Gerhard Weinberg, *A World at Arms: A Global History of World War II* (Cambridge: Cambridge University Press, 1994); and Earl F. Ziemke, *Stalingrad to Berlin: The German Defeat in the East* (Washington, DC: Office of the Chief of Military History, U.S. Army, 1968).

and in the air—that is the balance sheet of the regime destined to destroy the German people and to burden it with a testimony of an immense and everlasting infamy.

JANUARY 31

In the face of millions of victims, I do not know whether I should mention the tragedy that just took place in the nearby village of Janczyn. Yesterday the news arrived that the Jewish families who had stayed there by virtue of a permit from the rural Commissar were delivered by the Ukrainian militia to Lwów, where they were all shot. Among them, three families from Przemyślany fell— the Alwaglows [Alwaylows?], the Zimmers, and the Hochbergs.[41] They all had permits to stay in the village. The rural Commissar [*Landkommissar*] himself intervened by phone on their behalf, without success. For two months these families had tried to live legally in the village, in accordance with German law, and now had paid for it with their lives.

The other day the priest Kowcz [Kovch] was taken away, apparently to the Janowska camp in Lwów.[42] No one knows why. But I mention him with

41. Frida Hochberg survived and provided testimony to Yad Vashem on behalf of rescuer Tadeusz Jankiewicz (see excerpts in document 11, part III of this book). Hochberg endured the Jaktorów camp and the Peremyshliany ghetto. While hiding in the forest, she witnessed Jankiewicz bringing food in baskets to Litman and other Jews. She explained that Jankiewicz pretended to be picking mushrooms and would crouch down and secretly place food under shrubs and bushes for the refugee Jews, who relied almost entirely on whatever he left for them. See Document G, Righteous Among the Nations Department, Yad Vashem, folder 158, Tadeusz Jankiewicz. A relative of Frida, Izio (Yehuda) Hochberg, organized escapes to the forest from the ghetto in 1943. See Jones, *Smoke in the Sand*, 311.

42. For more on Omelian Kovch, see Biographies and Anna Maria Kovch-Baran [Kowcz-Baran], *For God's Truth and Human Rights*, ed. Emil and Olena Baran (1994; Ottawa: Baran, 2006). Kovch's activities are also mentioned in Friedman, "Ukrainian-Jewish Relations," 176–208. On the role of the Catholic Church in the rescue of Jews in Poland and Ukraine, see Ewa Kurek, *Your Life Is Worth Mine: How Polish Nuns Saved Hundreds of Jewish Children in German-Occupied Poland, 1939–1945*, with an introduction by Jan Karski (New York: Hippocrene, 1997); Andrii Krawchuk, *Christian Social Ethics in Ukraine: The Legacy of Andrei Sheptytsky* (Toronto: Canadian Institute of Ukrainian Studies Press, 1997); and Peter Potichnyj and Howard Aster, eds., *Ukrainian-Jewish Relations in Historical Perspective* (Edmonton: Canadian Institute of Ukrainian Studies, University of Alberta, 1998). Rescue of Jews by priests and monks in the Lviv region is documented in the papers of Kurt I. Lewin (son of Rabbi Lewin), who was assisted by the Sheptytsky brothers; see USHMMA Acc. 1997.A.0076, Kurt I. Lewin collection. The Janowska camp was located on Janowska Street on the outskirts of Lwów (Lviv). Janowska was established in September 1941 as a forced labor camp where mostly Jews did armaments-related work.

a genuine feeling of sympathy because he offered baptism to many despairing Jews, giving them a possibility to save themselves, doing so without ceremony, *in articulo mortis*, and without any remuneration, which in itself is quite exceptional nowadays.[43] And he baptized openly despite the fact that the authorities prohibited this. He responded to this matter with deep understanding, showing a rare nobleness. I remember his words at the time of the act. He stripped illusions and emphasized the difficulties. He discouraged. He did not, however, reject the hope of rescue and thereby gained many converts. In these terrible times, this priest measured up to the enormity of the task. One cannot say the same about so many other clergymen.

Baptism became the last, if quite illusory, lifeline that Jews grasped in their mortal dread of the ghetto. Among the converted were god-fearing old Jewish men, old Jewish women, as well as little children, but mainly women. One invoked the times of the Spanish Inquisition and utilized the remedy used in the Middle Ages to stifle the fanaticism [illeg.] and allay the cruelty of the crusaders. However, the modern barbarians are themselves blasphemers whom the word of God does not reach.

The converted Jews live in the ghetto. Only a small percentage, mainly the village girls whose looks are definitely nonsemitic, move around freely. They go to church and pray fervently. They are Catholic and will never return to Judaism [*żydostwo*]. Some of the girls volunteered to go to Germany as part of the [labor] "contingent," where they share the fate of millions of other foreign workers carrying their national dramas imprinted with blood in their hearts.

It later served as a transit camp for Jews and other prisoners sent to killing centers in Poland. The liquidation of the camp began in November 1943, when members of the SS and police charged with hiding all traces of Nazi atrocities (Commando 1005) brutally killed thousands of prisoners held there. See Leon Weliczker Wells, *Death Brigade (The Janowska Road)* (New York: Holocaust Library, 1978). A few of the German SS and police at Janowska were tried after the war in Stuttgart, Germany, at the Lemberg Trial of 1961. The senior commander of this camp, Friedrich Warzok (mentioned in Golfard's diary as Warzuk), was last seen in March 1945 and was rumored to have fled to Cairo after the war. See BAL Stuttgart Trial Materials (StA Stgt: 2 Js 61533/97); and Pohl, *Nationalsozialistische Judenverfolgung in Ostgalizien*, 422.

43. The Latin phrase *in articulo mortis*, meaning "at point of death," is commonly associated with the history of indulgences (remission for one's temporal sins) granted just before death. A more cynical view of Kovch was offered by Samuel Golfard's friend, Jacob Litman, who described him as "a simple priest who meant to let Jews reach the other world as saved Christians rather than as cursed Jews." See introductory comments by Jacob Litman in his English translation of the Golfard diary, *Samek's Testimony* (1983), 15, USHMMA Acc. 2008.316, Litman family collection.

FEBRUARY 1, 1943

A month has passed again. Those who will endure will know perfectly well what such a period of time means in our life, they will be able to give testimony. One is in touch with death every moment, one trifles with it. It has become an everyday game, like bitter daily bread.

~~I work in~~ Every day I meet Poles outside the ghetto. A sort of friendship has even brought me close to one Polish family.[44] Mrs. X, of Czech descent but a passionate Pole, treats me as if there were no racism in Hitler's regime. She displays the kind of tact that one seldom sees these days in relation to us.

~~Today she said~~ [illeg.] I have noticed that she has a certain fear of me, and the reason for it occurred to me today. It seems she is afraid that I may soon share the fate of other Jews, and she therefore guards against our becoming friends in order not to have painful memories about me. She has made it clear to me in so many words.

Today news arrived about the capture of Jews hidden in the countryside. They were taken to the woods and were shot there. A horror seized the town with the realization that the last chance of rescue by running to the countryside has collapsed.

A hiding place with Jews was uncovered in the woods of Lachodów. They had been holed up with their children since December. Deported to Złoczów, they were all shot in its castle. A friend of mine concealed his 18-month-old baby in the shack of a peasant woman in the village of Stanimierz. Denounced, the baby was taken away and shot.

The tragic conditions of Jews hiding in the countryside are no less life threatening than those in the ghetto. I visited one of those families. Emaciated and frightened, they go on with their confined lives in stables, garrets, and in

---

44. Golfard is referring to the Tadeusz Jankiewicz family. The Czech wife he mentions had a brother with the surname Swoboda (or Svobodah). Swoboda was a local forester who found hiding places in the forest for the Jews and brought them news of impending raids. After the war, Jankiewicz wrote about the forest in two private letters to Jacob Litman, sent from Lubaczów, Poland, to Litman in Union, New Jersey, on January 30, 1954, and October 28, 1981. Jankiewicz letters, copies in USHMMA Acc.2008.316, Litman family collection. On Jankiewicz's status as a Righteous Gentile (rescuer), see Sara Bender and Shmuel Krakowski, eds., *The Encyclopedia of the Righteous Among the Nations: Rescuers of Jews during the Holocaust, Poland* (Jerusalem: Yad Vashem, 2004), 2/1:300. Also see the detailed testimony on Jankiewicz in the Righteous Among the Nations Department at Yad Vashem. Jankiewicz received this honor in 1979 (see excerpts pp. 133–34).

the woods. The barking of a dog for whatever reason is enough to scare them to death. When the militia arrives in the village for the quotas, or when they come for the so-called peasant "catching" ["*łapanka*" *chłopów*], these Jews run to the forest, trudging in snow up to their knees. At times they must spend the night outside in the biting frost of the forest or, at best, in cold barns.

They hand over fabulous sums to stay in this kind of prison, fortunes in gold, everything they possess. It happens sometimes that persons who accept Jews with their belongings after a few days rob them and then drive them away from the village. It is worse when they are denounced, for they perish in such cases.

There are also peasants who consider it their duty to give shelter to their Jewish acquaintances without taking money, and what is more, they even cover their expenses. There are even Ukrainians among such people.[45]

FEBRUARY 27, 1943

I have not taken any notes for over two weeks. I mill about in non-Jewish surroundings and have allowed their prevailing cheerfulness to put me at ease. My nature, gnawed by anguish, wants to be well again. I rebel against the instinct of self-preservation, but that instinct is stronger.

~~Only yesterday~~ [illeg.] Yesterday I saw it in myself when I was again threatened with grave danger, which, however, passed quickly. The inmates in Czupernosów were taken to Jaktorów and thence to a camp near Złoczów. The butchery of Jaktorów is being shut down.[46] The camp in Czupernosów deserves special attention as yet another document [about?] the rule of the Jewish Council. Following my transfer from Jaktorów, I was assigned to this camp for a short while. It was an "open" camp because the inmates worked in quarries and could go home for the night to sleep. The boys quickly got used to the hard labor; some even liked it. One of my friends, a young teacher, talked with

---

45. This sentence, translated by Monika Adamczyk-Garbowska in 2007, is missing from the first (Litman) translation of 1983.

46. The Jaktorów camp was liquidated on July 22, 1943, as was the Kurowice camp in the days that followed. Pohl, *Nationalsozialistische Judenverfolgung in Ostgalizien*, 353. According to a wartime leaflet of the Polish underground, the four hundred Jewish laborers in Jaktorów and Kurowice mounted a resistance campaign either in anticipation of or during the liquidation. They tried to flee on the nights of July 20 and 21, but most were killed. See Marilyn J. Harran et al., *The Holocaust Chronicle* (Lincolnwood, IL: Publications International, 2000), 469; Lucyna Kulińska and Adam Roliński, *Kwestia ukraińska i eksterminacja ludności polskiej w Małopolsce Wschodniej: W świetle dokumentów Polskiego Państwa Podziemnego 1942–1944* (Kraków: Księgarnia Akademicka, 2004), 15.

delight about his work crushing stone. That did not prevent him from selling the hammers. He thus performed a civic duty at any rate.[47]

The Jewish Gestapo-men seek to turn every misfortune into a source of profit.[48] When an "action" is carried out, they miss no opportunity to plunder. When there is a seizure [mass roundup, selection, and deportation] to the forced labor camps, they take ransom money from the rich and consign the poor to death. The Czupernosów camp was an affair of a special kind.

One was mainly admitted there for money, as much as 1,000–2,000 złoty.[49] People were assured that the yellow camp patch with a stamp would provide complete safety. The number of inmates kept growing by the day. The chief of the Jewish Gestapomen[50] taking care of the camp had risen to the status of a hero.

Yesterday the camp commander arrived to take all camp workers away. As they walked to their work in the quarry in the morning, there was no singing among them as usual. Around 11 o'clock they were led to town under an armed escort and loaded onto trucks. The girls who came to offer them bread were taken away with them, and a deaf-mute Jew was shot. In the place of missing inmates who had been forewarned and escaped, their wives or sisters were taken.

FEBRUARY 28

It became known today that the captives were sent to a penal camp in Pluchów beyond Złoczów. They are working there in a lignite mine 15 meters under the ground. They get 200 grams of bread and half a liter of coffee without sugar and must live on it a whole day.

---

47. Here Golfard is referring to Jacob Litman.

48. The behavior of Jewish police auxiliaries so incensed Golfard that he condemned those Jews with the label "Gestapo-men," thus equating them with the much-feared German Secret State Police.

49. German authorities were supposed to pay Polish laborers four to five złoty per day. In the Warsaw ghetto in 1941, Jews could buy their "freedom" from a camp for two hundred złoty or a position in the police force for five hundred złoty; the price of bread in the ghetto was on average eleven złoty per kilo. At the end of 1942, Jews in the Warsaw ghettos received no wages. Thus the one to two thousand złoty rate to secure a spot in the forced labor camp at Czupernosów was astronomical. Emmanuel Ringelblum, *Notes from the Warsaw Ghetto: The Journal of Emmanuel Ringelblum* (New York: Schocken, 1958), 155–63, 318.

50. Golfard also used the term to refer to prisoners within the German camp system who were assigned to supervise other prisoners. Known as Kapos, these Jewish or other prisoners were expected by their German supervisors to perform their duties, but some seemed to have gone beyond even German expectations. See Eugen Kogon, *Theory and Practice of Hell: The German Concentration Camps and the System behind Them* (New York: Farrar, Straus and Cudahy, 1950).

The chairman of the Jewish Council was taken along with the captives to Pluchów. He stayed there a few days because he was ransomed for the price of delivering tens of new slaves. They are capturing [people] all week long, and ever new deliveries go to Pluchów.

Today came the news about the terrible slaughter of 1,200 Jews in the Wehrmacht camp of Mosty Wielkie. Following the eviction of Jews from this town, a camp was set up outside [of the] town. They [Jews] paid enormous sums to get the letter "*W*," which signified a laborer of the Wehrmacht. At a roundup of 1,300 people, on the tenth of last month, 1,200 were shot with machine guns.[51]

MARCH 3

Two days passed in dreadful anxiety. Yesterday night the ghetto was alerted to a forthcoming "action" at 3 o'clock in the morning. At 2 o'clock almost the entire ghetto made off to nearby woods, fields, barns, and wherever the eyes could see.[52] Many people sat out in the quaggy mud of the field till daybreak waiting for the events of the morning.

There were among them people sick with typhus fever as high as 40°C [104°F]. They knew that they would not be saved, that they would be the first to be shot. In the morning it turned out that the alarm was caused by a German SD man who, in a state of drunkenness, was prompted to show some sympathy to the Jews and forewarned them of the danger. News about "actions" is spreading again. There is talk about Drohobycz, Stanisławów, Stryj. Specific details are lacking.

We are beginning to measure our lives in terms of days rather than weeks. Hitler's latest declaration about the final destruction of Jews struck like thunder from the clear sky and left no illusions. The papers quote the speech of the prime minister of Slovakia about resettling the remaining 20% of Jews in

---

51. The camp was established and run primarily by a Wehrmacht sapper unit (*Pioniereinheit*). It grew to be the largest of the Jewish forced labor camps in the outskirts of the Lviv district (Kreis Lemberg-Land), with four thousand workers. The "*W*" insignia on their uniforms protected them from killing actions until 1943. In January 1943, the local military commander reckoned that the wages of the laborers were too much of an economic burden (the military paid the SS and police for the laborers, but the SS and police did not turn the wages over to the Jewish laborers). A month later, Katzmann's men, Friedrich Hildebrand and Willy Schulze, arrived at the camp and oversaw the mass killings of all the female and elderly laborers. Pohl, *Nationalsozialistische Judenverfolgung in Ostgalizien*, 237,249–50.

52. This is an eastern Galician idiom for going somewhere without a destination in mind.

March.[53] We know what "deportation—*Aussiedlung*" means. It is literally the murder of thousands by the most horrible tortures. Someone brought news of a large collective grave being dug near Zborów. From the same source came the news that 70% of the remaining population had been demanded in the Tarnopol district.

In Krosienko, a village 3 km away from here, 30 converted Jews were murdered. Only a few saved themselves by fleeing. The killing was carried out not by Gestapo men but by the local "Schupo" men, who sometimes feign pity toward Jews.[54]

The news from the battlefront has not been very reassuring recently. After the recapture of Kharkov, Kursk, Rostov, and Krasnodar, the front at the Dnieper was expected to break any day. We are very impatient, saying that the result of the war does not matter if we do not endure. Hence the denunciations that the English and the Americans intentionally delay the victory of the Soviets and, thus, our own liberation. A general conviction prevails that the allies of the Soviets wish to let Russia bleed in order to gain the fruits of victory more easily. This means our inevitable end. Each day of our lives holds hope for tomorrow, hope that depends on how rapidly the Soviets march forward or on something improbable happening. We have waited for the second front since last November, keeping in mind Molotov's declaration about the creation of a European second front back in 1942.

It seems probable that the Allies procrastinate in playing their last trump cards, wishing to define first their postwar relationships with the Soviets, which still appear to be quite hazy. Perhaps various laymen are right when they say that the war has already entered a phase in which the position of Germany has become secondary in relation to the coming big game between the Allied plutocracy and Bolshevism. If this should prove true, the war will undoubtedly be protracted, and the occupied nations will become the scapegoat of

---

53. Golfard may have meant a widely publicized address that Hitler had delivered in absentia on February 24, 1943, at the commemoration of the founding of the Nazi Party in Munich. See Max Domarus, *Hitler: Speeches and Proclamations 1932–1945 and Commentary by a Contemporary* (Wauconda, IL: Bolchazy-Carducci, 1992), 4:2761–64. The other reference is probably to a speech by Slovak minister of the interior Alexander Mach, given February 7, 1943, discussing "removal" of the remaining Jews. Wacław Długoborski, *The Tragedy of the Jews of Slovakia: 1938–1945* (Oświęcim: Auschwitz-Birkenau State Museum, 2002), 167; Ivan Kamenec, *On the Trail of Tragedy: The Holocaust in Slovakia* (Bratislava: H&H, 2007), 283.

54. "Schupo" refers to the Schutzpolizei (Protective Police), part of the German Order Police stationed in the cities and larger towns and subordinated to Himmler as Reichsführer-SS and chief of the German police.

behind-the-scenes diplomatic games in which the lives of millions are an innocent plaything [*sic*].

MARCH 6

I realize that I should not write about politics. The sparse as well as one-sided information does not allow one to form an objective judgment on the situation of the world. Besides, no one is interested in my personal views.

I must, however, mention the conversation I had with an "expert" in Ukrainian affairs. He is an ardent Pole ~~for whom~~ rooted in these eastern borderlands [*kresy*], which represent to him more than a mere recollection of a historical text because he has witnessed the daily, at times bloody struggles of two peoples living together on these lands from the inception of their annals.

Just as the Allies, without having yet won the war, are already determining our borders, so does my interlocutor define the task of an Independent Poland in relation to its minorities, particularly its Ukrainian minority. He berates the former Polish government for its lenient policy toward the Ukrainians, recommending now as the best solution their mass resettlement, patterned on the forced resettlements organized by the Soviets. The accusation against Ukrainians includes valid points: disarming Polish soldiers in 1939, tracking Polish colonists during the Soviet rule, killings and plunder.

In principle I should approve of Mr. K.'s opinion.[55] Why, the injuries the Ukrainians have inflicted upon the Jews alone suffice to make the most severe accusations. The participation of Ukrainians in the murder of hundreds of thousands of Jews is beyond any dispute. To this day they carry out, often ruthlessly, the beastly Hitlerian orders. During the German invasion they themselves initiated terrible massacres compared to which even the cruelty of the Germans pales. It is a fact that the Germans took pictures of Jews being hurled into the flames of burning houses. In Przemyślany the perpetrators of this were the Ukrainians. Had they been allowed, they would even today take apart the entire ghetto in their passion for plunder.

However, I am neither a Polish nor a Jewish nationalist. In the face of such horrid, deadly injuries, I cannot for a moment equate a people with a bigger or smaller minority of its bandits. They can be found in each nation, even among the Jews, who in the past were famous for being repulsed by bloodshed. While

---

55. "Mr. K." was Dr. Jacob Katz, a revered lawyer who lived on the main street in town. Katz introduced Golfard to Litman. His name appears in an official directory of officials and professionals (under the grouping of the town's lawyers) in *Schematyzm woj. tarnopolskiego* (1934), 20.

in camp, I saw human beasts among Jewish group leaders [*grupenführerzy*], the Ukrainian militia, and the German Gestapomen. It is they who are guilty of letting loose man's most primitive animal instincts as the war made human life worthless and all morality a museum relic. People are embarrassed to affirm the former moral "superstitions," the day-to-day ethics of the prewar.

Every nation possesses its innate traits. The Hitlerites call them racial traits. With the Poles, that trait is their overly hot temperament and recklessness. With the Ukrainians, it is indisputably their hypocrisy and cruelty. These are hereditary traits but by no means constant. They developed in the psyche of the Ukrainian masses as a result of their political situation, always uncertain, and as a response to the methods of ruthlessness and violence that constituted their daily bread in our eastern lands from the times of Chmielnicki through the rule of the royal land magnates until the pacification.[56] The same element has always acted—the tenant peasant to whom the Pole was first of all an instrument of economic and political oppression. Despite its nationalistic appearance, the struggle in the eastern provinces has its base in class discrimination with the nationalist factor only as a secondary phenomenon aroused by political parties and foreign forces.

The Ukrainian peasant did not have it much worse than the Polish peasant. And the Polish peasant, too, rebelled. Not infrequently did he kill officials at the sequestration of his last cow, and he set fire to manorial estates surrounded by fields that lay fallow. During the twenty years of independence, the peasants did not once support the government, excluding the period of Witos's rule, even though he also did nothing good for them.[57] The Polish peasant, however,

---

56. Bohdan Khmel'nyts'kyi (ca. 1595–1657) in 1648 launched an uprising against the Polish lords who governed most of Ukraine in the sixteenth and early seventeenth centuries. Khmel'nyts'kyi initially succeeded in defeating the Polish army and unleashed a wave of violence in which Ukrainians (mainly peasants) and Cossacks massacred Polish nobility, priests, Uniate Ukrainians, and tens of thousands of Jews—estimates of Jewish victims range from sixty to one hundred thousand—perceived as allies of the Polish nobility. To secure Ukrainian autonomy as well as a victory over the Poles, Khmel'nyts'kyi turned to the Russian tsar for aid and signed a treaty with Russia at Pereyaslav in 1654. The war with Poland resulted in the partitioning of Ukraine between Poland and Russia, and Russification replaced Polonization as the more dominant trend. Subtelny, *Ukraine: A History*, 125–38; and Magocsi, *History of Ukraine*, 195–207, 212–16. The "pacification" to which Golfard refers is the 1930s Polish suppression of Ukrainian nationalism, which was so extreme that Ukrainians brought their case of persecution to the League of Nations.

57. Wincenty Witos (1874–1945) was born in Galicia, and as a leader of the Polish peasant party Piast was elected as a representative to the Polish parliament. He became premier of Poland in the early 1920s. In 1926, a coup by Marshall Józef Piłsudski ousted him. He was arrested and sentenced to prison but fled to Czechoslovakia in 1933 and later returned to Nazi-occupied Poland.

was bound to the notion of lordship [*Państwo*] by love for his native country, its language, tradition, and history. Here, in the eastern provinces, even the Polish peasant speaks Ukrainian; his wife or relatives are Ukrainians, and Polish culture reached out here very slowly. I talked with the Polish peasants of Świrz—the Wyspiańskis, the Lipskis, the Wojciechowskis, etc. They all recall Austria with greater reverence than Poland. In those times, they asserted, it was much better; one derived more from one's land. And these people are undoubtedly Polish patriots who belonged to the *Sokół* organization before the war.[58]

One must not simplify this problem. The concept of statehood in these lands is still inadequately worked out, with the possible exception of big cities like Lwów.

MARCH 30

I must hurry to write my last few words. There is blood all around us. Every day brings word of new victims. In Kimierz, a village populated by *Volksdeutsche* [ethnic Germans], 22 Jews were murdered.[59] They agonized with their children in forest hideaways for four months.[60] A raid was organized against them with Sujba, the *Volksdeutsche* snitch [*szpicel*], at the head and with the participation of the Ukrainian militia, as well as the German gendarmes. They were herded to one location, placed before an open pit, ordered to undress completely, then called one by one to the pit's edge and shot. One mother witnessed the death of her four children, one after the other, while a

---

58. On the *Sokół*, see part I, note 74.

59. German representatives from the Reich Commission for the Strengthening of Germandom (RKfDV), an agency created by Himmler, set up an office in Złoczów. There were two German colonies near Przemyślany: Uszkowice and Podusilna. See the report from the RKfDV, Złoczów, January 25, 1943, former Lviv Oblast Archive (USHMMA Acc. 1995.A.1086, reel 8).

60. According to the testimony of one forester in the region, Petro Pyasetsky, there were approximately seventeen hundred Jews hiding in the forests around Przemyślany. The extent to which Ukrainians helped them is unclear, though recent Ukrainian-led attempts to identify Ukrainian rescuers and gain recognition have compared Pyasetsky's rescue efforts to those of Swedish diplomat Raoul Wallenberg in Hungary. See Pyasetsky's "Testimony," in *Ukrainians and Jews*, ed. Walter Dushnyck (New York: Ukrainian Congress Committee of America, 1966), 135–36. The same figure of seventeen hundred Jews is also used by historian Frank Golczewski, "Shades of Grey," in *The Shoah in Ukraine: History, Testimony, Memorialization*, ed. Ray Brandon and Wendy Lower (Bloomington: Indiana University Press, 2008), 145.

A Polish witness who was questioned after the war identified a gendarme in this photograph as Seeman and the Jewish victim lying on the side-walk in Peremyshliany as a man named Chaskiel (courtesy of the Institute of National Memory, Kraków Branch Commission, shelf mark Ko 5/09, no. 26791).

husband [saw the same happen to] his wife and children. Some were allowed to stay in their underpants if they were no longer usable. Following this collective execution, Seemann, one of the German gendarmes, summoned the peasants and explained to them that it was all done for the harm suffered by the peasants under the Bolsheviks.[61] Eyewitnesses related what happened with tears. In Ciemierzyńce, 11 hidden Jews were caught and shot. Every day new victims, destined to be shot, are brought to Przemyślany. They walk to their death with a certain singular dignity and astounding calm. The captured Jews

---

61. In the original, the name of the German gendarme is underlined. The gendarme's name was actually Willi Seeman. He was identified by his fellow gendarme in Przemyślany, Bruno Sämisch, who was tried by the East Germans and convicted. See Sämisch testimony, February 3, 1951, at the BStU Berlin: BV Halle, Ast 5544, BStU# 00133–138.

are kept for a day or two in the local jail without food and in total awareness of the inevitability of being shot.

On Saturday I followed two victims up to the little birch woods, the point of execution; I could not perceive any despair in the eyes of these two young people, a husband and wife. They lost their children in Kimierz a few days before. ~~After~~ [illeg.] ~~their~~ The execution is carried out by the German gendarmes, none members of the [Nazi] party, who are undoubtedly quiet people as civilians, but who nonetheless become savage under Hitler's orders.

Yesterday, as a result of a very influential intervention, a woman and her three little children were released a few minutes before their impending execution. The woman talked about it with a dull indifference and no joy whatsoever.

A conscription of all males has been proclaimed for Friday. They intend to sort out all young men and carry them off to extermination camps. This affects men from 14 to 60.

Job-like reports about the massacre of 4,000 Jews in Lwów, in revenge for the killing of a Gestapo man, have not subsided as new bloody "actions" begin.[62] In Kraków the entire remaining population, with the exception of the workers barracked in Płaszów, was murdered.[63] In Żołkiew the women and children were quite likely killed after 600 men were carried off to camps.

~~In the face of those events~~ I look at the last pangs of tormented life of Jews whose fate I will soon share. A psychiatrist could probably write volumes every day. Every thought is poisoned by death. When taking a spoon of nourishment in my mouth, I see murdered acquaintances. I go to sleep with the knowledge that I will soon perish. I get up ~~with fear of~~ uncertain whether I will survive the day. I feel the air I breathe will bring my death. ~~I'm looking at~~ I stare at the sun that does not shine for me and that will soon be replaced by impenetrable darkness. No matter with whom one talks, whether Jew or Catholic, the conversation invariably turns to the basic question of life and death. The day is permeated with a mist of blood that invisibly whirls around us [illeg.]. Frantic, I cannot for one moment forget what awaits me. Every shot of vodka I take gives me the bitter taste of life. The numbers that I record in the firm's inventory book are saturated with my thoughts about the life and death of my nation.

---

62. On "Job-like," see note 19 above.

63. This slave labor camp was established in 1940, first housing Poles and later Jews. The camp's history, including the brutal actions of its commandant, Amon Goeth, was made famous by the film *Schindler's List*. For more information about the camp, see Geoffrey P. Megargee, ed., *The USHMM Encyclopedia of Camps and Ghettos, 1933–1945* (Bloomington: Indiana University Press in association with the USHMM, 2009), 1:861–66.

Every effort is twofold: I am cutting wood, but my mind is preoccupied with a profoundly real and no longer Hamletian question of "to be or not to be."

APRIL 2

Now there is no longer a universal date of good fortune, each day brings us a new tragedy. Yesterday's "prima aprilis" [April Fools' Day] passed by under the sign of terrible news.

200 girls from the Szwartz military factory in Lwów were shipped away. The girls wore the "*W*" emblem, which was supposed to protect them from being killed. The number of victims has been estimated at 1,500.[64]

On Thursday in Żółkiew, 600 Jews were carried off during the so-called *Überprüfung* (reexamination) administered these days. After a few days, an "action" was set in motion in which the remaining people were rounded up and murdered in the ghetto.

It seems that the last moment is drawing near. The insanity has again assumed blood thirsty forms. We just received word that a mass murder began in the ghetto of Złoczów and that the executioners may drop in here any minute.

I no longer despair. Despite the fact that from a certain point a new feeling has bloomed in my heart, I abhor life. I no longer mourn for my sisters and parents. I no longer weep over them, just as I no longer lament a friend whom I have lost recently. He luckily died in convulsions, having not regained consciousness. Died a rare civilian death—sick with typhus—at the age of 30.

It was pining for Mania that induced me to write these notes. Now I have in front of me your one and only photograph, the last trace of your existence, since all your things have been stolen. I do not believe in life beyond the grave, but if there is such a thing as an immortal soul that manifests itself in man, your soul must be blessed beyond words. You appear to me every day as a moving and acting who substitutes for you and to whom I become attached ever more strongly so that. Parting from life so for me right now in every moment right now would have twofold value. I will part with this life when I myself choose to do so. parted with

---

64. Wells, *Janowska Road*, 21, also mentions the assignment of the "*W*" emblem to laborers in Janowska. The firm Schwarz & Co. appears on the distribution list of a report issued by the SS and police headquarters in Lwów concerning the use of Jewish labor; see report of SSPF (SS and Police Leader) Friedrich Katzmann, October 23, 1942, reprinted in Andrzej Żbikowski, ed., *Rozwiązanie kwestii żydowskiej w Dystrykcie Galicja/Lösung der Judenfrage im Distrikt Galizien* (Warsaw: Instytut Pamięci Narodowej, 2001), 11–13.

Thoughts of suicide catch hold of me, perhaps because I fear that the dream that I have been longing for will cease to be. However, I can overcome that.

APRIL 5

The registration *"Überprüfung"* to recheck the Jewish population from the ages of 14 to 60 is over. Ludwig from the SD and Warzuk [Warzok], the chief of camps in the Złoczów district, arrived.[65] Unemployed and employed Jews had to register, and as a result many were taken away to unknown camps. I spent the day of registration in a village. I do not know whether they "enlisted" me in my absence. It seems that, based on the importance of my function, they exempted me. Many did not come, and all absent people were condemned to the camp by default.

Actually, there is a great "run" to camps. People are paying as much as 10,000 złoty to be taken to these slaughterhouses because people are losing their minds.

No sooner was the registration a thing of the past than a wave of "actions" spread through the land. Mass slaughters were carried out in Złoczów, Brzeżany, and Lwów. They will be here any minute. The fairness of the sunny sky today is veiled by a red glare. People do not sleep, nor do they eat. Bewildered, they move around with a death warrant imprinted on their faces. One talks only about life and death—whether to go into the woods, go to a camp, or take poison. But where could one get poison? In consultation with pharmacists? Embryonic bands are beginning to form. Sons abandon their mothers, and fathers leave their children. There are those who could perhaps save their own lives, but they are responsible for the little ones.

The Jewish Council is being dissolved. Those bandits, having done their duty, have finally recognized that it is time to leave. Instead of arming young people and sending them to the woods, they [have] consigned them until now to camps and a slow agony. They "saved" Jewry by taking contributions from them, rounding them up for the camps, and deploying the Jewish militia in the

---

65. According to the deputy district captain in the civil administration of Złoczów, Gerhard von Jordan, "In Złoczów there was a Sipo [Security Police] office, which reported to the office in Tarnopol. A Mr. Ludwig is in my memory as associated with that office." This may be the Ludwig mentioned by Golfard. For the von Jordan testimony, see BAL 162/19244, II ar No., 1422/1966. Von Jordan and his boss, Dr. Otto Wendt, appear in a German administrative staff listing, dated November 28, 1942, in records of the Lviv Oblast Archive, fond 12-opis 1-delo 104 (USHMMA Acc.1995.A.1086, reel 8). For Friedrich Warzok, see Biographies.

Lucy Laufer, a Jewish girl born in Peremyshliany, hid for two years. After sheltering for a time in the railway station, Lucy fled to the forest with her parents. Ukrainian partisans shot her a few days before liberation in July 1944. (USHMMPA WS# 67638, courtesy of Gisela Gross Gelin).

massacres, [continuing in this way] as long as there was no threat to themselves. They sacrificed their people for the price of their own lives. Now, fleeing with their moneybags, they disappear in the nick of time—leaving, at last, the few remaining Jews to their own inevitable fate.

I talked with several young people about forming a group in the woods. Every one of them still has some expectations of hiding in a peasant's hovel or somewhere else, and they continue to reject any collective actions that might save their own lives. They will meet the same fate as those who have perished.

What will become of me? I am not thinking about it at all. I look with deep despair at the young but gaunt faces of girls and boys. I see in the faces of the old, the young, and the women the same stamp of death; it weighs upon all. I avoid meeting friends. The thought that they are doomed to perish in a few days in mass slaughter brings me physical pain.

I no longer think about my family. I do not think about myself. One cannot count on anybody. We are left facing our own destiny.

It is a beautiful day. I sit down for a minute on the steps of the house. All around there is the screaming of children. One also hears the rattle of passing carts. The air is full of spring coming from the wet fields. The sun is shining strongly; its rays glide across my face. They caress and kiss me, I open my eyes. The expanse of fields stretches before me into the distance, somewhere touching the faraway sky. Nature is overflowing with freedom. The spring excitement of rustling tree branches that are still half bare and the subtle whisper of the sprouting grass.

Church bells toll the approach of Easter. Will my eyes then still embrace the beauty of the firmament, the greenness of the grass, the grayness of the branches?

SUNDAY, APRIL 11

And again several harrowing days have passed. As if to mock us, the days were beautiful, full of sun. The eyes could not have enough of it in the ghetto where the sun sneaked into the low-roofed buildings and bestowed its love on the most unfortunate in the world. The Gestapo and the gendarmes could do absolutely nothing against it. The sun is moving about the ghetto. It caresses and plays with the little children, who for much too long have not felt any warmth or any tenderness. To experience the bliss of the sun, one does not need a pass or any intervention by the Jewish Council.

The atmosphere is becoming increasingly heavy. The doomed are awaiting their execution, due to happen any day, with complete passivity. The majority are resigned [to their fate]. A handful of young people are beginning to rebel. There is much talk about weapons and gangs. Apparently, there are already many young Jews in the woods. But it is to comfort their own fearful hearts that people retell exaggerated news about the formation of Jewish bands—perhaps they will save themselves and avenge [those who have perished]. People wander along the narrow streets of the ghetto. In small groups, which form here and there, they recount the cruelties in Złoczów. A woman who escaped from a shelter connected to the municipal sewers tells of the ongoing slaughter.

She spent eight days in the sewer together with others. The gendarmes uncovered the sewers and threw in teargas bombs. Suspecting the gas to be poisonous, they committed suicide en masse to put an end to their torment. The gas was not of a kind that suffocates, but in the narrow space it had a very intense effect.

On the day of the "action," over 2,000 people were taken to the nearby woods. After a massacre they were all ordered to disrobe completely. Under threat of torture all had to lie down in the pits with their faces to the ground lengthwise and crosswise, and in this position, they were all shot. The piles of corpses grew. After ten days the ransacking of hideouts continues until today. Many willingly emerge from their shelters, since they have no means of taking their own lives. The German executioners are just waiting for them. The people place themselves in a row, and each in turn gets a bullet in the mouth. The corpses are stripped of their clothing, which is taken to workshops to be tailored for the German population.

Terrible scenes take place in the shelters. The female refugee from Złoczów told of having seen two burning homes whose flames were ignited by those people hiding within. They preferred to die in the flames together with their possessions than place themselves in the hands of the German killers.

During the "action" in Zborów on Thursday, 700 people were murdered. People comfort themselves with a report that someone is still alive in that town.

I read yesterday in the bulletin of a clandestine Polish organization about "the nightmarish days of the mass murder of Jews in Kraków and Łódź."[66] Recently Sikorski spoke in London about "the poisoning of Jews in chambers by German scientists."[67]

All this is mentioned rather marginally as a manifest symptom of German barbarity. The tragedy of Jews does not particularly occupy the thoughts of the politicians. The population allows for it by its silence. Rarely, very rarely, does

---

66. These Polish underground bulletins called for acts of revenge against German perpetrators and stressed Germans' brutal behavior, such as that of Commandant Epple in Kurowice. For similar Soviet examples see part III of this volume, documents 4 and 5.

67. On October 29, 1942, General Władysław Sikorski (1881–1943) spoke at a rally at the Royal Albert Hall, London. His speech was released to the Associated Press; on October 30, 1942, the *New York Times* featured the event and a few lines of the speech. Sikorski declared that the Germans would be punished for their crimes against Jews and other Poles and warned the latter that they would be prosecuted for mistreating Jews. Parts of Sikorski's speech were secretly distributed by the Relief Council for Jews (RPŻ), also known as Żegota. About twenty-five thousand copies were distributed in Poland, see Polish Institute and General Sikorski Museum, 20 Princes Gate, London SW7 1PT (PIMGS A 10.4/12). A native of Galicia, General Sikorski was a staunch Polish patriot who joined the underground as a youth in World War I fighting for the cause of Polish independence. In 1922 and 1923 he was prime minister of the Second Polish Republic and minister of military affairs. During the Nazi occupation of Poland in World War II, he became the prime minister of the Polish government-in-exile and commander in chief of the Polish armed forces. The speech Golfard references occurred in the months preceding Sikorski's tragic death in a plane crash on July 4, 1943, near Gibraltar.

one see an active expression of sympathy on the part of the population. The majority of the populace continues to persist in its aversion to Jews despite scenes of martyrdom, the likes of which the world has never yet witnessed.

The tombs and graves of people murdered in martyrdom are ever increasing all over the country. Every village and town, every forest abounds with graves looming from a distance as a historical lesson and a warning. Once the living witnesses are gone, then those graves will speak volumes. They will accuse the whole world and more, with an eloquence a hundredfold mightier, of having committed or having failed to act against the cruelest of crimes.

WEDNESDAY, APRIL 14

The small town of Bóbrka lies about 20 km. from Przemyślany. After various camp actions and massacres, about 1,200 Jews remained there. Yesterday, this remnant in one of the last Jewish settlements was liquidated. Hardly any one escaped. The town was surrounded at midnight. The local gendarmes captured the few Jews living outside the ghetto and brought them to the assembly point. Although the Jews in the ghetto had been on the watch day and night for several weeks, they were taken by surprise at 4:00 in the morning with an action in which a few hundred Schupo men [szupowcy] and the notorious brigade of Jewish militiamen participated. At noon the Jews who have been rounded up are taken to their place of doom in the woods known as Wałowy. Only the healthiest 40 men were selected to go to the murderous Janowska camp, where they will inevitably perish. Before the execution, the Jews were stripped and deprived of all the money they had. A certain group of Jews, hidden in one of the shelters, had on them 58 thous. dollars, so I was told by one of the escapees from Bóbrka. The Germans lined their pockets with enormous amounts of loot. Jews converted all of their assets into currency, which they now carry on them in the hope of saving themselves. This explains why the Germans murder them in the nude and take away their clothing.

Today I received the details of an execution from an eyewitness. 6 Jews, 3 men and 3 women, caught in the village of Podusów, were shot in the Przemyślany woods. The executions were carried out by the local gendarmes under their lieutenant, with the participation of the bloody gendarme Sumann [Seeman], as well as the Ukrainian militiamen. The people were murdered naked. As a punishment for one of the condemned who ran away on the verge of the execution, the others were buried half alive. Gruder, a Jew from Hanaczów taken to bury the murdered people, testified that terrible screams of the suffocating victims came up from the pits. The earth above them was heaving and sinking, showing their horrible torment.

Beastly details of murder from other places verify this report. The Hitler murderers torture their victims, especially the women. Few are lucky enough to get some compassion and be shot at once. They let their victims suffer and do not always shoot in the temple or skull.

News gets in about the liquidation of all so-called subcamps [*Nebeu-lagerów*]. These [liquidations] are supposed to take place to discourage notice-able sabotage among Jews [*sic*]. The SS is therefore afraid of allowing so-called free camps. Indeed, there are presently more and more young armed people in the woods. For the time being, the groups are small and lacking in organization and means. The disintegration of the Jewish Council has increased the resis-tance. Unfortunately, it is too late for a mass rescue from evil. People are weary. They want an end to their torment as quickly as possible.

The participation of a Jewish gang from Lwów in the actions is the most contrived device of the Nazi murderers. The Germans believe that this will vindicate them in the eyes of the world. The Golliger gang from Lwów is the epitome of the utmost disgrace. The Germans take pictures of Jewish gangsters chopping down Jewish shelters. It is supposed to show that Jews murder each other.

It is simply too early to speak in defense of those who helped the Nazi murderers. The Germans brought the Jewish people to a state of degradation in which humanity vanishes because minute by minute one must wage a war for one's life, the life of one's children, etc. [Those who perform] deeds of hero-ism and devotion are stripped of any glory. The entire Jewish community pays a collective price for the devotion shown by one Jew in defense of another. For one Gestapo man killed, Jews are murdered in the thousands or tens of thousands. Whole families are killed for resisting German authority. Heroism under such circumstances seems to amount to a lack of common sense, and it is condemned by everyone, even the best people. The only thing left to do is either hide in a shelter, in the woods, or live out in the open and murder [illeg.] one's own.

The Jewish Council has done its job. It enabled the Nazi murderers to liquidate the Jews economically and physically. Now its members are no longer needed. Therefore they are the first to be shot. The same fate is shared by the Jewish militia.

Here and there, the Ukrainian militia participates in the "actions," and in nearby villages they play leading roles in disclosing Jews, next to the peasants.

I should like to summarize briefly the sense of these notes, for I must bring them, and my young life, to a close. I have endured almost 2 years of Hitler's hell, the worst two years. I have lost everything during that time, whatever was dearest to me. I have suffered terrible hunger. I have borne the most dreadful humiliation. I have seen the agonizing torment of people on the gallows and of those in mass graves. I myself have suffered such physical and moral agony that I shudder at the very thought of having to describe it.

But I have never debased myself by cooperating with the Germans. While working at the collection point for scrap and metals, I used to sabotage the job to the greatest extent [possible]. I have rejected, even in the worst moments, any thought of donning the cap of a militiaman or any other form of collaboration with the Germans.

Everything presently taking place before our eyes is undoubtedly a contrived form of madness, driven to a frenzy. No one has the right to raise the question of Jewish guilt. They have been doomed to martyrdom, and in this respect, they endured to the last in the manner of the first martyrs of Christianity. There have been no favorable conditions for opposition. No nation should be critical of Jewish behavior in these horrible times. No nation has the moral right to do that, just as no [non-Jewish] persons can excuse themselves by citing the [fear of the Nazi] terror. ~~The terror did not go so far that it forced the Jews~~ The fact is that the denouncer peasants delivered Jews in hiding en masse in hopes of robbing them of their possessions. The fact is that they cooperated with the Germans in murdering the defenseless. Ukrainians in greater numbers, but Poles as well, would rather send helpless ones to death, even when extending some help posed no threat to them. In the face of this most terrible tragedy, the various nations behaved at best neutrally, without deriving any lessons from the atrocities. To Catholic children, the unfortunate were an object of scorn. The church did not use these tragedies to evoke compassion for "Israel, the older brother." As for the Germans, let their judgment be cast by the thousands of graves of the murdered. Let the German people be cursed forever. Let the damnation of the murdered mothers, children, and elderly pursue the German people to their own ultimate destruction. I pity the German mothers who brought such sons into the world. I find it difficult to sustain a hatred for them. Perhaps they are unaware of their sons' crimes. Perhaps they themselves will curse their own sons.

Not only must the Nazi system and any other form of fascism disappear, but any form of cruelty must also be forever eliminated from the soul of nations. The Germans are not alone guilty of our tragic fate. The English and the Americans who tolerated the acts of the German nation are also guilty. They fattened Hitler and nurtured the present regime in Germany.

Despite everything, the Jewish nation's honor has remained intact. If anything, it will preserve contempt for the world's cowardice and heartlessness.

* * * * *

[illeg.] despite everything that [illeg.] good [illeg.]. Evil and cruelty are the result of upbringing and [fostered by one's] regime. Therefore, mankind may still have a future if it will condemn regimes that feed on animal instincts, since it is so easy to arouse such instincts.

I do believe in the goodness of [people?]. I was like a stray dog, humiliated and maltreated, when I unexpectedly experienced kindness and friendship from people to whom I could offer nothing in return. Perhaps there are more people like that. Maybe more are like that, ready and fearless enough to acknowledge the human rights [of those] who have been bereft of all humanity. Bearing in mind the example of their culture and dignity, I am inclined to believe it.[68]

It is no coincidence that such people to whom I refer are Polish. Among the Polish people there has always existed an immeasurable wealth of kindheartedness, which has been purposely stifled. These Poles [who have helped me] have restored my faith in the Polish people, and let it be to their credit.

In the last moments of my life, I have experienced genuine kindness and friendship from the Jankiewicz family of Przemyślany. May happiness, as well as the affection of the most oppressed, accompany their lives and the lives of their children always.[69]

---

68. Alongside this paragraph, Golfard writes, "In the last mome[nts?]" without concluding the sentence.

69. Although earlier in the diary Golfard does not identify his helper and friend Jankiewicz, here he reveals his name in the last sentence.

PART III

RELATED DOCUMENTS

WARTIME DOCUMENTS

Samuel Golfard's diary provides one perspective on the Holocaust, albeit an extraordinarily graphic and moving one. But historical reconstructions of events and explanations for their occurrence require that we compare the views and behavior of the multitude of persons who were involved. In Holocaust history, as it occurred in Ukraine, Poland, and the rest of eastern Europe, the central event was a crime: the mass murder of Jews. As such, the main actors have been categorized in legal terminology as perpetrators, victims, and bystanders. While there are inherent problems in constructing biographies with these morally charged typologies, the fact is that in places like the ghetto of Peremyshliany and the camps of Kurowice and Jaktorów, repeated public acts of murder happened, and persons at the time occupied the roles of killer, victim, bystander, collaborator, or witness. After the war the collection of testimonies to convict or exonerate individuals added to the documentary record, making it possible to write the history of the Holocaust in Galicia and smaller localities such as Peremyshliany. The act of "bearing witness" continued after the war in the courtroom, in oral history projects, and in various symbolic forms such as memorials. The documents below represent the wartime and postwar perspectives of other victims, perpetrators, and bystanders, providing a larger context for understanding Golfard's experiences and offering different vantage points from which to explain the Holocaust in Peremyshliany and its aftermath.

The memorandum presented in document 1 summarizes what transpired during a meeting of senior administrators with SS and police leaders in charge of the "Final Solution" in the Galicia District of the Generalgouvernement (Nazi-occupied Poland, present-day Ukraine). The participants were Dr. Ludwig Losacker (1906–1991), chief of staff of the General Galicia District administration, who was also an SS lieutenant colonel (Obersturmbannführer) and active in the SD; SS Brigadier General (Brigadeführer) Friedrich (Fritz) Katzmann (1906–1957), senior SS and police leader of the Galicia District; Judge Otto Bauer (1888–1944), chief of internal affairs of the General Galicia District Administration (his department oversaw "Jewish measures" in the region); Dr. Hanns Gareis (1896–1972), chief of the agricultural economy department; and the signatory to the memo, a department chief named Dr. Hans-Georg Neumann, head of the Generalgouvernement's presidential department (Präsidialabteilung).

In the weeks preceding this meeting, Katzmann had received orders that the Jews must be totally resettled from the Galicia District. Even with the considerable demand placed on the railways to facilitate the German army's summer 1942 offensives, Nazi leaders initiated mass deportations of Jews to the expanded killing center of Bełżec. Although Katzmann had already prepared his district SS and police leaders and deportations had begun while this meeting took place, he wanted to maintain the upper hand in Jewish matters. The meeting is significant evidence of the regional planning and implementation of the "Final Solution" and of the negotiations among local German leaders over labor shortages that resulted from mass murder. The timing of this meeting coincides with the deportations from Peremyshliany that took Golfard's sister Mania to Bełżec and the retention of laborers, such as Golfard, who remained in the dwindling ghettos and camps in and around the town.

Interpretations of the history of the Nazi "Final Solution" vary in the emphasis placed on the influence of regional leaders such as Katzmann and central authorities, namely, Heinrich Himmler. Where does one place the locus of power in the history of radicalization, at the center or the periphery? Did Nazi anti-Jewish measures escalate in a linear manner because there was strong consensus among lower- and higher-level administrators that genocide was necessary and possible? Or were certain ad hoc compromises reached about retaining Jewish laborers in an effort to slow the process of destruction? In this document and the more detailed one that follows (the Katzmann Report, document 2), one sees how the most extreme forms of antisemitism unfolded in the shadow of the war, fear of epidemics, and labor needs.

DOCUMENT 1: Memorandum concerning a "Conference on Jewish Relocation" held by German administrators and SS officers in Galicia, August 6, 1942, USHMMA Acc. 1995.A.1086, Lviv Oblast Archive, reel 8 (translated from German).

70

Lemberg, den 6.8.1942

G e h e i m !

V e r m e r k

Betrifft: Besprechung über die Judenaussiedlung.

Anwesend: Der Chef des Amtes, Dr. Losacker,
           SS Brigadeführer Katzmann
           Abteilungsleiter Bauer
           Abteilungsleiter Dr. Gareis
           Der Unterzeichnete.

Brigadeführer Katzmann machte Mitteilung, dass es innerhalb eines halben Jahres im Generalgouvernement keinen freien Juden mehr geben wird. Die Leute werden teils ausgesiedelt, teils in Lager verbracht. Die vereinzelt auf dem Lande lebenden Juden werden von Einzelkommandos umgebracht. Die in den Städten konzentrierten Juden werden in Grossaktionen teils liquidiert, teils ausgesiedelt, teils in Arbeitslager zusammengefasst.

Die übrigen Anwesenden machten ihre Bedenken wegen des gänzlichen Mangels ans ausgebildeten nichtjüdischen Arbeitskräften geltend. Es ist völlig ausgeschlossen, innerhalb eines derartig kurzen Zeitraumes die nötigen ukrainischen und polnischen Handwerker nachzuziehen. Brigadeführer Katzmann erklärt, diesem Übel dadurch abhelfen zu wollen, dass in jedem Kreis ein Judenlager errichtet wird, in dem ein möglichst wohl asortiertes Lager aller notwendigen Handwerker gehalten werden soll.

Lemberg, August 6, 1942

<u>Secret!</u>

Memorandum

Regarding: Discussion of Jewish relocation [*Judenaussiedlung*]

In Attendance: Director of the Department, Dr. Losacker
SS Brigadeführer Katzmann
Division Head Bauer
Division Head Dr. Gareis

The undersigned [Dr. Hans-Georg Neumann]

Brigadeführer Katzmann reported that within half a year no Jew would remain at large in the Generalgouvernement. The people [Jews] will be in part relocated, in part brought to camps. Jews living here and there in the countryside will be killed by individual commandos. Some of those concentrated in the cities will be liquidated through large actions, some relocated, some concentrated in work camps.

The others present expressed their concern about the complete shortage of skilled non-Jewish labor. Training the necessary Ukrainian and Polish craftsmen within such a short time frame is completely out of the question. Brigadeführer Katzmann maintains that he intends to address this grievance by erecting a Jewish camp in each district in which, to the extent possible, a good assortment of all necessary craftsmen will be kept.

The Katzmann Report is one of the most significant German documents of the Holocaust to have survived the war. It was used as evidence of Nazi atrocities in the Nuremberg Trials (USA No. L-18, Exhibit-277) and in numerous U.S., German, and Polish investigations and legal proceedings against former German SS and policemen and Ukrainian auxiliaries. The sixty-four-page illustrated report, titled "The Solution of the Jewish Question in the District Galicia," was originally submitted by SS and Police Leader of Galicia Fritz Katzmann to his superior, Higher SS and Police Leader for the Generalgouvernement Friedrich-Wilhelm Krüger. According to Katzmann's calculations, 434,329 Jews had been killed, and about 28,000 workers were scattered in twenty-one labor camps in the spring of 1943. The excerpts and photographs here illustrate the thoroughness of German genocidal policy, the systems of persecutions, and the official, bureaucratic manner in which Nazi perpetrators recorded their "fulfillment" of the "Final Solution." The extensive list of confiscated Jewish belongings, including wedding rings, pocket watches, cameras, and stamp collections, also documents the widespread plundering and profiteering that accompanied and in many cases motivated the destruction of Jewish communities.

Many of the details found in the Katzmann Report, such as the establishment of the forced labor camps, the photos of Jaktorów, and the photos of Friedrich Warzok, corroborate and illustrate Golfard's story and description of events. Katzmann states that all ghettos were liquidated by June 23, 1943, and except for those Jews in the labor camps, the region could be declared *judenfrei*: free of Jews. Golfard was among the victims of these mass-murder operations in June 1943. For German SS and policemen, including Katzmann, such reports showed off to superiors that they had done their job of achieving a "Jew-free" district in a thorough manner (hence the focus on numbers in Katzmann's report). Like the Stroop Report, which praised the German "victory" over the Warsaw ghetto, Katzmann's report exaggerated the Jewish "threat" to legitimate the extreme Nazi policy of total annihilation.[1] Furthermore, the careerist, fanatical Katzmann presented his "accomplishment" with visual proof. His report is also a photo album depicting the typical Nazi tropes and antisemitic stereotypes of a conqueror committing genocide. Individual Jewish victims appear not with names but with captioned labels, designations such as "criminal," "saboteur," "vermin." The photographs of the labor camps, such as Jaktorów where Golfard was a prisoner (see p. 65), disguise the terror and sadism that reigned there. The camps appear to be peaceful, orderly systems run by enthusiastic collaborators. There are few prisoners in the photographs.

DOCUMENT 2: **"Report by the SS and Police Leader for the District of Galicia, June 30, 1943: Mass Killings of Jews in Galicia" (Katzmann Report), partial English translation (document L-18) reprinted in the Office of United States Chief of Counsel for Prosecution of Axis Criminality, *Nazi Conspiracy and Aggression* (Washington, DC: U.S. Government Printing Office, 1946), 7:755–70.**[2]

State Secret
The SS & Police Leader
In the District of Galicia

June 30th 1943

Ref. 42/43 g.R.-Ch/Fr

2 Copies
1st copy

---

1. On the Stroop report, see Sybil Milton, ed., *The Stroop Report: The Jewish Quarter of Warsaw Is No More!* (New York: Pantheon Books, 1979).

2. The German version is reprinted as document 018-L in *Trial of the Major War Criminals before the International Military Tribunal, Nuremberg, 14 November 1945–1 October 1946* (Nuremberg: International Military Tribunal, 1949), 37:391–431.

Re: Solution of the Jewish Question in Galicia
Concerning: Enclosed Report
Enclosure: 1 Report (executed in triplicate)
                     1 bound Copy
To: The Higher SS and Police Leader East, SS Obergruppenführer
       and General of Police Krüger or his official representative
                                   Cracow [Kraków]
Enclosed I am submitting the lst copy of the Final Report on the
Solution of the Jewish Question in the District of Galicia for your
information.

[Signed] Katzmann
SS Gruppenführer and Lt. Gen. of Police

SOLUTION OF THE JEWISH PROBLEM IN THE DISTRICT OF GALICIA

Owing to the term "Galician Jew," Galicia probably was the spot on
earth which was best known and most frequently mentioned in connection
with Jewry. Here they lived in immense multitudes, forming a world of their
own, out of which the rising generations of world-Jewry were supplied. In
all parts of Galicia, one found Jews in their hundreds of thousands.

According to obsolete statistics of 1931, the number of Jews then was
about 502,000. This number should not have decreased from 1931 up to
the summer of 1941. Precise statements on the number of Jews present
at the time when the German troops invaded Galicia are not available.
By the Committees of Jews the number was stated to have been 350,000
at the end of 1941. That this statement was incorrect will be seen from
the statement at the end of this report with regard to the evacuation of
Jews. The town of Lemberg alone had about 160,000 Jewish inhabitants
in July–August 1941. [. . .]

Our first measure consisted of marking every Jew by a white armlet
bearing the Star of David in blue. By virtue of a decree of the Governor
General the Department of the Interior was responsible for the marking
and registration of Jews as well as for the formation of Committees of
Jews. Our task, that of the Police, was first of all to counter effectively the
immense black market carried on by Jews throughout the entire district
and especially to take measures against loafing idlers and vagabonds.

The best remedy consisted of the formation, by the SS and Police
Leader, of Forced Labor Camps. The best opportunities for labor were

offered by the necessity to complete the Dg. 4[3] road which was extremely important and necessary for the whole of the southern part of the front, and which was in a catastrophically bad condition. On October 15, 1941, the establishment of camps along the road was commenced, and despite considerable difficulties there existed, after a few weeks, only seven camps containing 4,000 Jews.

Soon more camps followed these first ones, so that after a very short time the completion of 15 camps of this kind could be reported to the Higher SS and Police Leader. In the course of time about 20,000 Jewish labourers passed through these camps. Despite the hardly imaginable difficulties occurring at this work I can report today that about 160 km of the road are completed. [. . .]

* * * * * *

At the same time all other Jews fit for work were registered and distributed for useful work by the labor agencies. When the Jews were marked by the Star of David as well as when they were registered by the labor agencies, the first symptoms appeared of their attempts to dodge the orders of the authorities. The measures which were introduced thereupon led to thousands of arrests. It became more and more apparent that the Civil Administration was not in a position to solve the Jewish problem in an approximately satisfactory manner. When, for instance, the Municipal Administration in Lwow [Lwów] had no success in their attempts to house the Jews within a close district which would be inhabited only by Jews, this question too was solved quickly by the SS and Police Leader through his subordinate officials. This measure became the more urgent as in winter 1941 big centres of spotted fever were noted in many parts of the town whereby not only the native population was endangered but also, and to a greater extent, the troops themselves, those stationed there as well as those passing through. [. . .]

[O]wing to the peculiar fact that almost 90% of artisans working in Galicia were Jews, the task to be solved could be fulfilled only step by step, since an immediate evacuation would not have served the interest of war economy. With regard to those Jews, however, who had a place in the labor process, no real effect could be found of their work. They used their job mostly only as a means to an end, namely in order first to dodge the intensified measures against Jewry and secondly to be able to carry on their black market activities without interference. Only by continuous police

---

3. Durchgangsstrasse IV, or Thoroughfare IV (see above, p. 19).

interference was it possible to prevent these activities. After it had been found in more and more cases that Jews had succeeded in making themselves indispensable to their employers by providing them with goods in scarce supply etc., it was considered necessary to introduce really draconic measures. Unfortunately it had to be stated that the Germans employed in the district, especially so-called "Operational Firms" or the "ill-famed Trustees," carried on the most extravagant black market activities with Jews. Cases were discovered where Jews, in order to acquire any certificate of labor, not only renounced all wages, but even paid money themselves. Moreover, the "organizing" of Jews for the benefit of their "employers" grew to so catastrophical extents [*sic*] that it was deemed necessary to interfere in the most energetic manner for the benefit of the German name.

Since the Administration was not in a position and showed itself too weak to master this chaos, the SS and Police Leader simply took over the entire disposition of labor for Jews. The Jewish Labor Agencies, which were manned by hundreds of Jews, were dissolved. All certificates of labor given by firms or administrative offices were declared invalid, and the cards given to the Jews by the Labor Agencies were revalidated by the Police Offices by stamping them.

In the course of this action again thousands of Jews were caught who were in possession of forged certificates or who had obtained surreptitiously certificates of labor by all kinds of pretexts. These Jews also were exposed to special treatment.

Army administration offices in particular had countenanced Jewish parasitism by giving special certificates to an uncontrollable extent. [. . .]

There were cases when arrested Jews were in possession of 10 to 20 of such certificates.

Where Jews were arrested in the course of these check-ups most of their employers thought it necessary to intervene in favor of the Jews. This often happened in a manner which had to be called deeply shameful. [. . .]

Despite all these measures concerning the employment of Jews their evacuation [*Aussiedlung*] from the district of Galicia was commenced in April 1942, and executed step by step.

When the Higher SS and Police Leader once again intervened in the solution of the Jewish problem by his Decree Concerning the Formation of Districts inhabited by Jews of [November 10,] 1942, already *254,989 Jews* had been evacuated [*ausgesiedelt*], resp. resettled [*umgesiedelt*].

Since the Higher SS and Police Leader gave the further order to accelerate the complete evacuation [*Aussiedlung*] of the Jews, again considerable work was necessary to regulate the status of those Jews who, for the time being were permitted to be left in the armaments factories. The Jews in question were declared Labor Prisoners of the Higher SS and Police Leader and they were put into barracks, either within the factories or in camps established for this purpose. For the town of Lwow [Lwów] a Giant Camp was established at the borders of the town, in which at the time of writing 8,000 Jewish Labor Prisoners are confined. The agreement with the Army concerning the disposition and treatment of these Labor Prisoners was executed in writing. [. . .]

In the meantime further evacuation [*Aussiedlung*] was executed with energy, so that with effect from 23 June 1943 all Jewish Residence Districts could be dissolved. Therewith I report that the District of Galicia, with the exception of those Jews living in the camps being under the control of the SS & Pol. Leader, is

Free from Jews

Jews still caught in small numbers are given special treatment [killed] by the competent detachments of Police and Gendarmerie.

Up to 27 June 1943 altogether 434,329 Jews have been evacuated [*ausgesiedelt*]. [. . .]

Together with the evacuated action, we executed the confiscation of Jewish property. Very high amounts were confiscated and paid over to the Special Staff "Reinhard." Apart from furniture and many textile goods, the following amounts were confiscated and turned over to Special Staff "Reinhard":

As per [30 June] 1943:

25,580	kg	Copper Coins
53,190	kg	Nickel Coins
97,581	kg	Gold Coins
82,600	kg	Necklaces—Silver
6,640	kg	Necklaces—Gold
432,780	kg	Broken Silver

[. . .; list continues]

[. . .] On the occasion of these actions, many more difficulties occurred owing to the fact that the Jews tried every means in order to dodge evacuation [*Aussiedlung*]. Not only did they try to flee, but they concealed themselves in every imaginable corner, in pipes, chimneys, even in sewers, etc. They built barricades in passages of catacombs, in cellars enlarged to dug-outs, in underground holes, in cunningly contrived hiding-places in attics and sheds, within furniture, etc.

The smaller the number of Jews remaining in the district, the harder their resistance. Arms of all kinds, among them those of Italian make, were used for defense. The Jews purchased these Italian arms from Italian soldiers stationed in the District for high sums in Zloty currency. [. . .]

Underground bunkers were found with entrances concealed in a masterly manner opening some times into flats, some times into the open. In most cases the entrances had only so much width that just one person could crawl through it. The access was concealed in such a manner that it could not be found by persons not acquainted with the locality. [. . .]

Since we received more and more alarming reports on the Jews becoming armed in an ever increasing manner, we started during the last fortnight in June 1943 an action throughout the whole of the district of Galicia with the intent to use strongest measures to destroy the Jewish gangsterdom. Special measures were found necessary during the action to dissolve the Ghetto in Lwow where the dug-outs mentioned above had been established. Here we had to act brutally from the beginning, in order to avoid losses on our side; we had to blow up or to burn down several houses. On this occasion the surprising fact arose that we were able to catch about 20,000 Jews instead of 12,000 Jews who had registered. We had to pull at least 3,000 Jewish corpses out of every kind of hiding places; they had committed suicide by taking poison. [. . .]

Despite the extraordinary burden heaped upon every single SS-Police Officer during these actions, mood and spirit of the men were extraordinarily good and praiseworthy from the first to the last day.

Only thanks to the sense of duty of every single leader and man have we succeeded in getting rid of this PLAGUE in so short a time. [. . .]

The propaganda machinery of the Third Reich effectively mobilized Germans to wage a genocidal war in the east. One of the recurring themes that blared from loudspeakers and radios and was pictured in film, on street posters, and in school textbooks was that the Jewish "enemy" threatened Germany's existence. On the tenth anniversary of Hitler's appointment as chancellor, Nazi leaders planned elaborate celebrations and ceremonies and broadcast speeches around the country, to the troops on the front, and in the occupied territories. On January 31, 1943, Golfard wrote in his diary, "Yesterday, ten years passed since Hitler's regime prevailed. An address by Hitler was expected, but only Goebbels and Goering spoke." Golfard was right about the mysterious absence of Hitler, who did not speak at the Berlin rally. The first daylight raids of British Mosquito bombers had delayed and interrupted the rally, and, as a British press correspondent wrote, "crashed Hitler's gloomy tenth anniversary party." On February 18, 1943, Propaganda Minister Joseph Goebbels was back on the airwaves broadcasting his famous "total war" speech, in which he urged Germans to "rise up and let the storm break loose" and argued that the Bolshevik threat from the east could only be defeated by a total effort. In this speech and during the earlier tenth anniversary celebrations, Nazi leaders propagated a sinister, fanatical resolve in the face of possible defeat. As the British reported, Goebbels warned that "severe penalties" would be meted out to those who sabotaged the German war effort. This was not an empty threat and was aimed at all, especially the Jews, who were branded collectively as saboteurs and an enemy race.[4]

One of the central questions in the history of Nazi Germany and the Holocaust concerns the knowledge of ordinary Germans about the genocide in the east. After the war most Germans, shocked by the atrocities, demoralized, ashamed, and afraid of prosecution, asserted that they did not know what was happening, often reflexively blurting out to inquisitors, "Davon habe ich nichts gewusst" (I knew nothing about that). Such a reaction begs the question, What exactly was "that" of which one knew nothing? When could one know what exactly? Historians such as Peter Longerich, Robert Gellately, and Jeffrey Herf have found that by early 1943, the period of Golfard's diary, the systematic mass murder of the Jews deported to the east was well-known in continental Europe and abroad. Allied broadcasts of speeches, newspaper accounts, and information shared by German soldiers and policemen who arrived home from the eastern front presented a grim picture of the fate of Jews.[5]

Jews in the areas under German control were confronted with the daily manifestations of murderous intent, yet had few opportunities to incorporate their experiences into the bigger picture. News reports about military and political events blended with rumors, forming an uneven, contradictory

4. In fact, in his broadcasted speech, Goebbels hinted at the physical elimination of the Jews as he uttered the first two syllables of the German equivalent of "extermination" (*Ausrottung*), quickly correcting himself to the less obvious "exclusion" (*Ausschaltung*). See Bernward Dörner, *Die Deutschen und der Holocaust: Was niemand wissen wollte, aber jeder wissen konnte* (Berlin: Ullstein, 2007), 142.

5. Peter Longerich, *"Davon haben wir nichts gewusst!" Die Deutschen und die Judenverfolgung 1933–1945* (Munich: Siedler, 2006); Jeffrey Herf, *The Jewish Enemy: Nazi Propaganda during World War II and the Holocaust* (Cambridge, MA: Harvard University Press, 2006); Robert Gellately, *Backing Hitler: Consent and Coercion in Nazi Germany, 1933–1945* (New York: Oxford University Press, 2001); Frank Bajohr and Dieter Pohl, *Der Holocaust als offenes Geheimnis: Die Deutschen, die NS-Führung und die Alliierten* (Munich: C. H. Beck, 2006).

image of the situation. Golfard received information about Gen. Władysław Sikorski's protest of Nazi atrocities launched from London, but while Jews under Nazi domination did not know what was going on in the outside world, public opinion abroad lacked awareness of what German anti-Jewish measures amounted to.[6] The British propaganda about the Nazi crusade, as seen and reported from London in document 3, did not address the plight of the Jews specifically or atrocities in general. The Allied aim of defeating Nazi Germany was a military endeavor, not a humanitarian cause undertaken on behalf of the victimized Jews.

DOCUMENT 3: "The Gate-Crashers," excerpt from *Washington Post* coverage of the tenth anniversary of Hitler's accession to power, January 31, 1943, 1–2.

Bombs Fall Just as Goering Opens Speech; Hitler Is Absent [. . .]

The Gate-Crashers

London: Jan. 30.—British planes making their first daylight raid in history on Berlin today twice crashed Hitler's gloomy tenth anniversary party, and their bombs upset the broadcast explanations of Reichsmarshal Goering and Propaganda Minister Goebbels as to why German armies are meeting reverses in Russia.

Hitler—perhaps guided by his intuition—was reported to be off somewhere "with his soldiers" when the R.A.F.'s fast Mosquito bombers struck precisely at 11 a.m., Berlin time, as the bemedaled Goering was ready to talk at the Air Ministry in the heart of Berlin.

Explosions could be heard over the Berlin radio here in London. There were shouts, too, indicating turmoil within the ministry as the plump Goering and his audience scrambled for shelter.

The Berlin radio remained on the air to advise listeners from time to time that "there will be a few more minutes' delay in Marshal Goering's speech."

Delay Lasts Till Noon

The delay lasted until noon, an hour later.

---

6. See the report on Sikorski's speech mentioned by Golfard in his diary (see above, p. 91).

Then at 4 p.m., the Mosquitoes struck again, this time as Goebbels was beginning to talk in the Sportspalast. The propaganda minister had been delegated by Hitler to read a proclamation on one of the rare occasions when Hitler has not personally spoken to his people on the anniversary of his rise to power in 1933.

No British planes were lost in the first raid, and only one was missing after the second attack.

The R.A.F. pilots roared over Berlin at a high level instead of usual rooftop height employed by these swift bombers that can carry four 500-pound bombs and attain speeds up to 400 miles an hour.

The British raids apparently were heavy only in a psychological way. Berliners were kept busy running to shelter and keeping an eye on the sky while listening to their leaders simultaneously spur them to total effort and threaten death to shirkers.

Hitler's "Intuition" Again

Neither Hitler, Goering, nor Goebbels tried to predict when the promised German victory would come. Goering dwelt for some time in his 90-minute talk on why Germany never attacked Russia in the first place, finally attributing it to Hitler's "intuition."

He said the Russians had grossly "camouflaged" their inept 1939-40 winter war against Finland, then in an apparent contradiction of himself later said that Germany knew the true Soviet strength when the Nazis invaded Russia.

Goebbels made a long speech promising severe penalties for any attempted sabotage of the German war effort before reading Hitler's proclamation. Even while he was speaking a Reuters dispatch from Zurich said 17 German workers at Dusseldorf had been condemned to death for sabotage.

The second raid did not delay Goebbels' speech and the reading of Hitler's proclamation as far as could be determined here. British listeners heard nothing to compare with the confusion caused by the first raid.

Britons Are Jubilant

Britons, of course, were jubilant over the double slap at the Germans which was timed perfectly for its most embarrassing effect on Nazi leaders.

One returning pilot, Sergt. J. Massey, was quoted by the Air Ministry as saying: "We made for the center of Berlin and bombed. Only one thing startled me—the stillness over Berlin. We saw only one squirt of flak on the way out." [. . .]

What do communist propaganda leaflets reveal about the Soviet approach to mobilizing and unifying supporters, as compared to the Allied reports and Nazi speeches in the previous documents? While much is known about British, U.S., and German propaganda and wartime knowledge of the Holocaust, comparatively little has been uncovered and published about the Soviet side of this story. This is mainly because scholars have not accessed Soviet intelligence documentation from the war, including central orders or meeting reports from Stalin's besieged Moscow. Since the collapse of the Soviet Union, scholars have been able to conduct research in the provincial capitals of the newly independent states such as Ukraine and their regional and local archives. Thus, one can work from the "bottom up" by collecting evidence from operations in the field and looking for patterns that might point to a central Soviet policy, while revealing the specific influences and contexts of local conditions.

The Soviet communist propaganda leaflets presented in documents 4 and 5, found in the Ukrainian Central State Archives in Kiev, were part of a regional Soviet propaganda campaign around Peremyshliany. They are remarkable for several reasons. First, one is struck in the first lines by the reference to "forthcoming generations" and sacrifices of Soviet peoples in the "Great Patriotic War." According to historian Amir Weiner's research on the region of Vinnytsia during and after the war, Soviet leaders were well aware that the Nazi occupation and Red Army defeats in 1941–1942 had undermined popular support for Stalinism and that propaganda had to mobilize people on the front and behind the lines by "making sense of the war" with a counternarrative to the one offered by the Nazis, which stressed the evils and failings of Bolshevism. To expel Nazi conquerors from Stalin's empire, the "peoples of the great Soviet Union" had to be unified and demonstrate their loyalty to Moscow. In reality, however, disunity reigned among civilians and various partisan units that operated in the occupied territories. In fact, the Nazi occupation seeded new antagonisms and solidified old ones. Nazi "ethnic cleansing" and racial policies stoked interethnic warfare among Ukrainians, Poles, ethnic Germans, Russians, and Jews in the forests of Galicia and Volhynia. Since survival in the face of unfettered violence was the immediate concern of most, people switched sides in this maelstrom of overlapping nationalist, communist, anti-Nazi, anti-Soviet, and anti-Jewish warfare.

Second, the leaflets candidly relate in vivid detail the unique plight of Jews under Nazi rule. This would later be suppressed under the patriotic slogan that all peaceful Soviet citizens suffered equally. The depiction of Ukrainian policemen and "Galician scoundrels" as bloodthirsty, traitorous "proxies" of the Germans remained a mainstay of Soviet propaganda and fueled the massive repression of Ukrainian nationalism, as well as tens of thousands of postwar investigations and trials of Ukrainian "traitors to the homeland."

Third, the timing and detailed content of the leaflets suggest that the Soviets had people on the ground who were collecting information as events unfolded. The full description of the deportations to Bełżec from Peremyshliany fills in many details that are missing from Golfard's account of his sister's deportation at this time. This Soviet version, dated September 25, 1942, was written as the events occurred and distributed in their immediate aftermath. Were similar leaflets distributed in neighboring towns where such events also occurred? How vast and well-organized was this Soviet information network and propaganda machinery? The specifics about the deportations and atrocities appear in a digested form, not as cryptic reportage but in a literary style full of indignation and poetic references to nature. The images of the Jewish victims are of women and children; though not a distortion of fact, the obvious stress here was probably intended to evoke more sympathy and outrage from the reader. The text is presented in Ukrainian, not Russian, to appeal to the majority of the population. The leaflet about Commandant Ernst Epple begins with a nod to Pavlo Tychyna (1891–1967), a famous Ukrainian poet, director of the Institute of Ukrainian Literature, minister of education, and member of the Ukrainian Academy of Sciences of the Soviet Socialist Republic, who is merely mentioned for labeling Hitler "the swine of all swines." While most of the leaflet quotes a local source, it excerpts at length a diary entry from November 1942. Who was this diarist, and what happened to the diary, which was shared with, seized, or discovered by Soviet operatives? Its author seems to be one of the "witnesses" who observed Jewish suffering on the road construction project and the spectacle of violence in Epple's Kurowice camp. The scenes that the diarist re-creates of onlookers plugging their ears to muffle the "howls of the hanged man" and of the "fear" that descended on the village are important to keep in mind when one analyzes, and is tempted to judge, the inaction of bystanders as a whole during the Holocaust. Resorting to such a blanket condemnation, the Soviet leaflet concludes that "Galician renegades [. . .] enjoy watching the human tragedy."

DOCUMENT 4: **"Epple Plays Around," Soviet wartime underground leaflet describing the cruelties at the Kurowice camp perpetrated by Commandant Ernst Epple and similar atrocities committed at Jaktorów, January 4, 1943, Central State Archives of Public Organizations of Ukraine, Kiev, TsDAHO P-57/4/237 (translated from Ukrainian).**

Once years and decades have passed, our historians and writers will vividly describe the times when the Hitlerite bandits dominated the lands of our Great Motherland. Future generations of historians and artists will learn the realities of this epoch, the Second War for the Motherland, when the peoples of the great Soviet Union waged a heroic struggle like none before it in history, against vandals of the 20th century, those troops of the Hitlerite conquerors whom Hitler—the "Little Napoleon"—ordered to invade our land. Ukrainian poet P[avlo] Tychyna called Hitler "a Pig-Napoleonchik, or the most swinish swine of all hogs." This bandit will for centuries to come be infamous for his cruelty, surpassing all cruelty, in bestiality surpassing all possible bestiality. This monster together with a gang of his bandits has, based on some "racial theory," determined that the Germans belong to the "superior" race and are entitled to govern over the whole world, while all other peoples are to become their slaves. Convinced in his deluded head that the Germans are going to win the war, he began to annihilate mankind: first the Jews, then the Ukrainians and the Poles. This annihilation is carried out by the Hitlerites in various ways: by sudden roundups, mass arrests of people, and deportations of many tens of thousands to Belz [Bełżec]; mass arrests and deportations to the [labor] camps or shootings on the spot; and finally, by starvation to death or shootings and hanging in the camps.

One cannot explain it—there are no words to describe all the images of horror, the atrocities, the pain inflicted on the Jews and on anybody who is sent to a camp, who suffers at the hands of the German executioners and their collaborators, Ukrainian policemen. These Hitlerite dogs, bribed to the extreme, were always drunk and corrupt, stained by human blood, they tortured people worse than cattle, uncontrollably and with impunity. For them, murdering a person is like an amusement and a bestial pleasure. After having his meal, Grzymyk[7]—the commandant of the camp at Hrushka [Jaktorów]—makes a sport out of shooting people in the head from a certain range. He says he cannot get a good night's sleep if he does not kill 10–20 Jews daily. The commandant of the camp in the

---

7. For Josef Grzimek, see Biographies.

village of Kurowice, Epple (also a German), amuses himself in this manner: he hangs a person loosely in order to prolong his suffering before death, he lets his dogs attack and bite the person who is still alive, inflicting additional pain on the poor victim.

One of the eyewitnesses passing through Kurowice noted the following in his diary:

> November 1942. It was a cold autumn day. A drizzling rain fell all around. The ground underfoot turned into mud. Approaching the cathedral, we met a group of ragged, half-barefoot people with weary faces. The policemen escorted them. Whoever fell behind was mercilessly beaten with rubber sticks. People collapsed, pleaded, begged, but there was no one to help them. The response was to be whipped with a stick or a bullet to the head. Not even three minutes had passed when the policemen killed two Jews only for slightly falling out of line. Then they stopped the column, ordered them to line up and start marching in formation while singing one of the Jewish marching songs. These miserable human shadows, awaiting death at any moment, were even forced to sing. The column marched on. From a distance, one heard some unrecognizable sounds, like a crow's screeching, or the hollow creak of unlubricated wagon wheels. Yes. Perhaps, I was thinking, with all these sounds the song of "A New Europe" is being composed. We go on. Behind the column, there are three Jews; two of them move at a slow pace, holding a third one under his arm . . .
>
> In the course of life, people often see dead bodies and do not get scared.—They know that people get sick, their facial expression changes, and they die. More frightening are those dead who were sick for a long time with severe illnesses. But if a dead body lies there motionless, a living person, even if he feels some uneasiness at seeing this dead body, will not be frightened. However, if a dead man were to rise up and begin to move, then indeed the bravest person would be terribly frightened.
>
> This third person, who was carried under the arms by the two others, was a moving corpse. Only his legs jerked uncontrollably. He was not only being held upright by the two, but was carried by them. His drooping arms were motionless. He was half alive and half dead. It seemed that his bones were about to scatter onto the road, and only his dried, yellow, waxlike skin still kept them

together. His head, protruding from his stiff neck, was frozen. His deep, sunken eyes were gone. Instead of eyes, it seemed as if he had some round pieces of glass with which he stared into the distance, at one fixed point. And yet this man was being brought in a labor convoy to break stones. How he could work and for how long is unknown. However, the commandant Epple unexpectedly encountered and stopped these three. He made them go back to the camp, located near the church opposite the schoolyard. We had to go in the same direction, so we stopped to let these three pass. However, it was another horrible spectacle for us. We happened to arrive at the same time when Epple ordered the hanging of this Jew who was dying of starvation. They hung him by one arm and one leg so that he would not die quickly. Then Epple released his two big dogs and set them on the hanged man. The dogs attacked the victim, they growled, ripped his skin, tore his flesh to pieces. The miserable man screamed, writhed, pleaded for rescue. However, nobody dared or was able to save him. Passers-by (for this scene was by the road) were running away, unwilling to watch this horror. They plugged their ears to block out the terrifying and piercing howls of the hanged man. Meanwhile, Epple's children were running around the gallows, yelling to the dogs, and laughing gleefully. For them as well as for their father, all this was an amusement. The people of Kurowice say that Epple arranges such amusements almost every day. Then fear descends on the village of Kurowice. What is Kurowice, if the entire *Grossdeutschland* [Greater Germany] is one big camp?!

The Executioner rages. The Executioner is afraid in the face of his own demise. All this while the Galician renegades hide themselves and enjoy watching the human tragedy. Providing assistance to the occupiers, they do not see that the invader has already stretched his bloody hand out upon them.

DOCUMENT 5: **"A Sketch of Life in a 'New Europe,'" Soviet wartime underground leaflet describing the deportations to Bełżec from Peremyshliany, September 25, 1942, Central State Archives of Public Organizations of Ukraine, Kiev, TsDAHO P-57/4/237 (translated from Ukrainian).**

It was the end of August 1942. Evening settled in. Bright sunrays scorch the west, piercing through the branches of spruces and imprinting a final reflection of blood-red spots on the walls of houses. Tired at the end of the day, the sun went to rest. It was quiet.

Suddenly shots were heard. A commotion arose. Everyone fled wherever possible. Nobody knew what was happening. Finally, someone quietly said, "It is an 'Aktion' . . . against the Jews . . . There are many Gestapo in town." Another shot was heard, this time closer. The air shuddered and trembled. The Gestapo encircled the town. It seemed after a heavy silence that the wind began to rise, causing the trees to howl. Through the alarming howling, a terrifying sound came up. Yet these horrifying sounds did not come from the trees. These were human moans and screams—the Jews were being herded into the market square. These wretched people begged for mercy, they cried and moaned to no avail. The adamant knights of the "New Europe" silenced their victims by shooting them in the head or by whipping them.

An exhausted and completely weary mother of three children struggled with the youngest of them in her arms. Hungry and weak, she could not go any faster. A Gestapo man, like a beast in human form, snatched the baby from her arms and threw it to the other side of the street. Shattered pieces of brain and blood stained walls and the cobblestone road red.

A bit further, on the other side of the street, lay the body of a young and beautiful Jewish woman. Probably yesterday she did not think that she would die at such a young age. She might have had a younger brother and a sister for whom she cared. They hanged her father in the Kurowice camp, and her mother has disappeared, nobody knew to where. And today she is lying with closed lips and eyes wide open, gazing into the distance.

At the other side of the street, the Jewish policemen escorted an old man—a doctor. He was not able to run away, and he has nothing to offer to save himself. In the meantime, the [market] square filled with dozens, with hundreds of people who were a few hours away from their death in Belz [Bełżec].

Like wild hawks, the drunken Gestapo rushed from street to street, hunting their prey, while the "*Judenrat*" and Jewish police served them vodka and beer. The loyal dogs of the atrocious villain—"napoleonchik" Hitler—indulged themselves in a bloody banquet.[8]

Night came. Screams of despair were heard from various sides of the street. These screams blended with gunshots and with lights from

---

8. "Napoleonchik" is a diminutive form of Napoleon with a negative connotation.

flashlights, which resembled the glinting eyes of a pack of hungry wolves in the dark forest.

At about one o'clock in the morning, a dozen trucks were loaded with people whose lives would soon come to an end. The trucks left for Belz [Bełżec]. Indistinct sounds of groaning and moaning, pleas and curses, despair and prayers, screams and protests were heard in the sleepy town. These sounds converged into a solitary, sad, and sorrowful song echoing life in "The New Europe of Hitler."

On the next day, having done their work, the bloody vampires launched a feast: drinking vodka and beer, stuffing themselves with sandwiches.

In the meantime, the "*Judenrat*" and the Ukrainian Police, together with the Jewish Police, worked on filling the next Jewish quota bound for Belz [Bełżec]. They seized destitute people across the town, filling the jails with them.

This is how it was in Peremyshliany. Yet it was the same in all the towns and villages "liberated" by bloody Hitler.

I. Tyrsa

Town of Peremyshliany
25 September 1942[9]

POSTWAR DOCUMENTS

In the mid-1960s, West German state prosecutors conducted one of the largest trials against Nazi perpetrators to be held in the Federal Republic of Germany: the Lemberg (Lviv) Trial in the city of Stuttgart. At the end of proceedings, which included ten thousand pages of excerpted witness statements and eighty volumes of briefs and documents, only one life sentence was passed, in this case on Ernst Epple, former commandant of the Kurowice camp. Paul Fox, the former commandant at Jaktorów camp, whom Golfard identified by name, was acquitted. Of course, prosecutors did not have Golfard's diary to use as evidence in the trial. Prior to the judgment, the presiding judge asserted that it was not the task of the court in these proceedings to master Germany's past: it was the task of the entire nation, "whose conscience cannot be released and all

---

9. Certification at the end of the document: "Edition of 'The Committee of the Liberation of Motherland' or Committee: Liberation of Motherland. *Komitet 'Vyzvolennia Vitchyzny.'* 4 January 1943, City of Lviv." [Archival stamp and verification phrase and signature:] "This is true to the original. The Head of the Regional Party Archives of the Lviv Regional Party Committee of the Communist Party (Bolshevik) of Ukraine. Signature: Rostislava."

Ernst Epple, former commandant of Kurowice, arrested and photographed in West Germany in 1960 (Yad Vashem Photo Archive, A1584/209).

its stains wiped clean here in the court."[10] This statement epitomizes the view of a conservative judiciary that, on the one hand, understood the shameful magnitude of Germany's crimes but, on the other hand, distanced itself, courtroom defendants, and German society at large from personal responsibility for the crimes. The conviction rate for those who had blood on their hands was very low, despite suspension of the statute of limitations on murder committed during the Nazi era.[11]

Yet, trials such as the Lemberg Trial were not strictly national events. Although the defendants were German, the crimes had occurred outside of Germany, and the victims and many witnesses were mostly non-Germans. Held in the late 1960s, when the Eichmann Trial in Jerusalem, the Auschwitz Trial in Frankfurt, and the Anne Frank Trial in Munich had already sparked awareness of the Holocaust, the Lemberg Trial was part of a wave of post-Nuremberg proceedings that captured the attention of a much wider audience through the international media coverage accorded these trials. The presiding judge's statements were quoted in large-circulation newspapers such as the *New York Times*, as well as *Aufbau*, a more specialized, intellectual weekly catering to the German Jewish émigré community centered in New York.

---

10. Quoted from the German newspaper coverage of the trial, "Das Urteil im Lemberg Prozess," April 30, 1968, which was included in the Stuttgart prosecutor's press clipping file. BAL 162/4688 (208 AR-Z 294/59).

11. Annette Weinke, *Die Verfolgung von NS-Tätern im geteilten Deutschland. Vergangenheitsbewältigungen 1949–1969, oder: eine deutsch-deutsche Beziehungsgeschichte im Kalten Krieg* (Paderborn: Ferdinand Schöningh, 2002).

The article in *Aufbau* was among the more informed accounts because the newspaper had a deeper historical interest in the subject, and its author, Robert Kempner (1899–1993), was a prominent expert in German law and former prosecutor of Nazi war crimes at the Nuremberg Trials. The German-language newspaper, which first appeared in 1934, became a platform for intellectuals who publicized some of the earliest reports on the mass atrocities. Such eminent figures as Hannah Arendt, Albert Einstein, Theodor Adorno, and Thomas Mann were among those who emigrated or went into exile and wrote for *Aufbau*. After the war, the pages of the newspaper were often crowded with name lists of Jews who had survived in Europe and queries about family members who had gone missing in the war. In later years it regularly featured stories and commentaries on the war crimes trials and occasionally published announcements calling for Jewish survivors who could assist German prosecutors investigating Nazi crimes.

Robert Kempner remained a regular contributor to *Aufbau*. Prior to his emigration to America, Kempner had been a senior legal counsel in the police section of the Prussian Ministry of the Interior and a member of the Social Democratic Party. In February 1933 he was forced to resign his position; he later left Germany for Italy, eventually making his way to the United States in September 1939. Unlike most of the hundreds of thousands of German Jews who fled Nazi Germany in the 1930s, Kempner returned to Germany after the war, first to serve on the prosecution team at the International Military Tribunal at Nuremberg and as chief prosecutor at the eleventh Subsequent Nuremberg Trial (against members of the German Foreign Office and other Reich ministries, bank officials, and the Nazi Party hierarchy). Later he continued to practice law in his office in Frankfurt am Main, assisting survivors of Nazi persecution with restitution claims. Kempner remained an active publicist, who commented regularly in the German, Israeli, and American press about war crimes trials and the German legal system, particularly about the West German statute of limitations for Nazi war crimes.[12]

---

12. Hermann Weber, "Robert Kempner (geb. 1899). Vom Justitiar in der Polizeiabteilung des Preussischen Innenministeriums zum stellvertretenden US-Hauptankläger in Nürnberg," in *Deutsche Juristen jüdischer Herkunft*, ed. H. C. Helmut Heinrichs et al. (Munich: C. H. Beck'sche Verlagsbuchhandlung, 1993), 793–811.

DOCUMENT 6: R. M. W. Kempner, "'Genocide as Official Business': The Judgment in the Lemberg Trial," *Aufbau* (New York), May 10, 1968, 7 (translated from German).[13]

The most protracted of the trials of SS killers, the so-called Lemberg Trial in Stuttgart involving the murder of Jews in Galicia, has come to an end. After 144 days in court and examination of more than 200 witnesses, Ernst Epple, a crane operator from Reutlingen, was sentenced to life in prison on six counts of murder. The following members of murder squads received prison sentences of 2 1/2 to 8 years for being accessories to murder: Rudolf Röder, 10 years; Ernst Inquart, 9 years; Karl Wöbke, 9 years; Ernst Heinisch, 8 years; Roman Schönbach, 8 years; Adolf Kolonko, 7 years; Anton Löhnert, 7 years; Peter Blum, 6 1/2 years; Hans Sobotta, 2 1/2 years. Of a total of 15 defendants, four—Heinz Weber, Martin Büttner, Ernst Preuss, and Paul Fox—were acquitted, while defendant Karl Ulmer, though found guilty of being an accessory to murder, was not punished.

Chief prosecutor Rolf Sichting and prosecutor Karl-Heinz Ehni had requested only three acquittals and eight life sentences.

The most important piece of evidence was a report on the murders written by the higher SS and police leader in Galicia, Katzmann, which had already been introduced as evidence in the Nuremberg Trials. In this horror document, as Dr. Peter Pracht, the presiding judge, termed it, the extermination of the Jews of Galicia was described in detail. The finding of the court, the judge declared, was that in total at least 439,329 Jews were the victims here. Only 21,156 Jews survived.

As he read the verdict, the presiding judge declared with his voice raised that this was a case of "genocide as official business" and that the term "war crime" was not applicable. The guilt of individual murderers had to be established insofar as they could still be identified. These SS murderers had not acted under duress, he said; there were numerous instances in which individuals had refused to obey orders to fire without

13. Jürgen Matthäus, "'No Ordinary Criminal': Georg Heuser, Other Mass Murderers, and West German Justice", in *Atrocities on Trial: Historical Perspectives on the Politics of Prosecuting War Crimes*, ed. Patricia Heberer and Jürgen Matthäus (Lincoln: University of Nebraska Press in association with the USHMM, 2008), 187–209; Alexander Prusin, "Poland's Nuremberg: The Seven Court Cases of the Supreme National Tribunal, 1946–1948" (unpublished manuscript, paper delivered at the USHMM's summer workshop on war crimes trials, Washington, DC, June 6–17, 2005).

suffering any consequences. The convicted men had clearly done wrong:
even back then, murder was murder.

In the early 1970s in Poland, a regional prosecutor's office in Wrocław collected testimony on Nazi crimes committed in Peremyshliany. The investigation
began when a Polish citizen brought three atrocity photos from Peremyshliany
to the attention of the authorities. The photographs were published in the newspaper, and anyone with information about them was asked to report to the
Wrocław office. About ten testimonies were taken, but not enough evidence
was unearthed to indict suspects and hold a trial. Twenty years later, in post-
Soviet Poland, the case was reopened by the Institute of National Memory,
Main Commission for the Prosecution of Crimes against the Polish Nation
(IPN). Since the 1990s, this commission had a dual mandate: to investigate
crimes committed against Poles during both the Nazi and the communist eras.
In 1998 IPN officials contacted the German Central Investigative Office for
Nazi Crimes in Ludwigsburg and inquired about any additional information
related to the murder of four hundred Jews in Peremyshliany during 1942 and
1943. For the next three years, both governments kept the investigation open,
though little material was added to their files. The Germans found that the
primary suspects had died and closed the case in 2001. The Poles depended
heavily on the Germans for additional information, which was not provided in
a timely manner. Meanwhile, the IPN shifted its attention to the investigation
and prosecution of postwar Soviet-era crimes. In May 2005 the Poles disconti-
ued the Peremyshliany investigation. This failed attempt at justice is not surprising. Most investigations did not result in trials. Between the end of the war and
the early 1990s, the West Germans launched more than 103,000 investigations,
but fewer than 6,500 led to a conviction. Behind the Iron Curtain, according
to Alexander Prusin's research, "Polish courts tried more than 20,000 culprits,
including 5,450 German nationals, who were tried largely in the 1940s and
1950s."[14] The politics of the Cold War complicated legal investigations and collaboration across national borders.

At best a fraction of German perpetrators active in Peremyshliany were
investigated, and a handful (mainly the top persons) were tried and served time:
Commandant Josef Grzimek at the Jaktorów camp was tried by the Poles, sentenced to death, and died in prison in 1950. Commandant Friedrich Warzok

---

14. Jürgen Matthäus, "'No Ordinary Criminal'" in *Atrocities on Trial.* 187–209;
Alexander Prusin, "Poland's Nuremberg: The Seven Court Cases of the Supreme National
Tribunal, 1946–1948" (unpublished manuscript, paper delivered at the USHMM's summer
workshop on war crimes trials, Washington, DC, June 6–17, 2005).

escaped to Egypt after the war. Commandant Paul Fox was acquitted in the Lemberg Trial, whereas Commandant Ernst Epple got the maximum sentence of life in prison, where he died in 1976. Karl Kempka, commandant of the Kurowice camp, died in 1946 and was not tried.[15] In the early 1950s, East German authorities arrested two German gendarmes who participated in the November 1941 massacres in the Brzezina Forest; they let one go and amnestied the other after he had served half his sentence. The fates of the more numerous Ukrainian and ethnic German police collaborators who carried out ghetto liquidations and served as guards at the camps are difficult to trace, though it is clear that Soviet investigators rounded up suspected collaborators en masse and subjected them to deportations, with usually twenty-five years of hard labor; many were sentenced to death by kangaroo courts in 1944 and 1945. In fact, historian Tanja Penter estimates that as many as 80,500 collaborators were arrested by the NKVD in Ukraine between 1943 and 1953. Perhaps one or more of these collaborators committed crimes in Peremyshliany.[16]

In the summer of 2005, Dr. Vladimir Melamed (a historian of the Jews of Lviv) and I traveled to Peremyshliany to see the places mentioned in the diary and search for possible witnesses who might corroborate Golfard's account. Heading east on the main road from Lviv toward Zolochiv, the wartime route of Thoroughfare IV, we came upon the town of Kurowice. The site of the former Kurowice camp, now a *Prosvita* (cultural "enlightenment society" that was historically Ruthenian but is now Ukrainian), is extremely close to the local church, situated just opposite the camp on the same dirt road. At the roadside we discovered a small memorial erected by the Kirschner family. As we stood there wondering about the connection between the Kirschners and the Kurowice camp, a young man appeared in blue workman's overalls. He asked us why we were there. Then his parents emerged from the farmhouse and joined us. They explained that they had been asked by the Kirschner family to look after the memorial, to make sure the weeds around it were cut back and the engraved plaque protected from vandals. As they explained this to us, we could hear the mass being conducted at the Greek Catholic church behind us. That Sunday, as mostly elderly women exited the church, a group gathered and began to talk. The oldest one, who called herself Dziunia but did not offer a full name, had lived through the war and offered the most detailed eyewitness account. She identified the notorious Commandant Epple and also spoke about two incidents that had become part of the local oral history in this village. As we listened

---

15. For histories of these men, see the entries in Biographies.

16. Tanja Penter, "Collaboration on Trial: New Source Material on Soviet Postwar Trials against Collaborators," *Slavic Review* 64 (2005): 782–90.

and observed the other villagers, it became clear that Dziunia was one of the few wartime witnesses left and was revered as the local expert on this history. She had reported the events before, but people listened patiently. One younger woman tried to add to Dziunia's account, but the other villagers dismissed her. In any other situation Dziunia might have been passed over as "just an old peasant woman" telling stories from another era, but her matter-of-fact tone and stiffened posture emanated authority.

The excerpts presented in document 7 show how local storytelling turns individual events, often the most traumatic ones for the eyewitnesses, into legends and parables. Christian bystander Dziunia tried to make sense of Epple's evil in religious terms. She described the brutal hanging of one Jewish prisoner (corroborated in detail by the 1943 Soviet leaflet presented in document 4), but added that a thunderbolt struck the tree where the man was hanged. We had heard this story about the hanging before, but nothing about the lightning striking the tree. In her eyes, this cursed tree was a place of suffering and judgment. The Jewish man was a martyr. Thunder and lightning in the biblical sense signaled God's wrath or the apocalypse. Dziunia's casual testimony demonstrates that for historians (not prosecutors) factual veracity alone is not the sole measure of a testimony's value.

DOCUMENT 7: **Vladimir Melamed and author's interview with Dziunia, July 23, 2005, Kurowice, Ukraine.**

Kurowice, Ukraine, Sunday, July 23, 2005
Transcript from filmed interview.
Wendy Lower and Vladimir Melamed (VM) stand among a group of women next to the church. An older woman (Dziunia) begins to speak (in Ukrainian).
Dziunia: It was a German commandant Epple who was in charge of all Jews. He would come to the [Kurowice] camp at night to check on Jews, to do what he wanted with them. Once, when he hanged a Jewish man in the camp, he left him hanging on the tree for some time. Then they took him off. Soon after, a thunderbolt struck this tree, but the hanged man was no longer there.
VM: Do you remember when the camp was liquidated, when all the Jews were killed?
Dziunia: It was sometime in 1943.
VM: So now there are no signs or markers for those mass graves.

Dziunia: No, there is only a grave of a Jewess [Kirschner], that's it. Last year some people also came from abroad and asked about a monument. I directed them to this Kirschner grave.

VM: What happened to Epple? Was he arrested?

Dziunia: Nothing, he just left for Germany.

VM: Where was the commandant's office in Kurowice?

Dziunia: It was a gendarmerie unit [looks in the direction of the camp]. One Jewish prisoner said, "Someone must survive, and then, when all this will be over, we shall erect a house of sorrow on this site." And there was also a Jewess who was hiding here. First, she was hiding at someone's house; then she moved to the church attic.

VM: Was a priest aware of her hiding in the attic?

Dziunia: I do not know, maybe. The Germans discovered her. Realizing her fate, she asked to put on her best dress and then started walking on the road. She kept walking; then near the church she started to run and was killed [shot] while running. When the Germans entered Kurowice in 1941, there were eight to ten Jewish families. They were all killed on that roadside there.

JACOB LITMAN'S TESTIMONIES

As of 1947 Jacob Litman provided numerous testimonies in Yiddish, Hebrew, and English about his wartime experiences. His first sworn statement was given in defense of a militiaman from Peremyshliany, Zbigniew Kalinksi, who had been falsely accused as a perpetrator when in fact he had rescued Jews. Then, in 1979, Litman testified to Yad Vashem on behalf of Tadeusz Jankiewicz. At this point he revealed that his friend Golfard had been helped by Jankiewicz but was killed by the Germans, and he offered the Golfard diary as evidence to support the investigation of Jankiewicz's rescue activities. In a 1982 audio interview with his son, Julius Litman, in his 1983 introduction to his translation of the Golfard diary, in a 1995 videotaped interview (with his wife, Rita) for the Shoah Foundation, and in his 1997 memoir, Jacob Litman described how he suffered and survived the Holocaust in Ukraine and who Samuel Golfard was. Litman's accounts of Golfard provide the only information available about the possible causes of the diarist's death, his final moments, and the immediate repercussions of his death. These details emerged in the 1980s and early 1990s when Litman focused on recording his own story by providing testimony for his family and the public. As the U.S. Holocaust Memorial Museum prepared to

Jacob and Rita Honig Litman upon their arrival in the United States in 1949 (USHMMA Acc. 2008.316, Litman family collection).

open its doors in 1993, Jacob Litman considered donating the Golfard diary to its collections. Unfortunately, circumstances prevented the diary from becoming part of USHMM's archives for another decade during which time Litman's health deteriorated. In short, Jacob Litman made consistent efforts to document and share his story and Samuel Golfard's diary, at different times and for different reasons.

In the three versions of Litman's testimony presented in documents 8 to 10, one can see slight differences in the details that he remembers, his interpretation of events, and the style of his presentation. Penned in 1982 and 1983, the more formal introduction to the diary, which Litman hoped to publish, has a more detached, scholarly tone that is critical but not harsh. In his own autobiography, written more than a decade later, he judges Golfard's last act with more personal reflection and emotion. In the earlier introduction (and in the audio interview with his son Julius, which was recorded at the same time), Jacob derided Golfard's last act as senseless and impulsive. Yet, later he praised Golfard for committing what he believed was the only assassination attempt of a German commander by a Jew in eastern Galicia. In comparing the audio interview with the written testimonies, one can see that the interview taken by his son elicited from Jacob a more intimate description and judgment of Golfard. But it is in his last written autobiography that Litman revealed how he felt when he buried Golfard and expressed a sympathetic view of his fallen comrade. Although Litman refused to speculate about Golfard's frame of mind when he decided to pull out his gun, one can see in these testimonies that Litman did just that at the time and henceforth, culminating in his question, "Why . . . why . . . why?" Over the years, he struggled to make sense of the horror and senseless loss of life, just as Golfard did in his diary.

In document 8 Jacob Litman describes his first encounter with Samuel Golfard and their exchanges during the war, before he gives an account of Golfard's death.

DOCUMENT 8: Jacob Litman, introduction to *Golfard's Testimony* (1983), 5, USHMMA Acc. 2008.316, Litman family collection.

A few weeks after I came to live in the Katz's apartment [in August 1941], I was introduced there to Samek (Polish diminutive of Samuel) Golfard. He was about 8–10 years my senior, a sociable and well-spoken person who, with his lean figure, high forehead, receding copper-blond hair, and matching moustache, projected the image of an urbane, informed, and self-confident man. This image was reinforced by his wit, tinged with bits of sarcasm, which betrayed liberal-progressive-leftist convictions. Although not long in town, he already knew several individuals of the local "emancipated" Jewish intelligentsia and, at our first encounter, told me a few details about myself as well. I felt then, and for some time afterwards, a certain condescension on his part intimating a belief that I was faring well by luck rather than wits, a conclusion in which he may not have been altogether wrong. Although we talked during his frequent visits with the Katz family, we never really became close friends. After the ghetto was set up in Peremyshliany, we met occasionally and talked about the deteriorating situation, exchanging "news" about the war and rumors concerning our lot, the lot of Jews repeatedly denounced by the Nazis as the most monstrous adversary and the single most dangerous threat to Western civilization. [. . .]

[Some months prior to his death, Samek] came to fall into that category of the "productively employed." His rank and circumstances were even more propitious [than mine] in that he was the only Jew in the immediate territory to land a job with a German firm in charge of collecting scrap metals for recycling, an increasingly pressing task in maintaining the war operations. It was quite useless to speculate how of all the "influential" Jews still around, Samek—penniless, lone, and certainly an easier mark than others—could win such an enviable position. However, aware of his intelligence, his suave, thoughtful manner with people, and his practical cleverness, I personally was not surprised. Be that as it may, Samek became a garbage collector with no pay but with a tin badge on his chest to prove his special status. He was at liberty to roam about in the adjacent villages, buy or beg some food, get to know some Christians in the countryside and, most urgently, ascertain whether or not one of those Christians might, perhaps, be willing to defy danger for the sake of a wretched Jew.

In the first 3–4 months of 1943, when Samek spent most of his time outside the ghetto limits, the situation began to deteriorate more rapidly. Having completed the process of rounding up, caging, and isolating virtually all Jews in the area, the stage was set for the SS-Einsatzgruppe (SS-task force) operating in Eastern Galicia to carry out the ruthless "resettlement actions," a German euphemism for deportations to extermination camps. In the period between these ghastly brutalities, with the ghetto thinned out and conditions eased somewhat, the ever smaller number of survivors deluded themselves and were lulled by promising rumors. In reality, however, it had become obvious that the ghetto inhabitants were doomed. It was impossible to flee because in a climate of pervasive enmity, with fear and indifference all around, there was no place to go.

The annex labor camp in Czupernosów was liquidated. Luckily, I was still considered strong enough to be included in the small group of spared, able-bodied workers put to build prefabricated granaries at the railway station in town. Eventually, the group was ordered out of Peremyshliany and stationed in the main labor camp of Kurowice from which it was transported by trucks every day. But this arrangement did not last long.

On May 23, 1943 the SS-Einsatzgruppe swooped down upon the ghetto of Peremyshliany for the last time, putting a cruel end to its existence, and declaring the entire region *Judenrein*, clear of Jews.[17]

---

17. During the ghetto liquidation, members of the German Order Police, a company of the 1st Battalion, Police Regiment 23, killed two thousand Jews. Aleksandr Kruglov, "Przemyślany," in *The United States Holocaust Memorial Museum Encyclopedia of Camps and Ghettos, 1933–1945*, vol. 2: *Ghettos in German-Occupied Eastern Europe*, ed. Martin Dean (Bloomington: Indiana University Press in association with the USHMM, 2011), 817–19.

Immediately thereafter our group was transferred back to Peremyshliany and housed in a place which had belonged to a Jewish family. Located close to the outskirts of town, a short distance from the Jankiewicz house, the place had a main stucco dwelling, in which numerous wooden bunks had been tightly wedged, and a wooden cottage in the backyard which served as a kitchen. The German scheme in "accommodating" us once more in town, with hardly any surveillance, was shrewdly intended to kill three birds with one stone: to economize by eliminating the need to haul us in trucks, to speed up construction of the granaries, and—above all—to lure out all those Jews who remained in hiding in their own camouflaged holes or among the peasants in either case enduring unbelievable discomfort and constant fear of discovery.

As the Germans had hoped, our *nebenlager* (subcamp) soon became a "haven" for a bunch of desperate men, women, and children seeking hushed refuge under the cover of the legitimate camp inmates.[18] To the local German gendarmerie and Ukrainian police, who for weeks after the ghetto liquidation kept tracking down Jews all over, this influx of Jews was no secret, nor could it have been with the growing number of victims who now crowded the place.

One of the very first to find this "sanctuary" was Samek who had been summarily dismissed from his "protective" job. Now, for a period of three weeks or so, we were in close daily contact exchanging views on the foreboding situation and our chances to elude the deadly clench of the German SS. Inevitable as our fate seemed to be, we nonetheless hoped to make off at the earliest opportunity to the expansive forests of Czupernosów with the help of our mutual friend, Jankiewicz.

In this new and unreal situation, seemingly "relaxed" but diabolically deceptive, I was immediately picked out at a morning roll-call for the so-called Toten-Brigade (death squad)[19] which was ordered to go to work in the nearby Brzezina forest. The Toten-Brigade was assigned to the grueling chore of "facilitating" the last murderous acts of the German gendarmerie

---

18. This camp was established on March 21, 1943, and overseen by SS-Unterscharführer Karl Kempka. See Kruglov, "Przemyślany," in *The USHMM Encyclopedia of Camps and Ghettos*, 2:817–19. Survivor Stella Schneider Baum also confirmed the name of the camp commandant as Kempka during a telephone interview on August 24, 2005. The "camp" was actually the former home of the Freundlich family, which consisted of a stucco building and a wooden house, where bunks for fifty laborers were built. This minicompound was on a main street and surrounded by a fence.

19. This is Jacob Litman's translation of the term.

in carrying out the purging phase of the Judenrein proclamation. Jews, rounded up from their hiding places into the town's jail, were brought in groups of no less than 50 to the Brzezina where a pit, dug by the boys of the death squad, was ready.[20] We were always ordered to move away a hundred yards or so while the victims, having disrobed and lined up on opposite sides of the pit, were shot in the head by the brave slaughterers of the German master race. We then returned to cover the pit with the freshly excavated soil, now splattered with human blood and flesh.

Enduring at the time in close proximity of the residence of Jankiewicz, it was easier for me to be in touch with him. He advised me to get off to the woods at the first opportunity, regardless of any possible consequences to others. His brother-in-law, a former chief forester in the area, had already decided on a safe spot for me. But I, in respect of his pragmatic cleverness, deferred to Samek in deciding the exact circumstances and time of our escape. Noticing a touch of excitement in him during our brief and muted exchanges, I could not figure out why he continued to delay. His reason became clear one day when, apprehensively and hesitantly, he showed me a tiny pistol in his hand. Although I saw it for a fleeting moment, I knew that it was of doubtful quality and not much of a weapon. But Samek whispered, "Now we can get ready to run off . . ." The very next day, however, the unexpected happened.

I was already in the Brzezina, with the pit of that day almost covered, when a small wagon with some fresh corpses arrived. Among them was Samek's body which looked more like a sieve than a body. It seemed as if all the bullets given to the Germans that day to carry out their murderous order had been unloaded on poor Samek. Soon enough we learned what had come to pass from the eyewitnesses, the remaining boys at camp.

Right after the death squad left earlier that morning, the local German gendarmerie, reinforced by a number of SS-men, surrounded the camp. Their purpose, apparently, was to separate the "illegals" from the camp workers and carry them off, as part of the ongoing purge, to their final destination. Terror seized all inmates when everybody was ordered into a line-up. Standing in formation, faced by so many armed German brutes and believing that it was the end, Samek must have felt an overwhelming disdain surging in his mind and an indomitable, compelling self-respect moved him to die in a defiant manner. Even before the selection began, he suddenly drew out his little pistol and shot at one of the

---

20. Litman indicates here that the name Brzezina literally means "birch wood."

Germans . . . missing.[21] In return, a hail of bullets from all sides riddled his body killing some others as well. Having buried Samek, I, like the others in the death squad, had no doubt that our end was at hand right then and there, but we were shipped together with the other fit workers to the main labor camp in Kurowice later that same day.[22]

While Jacob Litman worked through his own past by translating Golfard's diary and writing an introduction, he also began to speak with his adult children about his experiences during the Holocaust. In the early 1980s, he agreed to record his own oral history in a taped interview with his son Julius and later wrote a memoir for his family. These rituals formalized what Elie Wiesel has described as second-generation witnessing: the story of the Holocaust survivor parent is passed down to the offspring, thus starting a genealogical chain of retelling and bearing witness. In the summer of 2008, Julius and his children traveled to Peremyshliany and retraced Jacob's wartime experiences based on his oral history and the Golfard diary. This trip marked the transmission of the history down to the next generation, Jacob Litman's grandchildren.

DOCUMENT 9: Interview with Jacob Litman conducted by his son, Julius Litman, tape no. 4, June 27, 1982, third session, USHMMA Acc. 2008.316, Litman family collection.

[. . .] Jacob Litman: Then one day while I was in the woods preparing a grave, all of a sudden we heard that something terrible happened in the *Nebenlager*, that the SS and the local gendarmerie surrounded the entire *Nebenlager* to call the people, and said no more *Nebenlager*. It's being liquidated, and we're going to take you to Kurowice. We happened to be in the woods because before it happened they took us to the woods.

21. In 1974, Tadeusz Jankiewicz wrote to Litman about the celebration of his fiftieth wedding anniversary, where old friends reminisced about the war. Among the stories recounted was "how Samka [Samek] was shooting at the officer" and questions about Golfard's diary. Jankiewicz letter to Litman family, September 9, 1974, Lubaczów, Poland, to Union, New Jersey.

22. This event may have occurred on June 28, 1943, when the camp was liquidated. In addition to Golfard and other prisoners who were around him and killed, 250 women were shot, and 200 men were sent to Kurowice at this time. See Kruglov, "Przemyślany," in *The USHMM Encyclopedia of Camps and Ghettos*, 2:817–19, which is based on Polish and Hebrew testimonies in the *Biuletyn Żydowskiego Instytutu Historycznego* 69 (1969): 45 and 61 (1967): 12; Eliyahu Iones, *Evrei L'vova v gody Vtoroĭ mirovoĭ voiny i Katastrofy evropeiskogo evreistva 1934–1944*, ed. S. Shenbrunn (Moscow and Jerusalem: Rossiiskaia biblioteka Kholokosta, 1999), 231.

Then we heard that Goldfarb, in the middle of being lined up, when they were all lined up, all put together, there were too many people there. There were lots of people that didn't belong there. But when they lined them up, Goldfarb decided to pull out a little pistol from his pocket and shoot at the commandant, the commander of the gendarmes. Of course he didn't hit anybody, but as soon as that happened, the German took cover, and they started to shoot at many people. They brought them to the forest, and then they brought Goldfarb to the forest. I carried him; he was like a sieve. Hundreds of holes in his body.

Julius Litman: You carried him to the grave?

Jacob Litman: They brought dead bodies on wagons. [. . .] I carried his body into the grave. We recognized that he made a big mistake because the fact was that the rest of the people they took to Kurowice. [. . .] So it was stupid on Goldfarb's part to jump the gun. He actually jumped the gun unnecessarily, but he did it. He did it, and that was it. It turned out to be a very small pistol, an old one too. How good it functioned I couldn't tell you. But that's what happened. We were very upset. I was very upset, obviously, and we didn't know what to do. But when we came back, they took us also to Kurowice. [. . .]

DOCUMENT 10: Jacob Litman, *Autobiography* (unpublished manuscript, 1997), 62–63, USHMMA Acc. 2008.316, Litman family collection.

The pit was just about covered and he had finished with his clothing sorting when all of a sudden a certain hushed agitation cropped up among the boys [of the *Totenbrigade,* which served as the burial squad]. Trying to see what was going on, I noticed a handcart being pulled toward us and soon saw a cargo of 5 corpses on it.

I did not expect Samek to be among them. I unloaded his meager, bloodless body, innumerably dotted with bullet holes, and placed the corpse in the nearly full grave wondering obsessively: why . . . why . . . why? As hardened as I had become after so many precedents of rabidly routinized iniquity, I was this time deeply affected myself. Shortly however, realizing that my emotions could only redound negatively, I did not let them take a hold of me.

It was useless to speculate on Samek's frame of mind at his moment of truth. A realist disposed to think rationally and seldom, if ever, given to illusions, he undoubtedly passed the ultimate and most crucial test of his life with remarkable courage. In all probability it would not be erroneous to state that his open attempt to kill an SS man was the first and only manifest act of armed defiance on the part of a Jew in the whole province of eastern Galicia.

RESCUE IN PEREMYSHLIANY: THE EXAMPLE OF TADEUSZ JANKIEWICZ AND HIS FAMILY

Applying the notion in the Talmudic phrase "The righteous among the nations of the world have a place in the world to come," Yad Vashem, the major center for Holocaust study and memorialization in Israel, recognizes and presents awards to those who risked their lives to save Jews during the Holocaust. Since the early 1960s a special commission has officiated over this process of identifying and documenting rescuers from forty-four countries. More than twenty-two thousand individuals have received this honor. Among the recipients is Tadeusz Jankiewicz. In the 1960s, Jewish survivors from Peremyshliany nominated Jankiewicz by testifying on his behalf. The commission reviewed the testimony and determined that he had aided and sheltered Jews, as well as secured their escape to the forests. He and his wife did this for altruistic reasons. They did not demand money from the Jews whom they helped, and they put themselves and their family members at great risk. According to Nazi occupation law, such aid to Jews was considered a crime, an act of sabotage against the German regime that was punishable by death. While there were exceptional cases of collective rescue in Europe, such as in Le Chambon, France, in Ukraine most rescue activity was conducted by individuals and families, as exemplified by the Jankiewicz household. In fact, analysis of the thousands of "Righteous files" held at Yad Vashem has not resulted in a rescuer typology. The Righteous do not fall into a neat category of rich or poor, intelligent or uneducated. Certainly different contexts informed different responses of bystanders, circumstances such as whether rescuers could act alone or discreetly, or what resources they had at their disposal. However varied or random, rescue was possible even in the worst and riskiest of conditions. Righteous individuals such as Jankiewicz listened to their conscience and acted to preserve and protect life, no matter whose life it was and no matter what the consequences were. These courageous people were few and far between. Many died for their noble deeds, and many remained silent after the war about their bravery.[23]

---

23. From a growing body of publications, see Nechama Tec, *When Light Pierced the Darkness: Christian Rescue of Jews in Nazi-Occupied Poland* (New York: Oxford University Press, 1986); Beate Kosmala and Georgi Verbeeck, *Facing the Catastrophe: Jews and Non-Jews in Europe during World War II* (Oxford: Berg, 2011).

Jankiewicz maintained contact with the Litmans after the war. Between 1954 and 1985 they exchanged annual letters. Photos were enclosed in these letters, including one of Golfard, which has been lost. In a letter dated November 1979, Jankiewicz wrote to Litman, "A month ago I received a diploma from Israel together with a letter and a very nice Medal of Justice [the Righteous Among the Nations Medal] in an ornate case made of olive tree wood. I was surprised when I received a telegram from Warsaw inviting me to take part in a ceremony during which I was to receive the medal from the hands of the Director of Yad Vashem, Dr. Arad."[24]

In fact, Litman testified on behalf of Jankiewicz, and in his statement to Yad Vashem, Litman also identified Golfard, stating, "Jankiewicz also helped and supported a young refugee by the name of Shimshon [*sic*] Goldfarb[?] who was killed by the Germans in the days of the liquidation of the ghetto of Przemyślany. This young man left a diary with the rescuer and it is now in his hands. This diary can be used to verify the efforts of Jankiewicz."[25]

Some thirty years later, contact between the Litman and Jankiewicz families was renewed in conjunction with the research for this book. In the summer of 2008, the children of Jacob and Rita Litman traveled to Peremyshliany, Ukraine, to see for themselves what their parents had spoken of, and to Lubaczów, Poland, to visit Jankiewicz's granddaughter. Jankiewicz saved Jacob Litman's life on several occasions, nursing him when he was ill, rescuing him from the Kurowice camp by bribing a Ukrainian guard, securing his flight to the forest and a hiding place there, and providing food while he was in the forest.

Who was Jankiewicz, and what happened to him? He was a town clerk prior to the war, and working as a surveyor, he probably had better knowledge of the terrain than most. His brother-in-law was the forester who also helped Jews find refuge. Jankiewicz was among a historically privileged minority in eastern Galicia that was targeted during the Soviet occupation (1939–1941) and the war. Threatened and terrorized by Ukrainian fascists who sought to clear western Ukraine of its minorities, he and his family were foced to leave Peremyshliany westward into central Poland. He died a poor man who had suffered the premature loss of his own daughter and the bitter disappointments and harsh realities of the Soviet system in Poland.

---

24. USHMMA Acc. 2008.316, Litman family collection. Yad Vashem recognized Jankiewicz on May 31, 1966, but it apparently took fourteen years to finally issue the award in Poland.

25. Litman testimony, Righteous Among the Nations Department, Yad Vashem, Tadeusz Jankiewicz file, folder 158.

So moved by and grateful for Jankiewicz's generosity was Golfard that, after devoting the bulk of his testimony to recording the cruel behavior of men and women, he reserved his last words for Jankiewicz, writing that he "unexpectedly experienced kindness and friendship from people to whom I could offer nothing in return. Perhaps there are more people like that. Maybe more are like that, ready and fearless enough to acknowledge the human rights [of those] who have been bereft of all humanity. [. . .] In the last moments of my life, I have experienced genuine kindness and friendship from the Jankiewicz family of Przemyślany. May happiness, as well as the affection of the most oppressed, accompany their lives and the lives of their children always." In a world where evil prevailed, the singular acts of kindness seemed miraculous and for Golfard affirmed the goodness of humanity.

DOCUMENT 11: Letters by Frida (Freda) Hochberg (1964) and Karolina Berger (1964) in support of Tadeusz Jankiewicz for his recognition as a Righteous Gentile by the Righteous Among the Nations Department, Yad Vashem, Jerusalem, Tadeusz Jankiewicz file, folder 158 (translated from Polish and Hebrew).

[Frida Hochberg account:]

I, the witness Hochberg, Frida, 43 years old, live in Ramat-Icchak at 26 Hasar Mosze Street, born [in Przemyślany], I also survived the war period in Przemyślany and the surrounding area. I spent some time in the lager [camp] Jachtorów [Jaktorów] and [Wicina?] [and] in the Przemyślany ghetto, and I was also in hiding in the forests near Przemyślany. There I had the opportunity to witness the acts of Mr. Tadeusz Jankiewicz. In the woods I was with a group of people who also included acquaintances of Mr. Jankiewicz, and I was an eyewitness to the fact that Mr. Jankiewicz was bringing food to them. In good and foul weather, I saw him creeping between the bushes with a basket in hand. This food was always covered with mushrooms, as if he was just out collecting mushrooms, in case he met someone. Mr. Jankiewicz endured much fear since he could get a bullet from the Germans for this type of activity. I know that help given was simply an angelic act, because I know that this group did not have money with which to pay, or [illegible] other connections. [. . .] He knew Litman because Litman lived for some time at Mr. Jankiewicz's. And he also knew the

Tadeusz Jankiewicz, 1970 (photograph provided, courtesy of Aleksandra Kobialka, Jankiewicz's granddaughter).

children of a certain Samuel Pfefer (they also called him Sztolcenberg) because they did not live far off. Two daughters of Pfefer remained alive—one, Krancia, presently Berger, lives in Ramat-Gan. The second, Libka, lives in America. The wife of Jankiewicz knew about this, because she too came with him once. Before the war Jankiewicz was a civil servant in the tax office in Przemyślany.[26]

[Karolina Berger account:]
   A) Details of the rescued witness
   1. Karolina Berger
   2. Year of birth: 1917
   3. Ramat Gan [and street address]
   4. Widow
   5. During the war in Przemyślany

B) Details of rescue
   The Berger family was on close friendly terms with the Pole, T. Jankewicz [Jankiewicz], even before the war. They also lived as neighbors.

C) Description of the activities of the rescuer
   Immediately with the entry of the Berger family to the Przemyślany ghetto, Mr. T. Jankewicz [Jankiewicz] sought to help them as much as was in his ability. He mainly brought them food and at no cost. The Pole T. Jankewicz did not give us any trouble. In 1942, with the liquidation of the ghetto in Przemyślany, I (Karolina Berger) escaped, with Lieba Goldberg (my sister), Ruzia Petzel (my cousin) to the forests. From there we got in touch with Mr. T. Jankewicz, and he promised to take care of us. At the next stage, he took us to meet my brother, Mordecai Feffer, whom he hid in a different place in the forest. There we built a bunker with the help of Mr. Jankewicz; he even proposed to hide us in his house, but this seemed too dangerous to us, and we preferred the forest. Mr. T. Jankewicz was the only one who took care of us, and he brought to [our] doorstep food and other necessary items (medicine, soap, etc.). Without T. Jankewicz there would have been no chance for us to remain alive. In the bunker with us were me, my sister, Ya'akov Litman (now in the USA), Eliyahu Yonas, Frieda Hochberg (now in Ramat Gan B', Shapira street). There were many other Jews whom T. Jankewicz helped, but they are no longer alive. Due to the pursuits of the Ukrainians, Mr. Jankewicz was forced to abandon his

---

26. A Hebrew-language account in the file provides additional biographical information about Frida (Freda) Hochberg.

home and leave for Poland, but before he left, he brought to us a large amount of food. It must be pointed out that all of Mr. Jankewicz's family knew about and helped in the rescue operation. His wife prepared the food that he brought to us. Even his brother-in-law, a guard in the forest, knew of our presence in the forest; he would not come to us, but in moments of danger would notify Tadeusz Jankewicz, who would come to warn us. The motives of T. Jankewicz were purely love of fellow man; he would not agree to receive any small gift if one of us offered it to him.

I hereby request that you bestow upon our rescuer Tadeusz Jankewicz the honor that he deserves, because it is only due to him that I am today alive.

Karolina Berger.

LIST OF DOCUMENTS

WARTIME DOCUMENTS

Document 1: Memorandum concerning a "Conference on Jewish Relocation" held by German administrators and SS officers in Galicia, August 6, 1942, USHMMA Acc. 1995.A.1086, Lviv Oblast Archive, reel 8 (translated from German).

Document 2: "Report by the SS and Police Leader for the District of Galicia, June 30, 1943: Mass Killings of Jews in Galicia" (Katzmann Report), partial English translation (document L-18) reprinted in Office of United States Chief of Counsel for Prosecution of Axis Criminality, *Nazi Conspiracy and Aggression* (Washington, DC: U.S. Government Printing Office, 1946), 7:755–70.

Document 3: "The Gate-Crashers," excerpt from *Washington Post* coverage of the tenth anniversary of Hitler's accession to power, January 31, 1943, 1–2.

Document 4: "Epple Plays Around," Soviet wartime underground leaflet describing the cruelties at the Kurowice camp perpetrated by Commandant Ernst Epple and similar atrocities committed at Jaktorów, January 4, 1943, Central State Archives of Public Organizations of Ukraine, Kiev, TsDAHO P-57/4/237 (translated from Ukrainian).

Document 5: "A Sketch of Life in a 'New Europe,'" Soviet wartime underground leaflet describing the deportations to Bełżec from Peremyshliany, September 25, 1942, Central State Archives of Public Organizations of Ukraine, Kiev, TsDAHO P-57/4/237 (translated from Ukrainian).

POSTWAR DOCUMENTS

Document 6: R. M. W. Kempner, "'Genocide as Official Business': The Judgment in the Lemberg Trial," *Aufbau* (New York), May 10, 1968, 7 (translated from German).

Document 7: Vladimir Melamed and author's interview with Dziunia, July 23, 2005, Kurowice, Ukraine.

JACOB LITMAN'S TESTIMONIES

Document 8: Jacob Litman, introduction to *Golfard's Testimony* (1983), 5, USHMMA Acc. 2008.316, Litman family collection.

Document 9: Interview with Jacob Litman conducted by his son, Julius Litman, tape no. 4, June 27, 1982, third session, USHMMA Acc. 2008.316, Litman family collection.

Document 10: Jacob Litman, *Autobiography* (unpublished manuscript, 1997), 62–63, USHMMA Acc. 2008.316, Litman family collection.

RESCUE IN PEREMYSHLIANY: THE EXAMPLE OF TADEUSZ JANKIEWICZ AND HIS FAMILY

Document 11: Letters by Frida (Freda) Hochberg (1964) and Karolina Berger (1964) in support of Tadeusz Jankiewicz for his recognition as a Righteous Gentile by the Righteous Among the Nations Department, Yad Vashem, Jerusalem, Tadeusz Jankiewicz file, folder 158 (translated from Polish and Hebrew).

Place Names Mentioned in the Diary

Wartime Polish Spelling	Current Ukrainian Spelling
Bóbrka	Bibrka
Brzeżany	Berezhany
Chlebowice	Glybovychi
Ciemierzyńce	Chemeryntsi
Czupernosów	Chuprynosiv
Drohobycz	Drohobych
Dunajów	Dunaiv
Gliniany	Hlyniany
Hanaczów	Ganachiv
Jaktorów	Iaktoriv
Janczyn	Ianchyn
Jaryczów Nowy	Novyi Iarychiv
Jaworów	Iavoriv
Kimirz	Kimezh
Krosienko	Krosenko
Kurowice	Kurowice
Lacki (Lackie Wielkie?)	Lyashky
Łahodów	Lachodiv
Lwów	Lviv
Mitulin	Mytulyn
Mosty Wielkie	Velyki Mosty

Narajewo	Naraiv
Płuhów	Pluhiv
Podusów	Podisiv
Przemyślany	Peremyshliany
Sądowa Wisznia	Sudova Vyshnia
Stanimierz	Stanymir
Stanisławów	Stanyslaviv, Stanislav (today, Ivano-Frankivs'k)
Stryj	Stryi
Świrz	Svirzh
Zborów	Zboriv
Złoczów	Zolochiv
Żółkiew	Zhovkva

BIBLIOGRAPHY

ARCHIVAL SOURCES

Austria

Simon Wiesenthal Archive, Vienna
- Correspondence, Senior Prosecutor Rolf Sichtig to Simon Wiesenthal, June 16, 1975 (crimes in Lviv)
- Correspondence, Simon Wiesenthal to Christian Broda, F.R.G. Federal Minister of Justice (June 1, 1964)

Germany

Bundesarchiv Ludwigsburg (BAL) (Federal Archives of Germany, Ludwigsburg branch)
- Interrogation of Przesluchania Swiadka, BAL 162/389 (208 AR-Z 38/98)
- "The Lemberg Trial," April 1968, BAL 162/2096; investigation of Walter K., Stuttgart 2 Js 6153/97
- Investigation of crimes in Złoczów, BAL 162/192444
- Indictment of Ernst Epple e.a., BAL 162/19230 (208 AR-Z 294/59)
- Indictment of Rudolf Röder e.a, BAL 162/4688 (AR-Z 294/59)

Bundesbeauftragte für die Unterlagen des Staatssicherheitsdienstes der ehemaligen Deutschen Demokratischen Republik (BStU), Berlin (Federal Commissioner for the Records of the State Security Service of the former German Democratic Republic)
- BV Halle, Ast 5544, BStU# 00133-138, verdict, "Strafsache gegen den Arbeiter Bruno Sämisch aus Mühlanger," Landgericht Dessau, and "Gründe," Fach Nr. 2052

International Tracing Service, Bad Arolsen
- Register of Forced Labor Camps of the SSPF (SS and Police Leader) in the District of Galicia, 1941–1943 (Stuttgart 12 Js 1464/61–Ks 5/65)
- Dr. Bruno Fischer, United Restitution Organization, "Report on the Concentration Camp as Prison Site" (March 1967)
- Prisoner registration cards, Jews from Radom (Główna Komisja Badania Zbrodni Hitlerowskich w Polsce, Warszawa)
- Survivor index cards, Przemyślany (Feffer, Mania, 226 947, document ID 46056577-8)

Israel

Yad Vashem, The Holocaust Martyrs' and Heroes' Remembrance Authority, Jerusalem
- Central Database of Shoah Victims' Names (www.yadvashem.org)
- Department of the Righteous Among the Nations, Tadeusz Jankiewicz file, folder 158
- Photo archive, images of Ernst Epple, file A1584/209
- Testimonies, Hochberg, Ptachiahu, Record Group 0.3, file 2230, 38 pp.

Poland

Instytut Pamięci Narodowej (Institute of National Memory; formerly Commission for the Prosecution of Crimes against the Polish Nation), Kraków Branch Commission
- Photo collection, shelf mark Ko 5/09, doc. 26791

Urząd Stanu Cywilnego, Urząd Miejski w Radomiu (Radom Town Hall, Registry Office)
- Registry records for people of the Jewish faith, 1826–1940

Ukraine

Lviv State Archives, Lviv
- Directories of Peremyshliany officials and businesses, *Schematyzm woj. tarnopolskiego* (1934)

Peremyshliany, Iaktoriv, Kurowice (fieldwork)
- Interviews with Ivan Fuglevych, July 23, 2005, and October 8, 2010; Bogdan Girs'ky, July 23, 2005; Dzunia, July 23, 2005.
- Materials and oral testimonies collected by Wendy Lower from wartime survivors and former camp sites

Central State Archive of Public Organizations of Ukraine (TsDAHO), Kiev
- P-57/4/237, Document collection on the history of the war, 1941–1945

USA

USC Shoah Foundation Institute for Visual History and Education, Los Angeles
- Testimonies by survivors from Peremyshliany, Iaktoriv, and Kurowice
  Henry C., 1996, Warsaw, interview code 14823
  Ida K., 1996, West Orange, New Jersey, interview code 20097
  Basia K., 1997, Brooklyn, interview code 6510
  Leopold K., 1995, Kraków, Poland, and Kurowice, Ukraine, interview code 700
  Mayer K., 1997, Palm Beach, Florida, interview code 26616
  Esther L., 1995, Brooklyn, interview code 8357
  Israel L., 1995, Brooklyn, interview code 8358
  Yetta L., 1999, Margate, New Jersey, interview code 50384
  Faina L., 1998, Peremyshliany, Ukraine, interview code 45446
  Jacob L., 1995, Union, New Jersey, interview code 3179
  Rita L., 1995, Union, New Jersey, interview code 3181
  Regina P., 1995, Miami Beach, interview code 9289
  Leon S., 1996, La Canada, California, interview code 21004
  Michal S., 1997, Warsaw, interview code 38053
  Mark S., 1996, Brooklyn, interview code 18607
  Mark T., 2001, Chicago, interview code 51758
  Lynn W., 2001, Delray Beach, Florida, interview code 51773

United States Holocaust Memorial Museum Archives (USHMMA), Washington, DC
- Acc.1995.A.1086, Selected Records from the Lviv Oblast Archive, reel 8
- Acc.1997.A.0076, Kurt I. Lewin collection
- Acc.2008.316, Litman family collection
- RG 02.208M, Memoirs of Jews collected by the Central Jewish Historical Commission, Poland, predecessor of the Jewish Historical Institute (Żydowski Instytut Historyczny), Warsaw (302 series)
- RG 15.084M, Holocaust Survivor Testimonies, 1945–1946, from the Jewish Historical Institute (Żydowski Instytut Historyczny), Warsaw (301 series)
- RG 15.112M, Records from the State Archives in Radom, reels 5, 6, 7; State Archives in Radom, fond 417
- RG 17.003M, Viennese Postwar Trials of Nazi War Crimes, reel 98, Karl Kempka et al., LG Wien Vg 8e Vr 847/55, DÖW shelf mark V475/1-7

United States Holocaust Memorial Museum Photo Archive (USHMMPA)

United States Holocaust Memorial Museum (USHMM), Holocaust Survivors and Victims Resource Center, Washington, DC

PRIMARY SOURCES AND MEMOIRS

Czerniaków, Adam. *Warsaw Diary of Adam Czerniakow*. Edited by Raul Hilberg, Stanislaw Staron, and Josef Kermisz. New York: Stein and Day, 1979.

Diment, Michael. *The Lone Survivor: A Diary of the Lukacz Ghetto.* New York: Holocaust Library, 1991.

Frank, Anne. *The Diary of a Young Girl: The Definitive Edition.* Edited by Otto H. Frank and Mirjam Pressler. New York: Anchor Books Doubleday, 1995.

Gold, Ben-Zion. *The Life of Jews in Poland before the Holocaust: A Memoir.* Lincoln: University of Nebraska Press, 2007.

Gross [Raubvogel], Lucy. *Memoir.* Unpublished Hebrew-language manuscript.

Heyman, Eva. *The Diary of Eva Heyman.* Jerusalem: Yad Vashem, 1974.

Kahane, David. *Lvov Ghetto Diary.* Amherst: University of Massachusetts Press, 1990.

Kaplan, Chaim A. *Scroll of Agony: The Warsaw Diary of Chaim A. Kaplan.* Edited by Abraham I. Katsh. Rev. ed. Bloomington: Indiana University Press in association with USHMM, 1999.

Katznelson, Itzhak. *Vittel Diary, 1943.* Tel Aviv: Ghetto Fighters' House, 1964.

Klemperer, Victor. *I Will Bear Witness: A Diary of the Nazi Years, 1933–1941.* New York: Random House, 1998.

———. *I Will Bear Witness: A Diary of the Nazi Years, 1942–1945.* New York: Random House, 1999.

Klukowski, Zygmunt. *Dziennik z lat okupacji Zamojszczyzny 1939–1944.* Lublin: Lubelska Spółdzielnia Wydawnicza, 1958.

Kulińska, Lucyna, and Adam Roliński. *Kwestia ukraińska i eksterminacja ludności polskiej w Małopolsce Wschodniej: W świetle dokumentów Polskiego Państwa Podziemnego 1942–1944* [*The Ukrainian question and the extermination of the Polish population in eastern Galicia in light of documents from the Polish Underground Government, 1942–1944*]. Kraków: Księgarnia Akademicka, 2004.

Lipson, Alfred, ed. *The Book of Radom: The Story of a Jewish Community in Poland Destroyed by the Nazis.* New York: United Radomer Relief of the United States and Canada, Inc., 1963.

Litman, Jacob. *Autobiography.* Unpublished manuscript, 1997.

Perechodnik, Calel. *Am I a Murderer? Testament of a Jewish Ghetto Policeman.* Edited by Frank Fox. Boulder, CO: Westview Press, 1996.

Redlich, Shimon. *Together and Apart in Brzezany: Poles, Jews, and Ukrainians, 1919–1945.* Bloomington: Indiana University Press, 2002.

Ringelblum, Emanuel. *Notes From the Warsaw Ghetto: The Journal of Emmanuel Ringelblum.* Edited by Jacob Sloan. New York: McGraw Hill, 1974.

Rubenstein, Joshua, and Ilya Altman, eds. *The Unknown Black Book: The Holocaust in the German-Occupied Soviet Territories.* Bloomington: Indiana University Press in association with USHMM, 2007.

Sierakowiak, David. *Five Notebooks from the Lodz Ghetto.* New York: Oxford University Press, 1996.

Sten, Ephraim F. *1111 Days in My Life Plus Four.* Takoma Park, MD: Dryad Press, 2006.

Wells, Leon Weliczker. *The Janowska Road.* Washington, DC: USHMM, 1999.

Yones, Eliyahu. *Smoke in the Sand: The Jews of Lwow during the War, 1939–1944.* Jerusalem: Yad Vashem, 2001.

Zapruder, Alexandra. *Salvaged Pages: Young Writers' Diaries of the Holocaust.* New Haven, CT: Yale University Press, 2002.

MONOGRAPH STUDIES, EDITED VOLUMES, AND ARTICLES

Arad, Yitzhak. *Belzec, Sobibor, Treblinka: The Operation Reinhard Death Camps*. Bloomington: Indiana University Press, 1987.

Andlauer, Teresa. *Die jüdische Bevölkerung im Modernisierungsprozess Galiziens (1867–1914)*. Berlin: Peter Lang, 2001.

Bacon, Gershon. "Warsaw-Radom-Vilna: Three Disputes over Rabbinical Posts in Interwar Poland and their Implications for the Change in Jewish Public Discourse." *Jewish History* 13 (March 1999): 103–26.

Barkan, Elazar, Elizabeth A. Cole, and Kai Struve. *Shared History—Divided Memory: Jews and Others in Soviet-Occupied Poland, 1939–1941*. Leipzig: Leipziger Universitätsverlag, 2007.

Bartov, Omer. *Erased: Vanishing Traces of Jewish Galicia in Present-Day Ukraine*. Princeton, NJ: Princeton University Press, 2007.

Bender, Sara, and Shmuel Krakowski, eds. *The Encyclopedia of the Righteous Among the Nations: Rescuers of Jews during the Holocaust, Poland*. Vol. 2/1. Jerusalem: Yad Vashem, 2004.

Bergen, Doris. *War & Genocide: A Concise History of the Holocaust*. Lanham, MD: Rowman & Littlefield, 2009.

Berkhoff, Karel. *Harvest of Despair: Life and Death in Ukraine, 1941–1944*. Cambridge, MA: Harvard University Press, 2004.

Berkhoff, Karel C., and Marco Carynnyk. "The Organization of Ukrainian Nationalists and Its Attitude toward Germans and Jews: Iaroslav Stets'ko's 1941 *Zhyttiepys*." *Harvard Ukrainian Studies* 23 (2002): 149–84.

Bishop, Marion C. "Witnessing Resistance in the Diaries of Mary Perkes, Alice James, and Anne Frank." PhD diss., New York University, 1998.

Boll, Bernd. "Złoczów, July 1941: The Wehrmacht and the Beginning of the Holocaust in Galicia: From a Criticism of Photographs to a Revision of the Past." In *Crimes of War: Guilt and Denial in the Twentieth Century*, edited by Omer Bartov, Atina Grossman, and Mary Nolan, 61–99. New York: Berghahn Press, 2002.

Brandon, Ray, and Wendy Lower, eds. *The Shoah in Ukraine: History, Testimony, Memorialization*. Bloomington: Indiana University Press in association with the USHMM, 2008.

Breitman, Richard. *Official Secrets: What the Nazis Planned, What the British and Americans Knew*. New York: Hill & Wang, 1988.

Browning, Christopher with contributions by Jürgen Matthäus. *The Origins of the Final Solution: The Evolution of Nazi Jewish Policy, September 1939–March 1942*. Lincoln: University of Nebraska Press, 2007.

Bruder, Franziska. *"Den ukrainischen Staat erkämpfen order sterben!" Die Organisation Ukrainischer Nationalisten (OUN) 1929–1948*. Berlin: Metropol, 2007.

Burds, Jeffrey. "AGENTURA: Soviet Informants' Networks and the Ukrainian Underground in Galicia, 1944–1948." *East European Politics and Societies* 11, no. 1 (winter 1997): 89–130.

Cała, Alina. *Żydowskie periodyki i druki okazjonalne w języku polskim: Bibliografia*. Warsaw: Biblioteka Narodowa, 2005.

Cole, Tim. "Writing 'Bystanders' into Holocaust History in More Active Ways: 'Non-Jewish' Engagement with Ghettoisation, Hungary 1944." *Holocaust Studies* 11, no. 1. (summer 2005): 55–74.

Corni, Gustavo. *Hitler's Ghettos: Voices from a Beleaguered Society, 1939–1944*. London: Arnold, 2002.

Dabrowska, Danuta, Avraham Wein, and Aahron Weiss, eds. *Pinkas ha-kehilot: Encyclopedia of Jewish Communities, Poland, Eastern Galicia*. Vol. 2. Jerusalem: Yad Vashem, 1980.

Davies, Norman. *God's Playground: A History of Poland*. Vol. 2: *1795 to the Present*. New York: Columbia University Press, 1982.

Dean, Martin. *Collaboration in the Holocaust: Crimes of the Local Police in Ukraine and Belorussia*. New York: St. Martin's Press, 2000.

Desbois, Patrick. *The Holocaust by Bullets: A Priest's Journey to Uncover the Truth Behind the Murder of 1.5 Million Jews*. New York: Macmillan, 2008.

Dietsch, Johan. *Making Sense of Suffering: Holocaust and Holodomor in Ukrainian Historical Culture*. Lund: Lund University Press, 2006.

Dobroszycki, Lucjan, and Jeffrey Gurock, eds. *The Holocaust in the Soviet Union: Studies and Sources on the Destruction of the Jews in the Nazi-Occupied Territories, 1941–1945*. New York: M. E. Sharpe, 1993.

Friedlander, Henry. *The Origins of Nazi Genocide: From Euthanasia to the Final Solution*. Chapel Hill: University of North Carolina Press, 1995.

Friedländer, Saul. *Kurt Gerstein: The Ambiguity of Good*. New York: Alfred A. Knopf, 1969.

Friedman, Philip. *Road to Extinction: Essays on the Holocaust*. Edited by Ada June Friedman. New York: Jewish Publication Society of America, 1980.

Garbarini, Alexandra. "To 'bear witness where witness needs to be borne': Diary Writing and the Holocaust, 1939–1945." PhD diss., University of California, Los Angeles, 2003.

———. *Numbered Days: Diaries and the Holocaust*. New Haven, CT: Yale University Press, 2006.

Gellately, Robert. *Backing Hitler: Consent and Coercion in Nazi Germany, 1933–1945*. New York: Oxford University Press, 2001.

Gitelman, Zvi, ed. *Bitter Legacy: Confronting the Holocaust in the USSR*. Bloomington: Indiana University Press, 1997.

———. *A Century of Ambivalence: The Jews in Russia and the Soviet Union, 1881 to the Present*. 2nd ed. Bloomington: Indiana University Press, 2001.

Goldberg, Amos. "'If This Is a Man': The Image of Man in Autobiographical and Historical Writing During and After the Holocaust." *Yad Vashem Studies* 33 (2004): 381–429.

———. *Holocaust Diaries as "Life Stories."* Search and Research—Lectures and Papers 5. Jerusalem: Yad Vashem, 2004.

Gross, Jan T. *Neighbors: The Destruction of the Jewish Community in Jedwabne, Poland*. Princeton, NJ: Princeton University Press, 2000.

———. *Revolution from Abroad: The Soviet Conquest of Poland's Western Ukraine and Western Belorussia*. Exp. ed. Princeton, NJ: Princeton University Press, 2002.

Gruner, Wolf. *Jewish Forced Labor under the Nazis: Economic Needs and Racial Aims, 1938–1945*. New York: Cambridge University Press in association with the USHMM, 2006.

Hagen, William. "The Moral Economy of Ethnic Violence: The Pogrom in Lwow, November 1918." In *Antisemitism and Its Opponents in Modern Poland*, edited by Robert Blobaum, 124–47. Ithaca, NY: Cornell University Press, 2005.

Hann, Christopher, and Paul Robert Magosci, eds. *Galicia: A Multicultured Land.* Toronto: University of Toronto Press, 2005.

Hellbeck, Jochen. *Revolution on My Mind: Writing a Diary under Stalin.* Cambridge, MA: Harvard University Press, 2006.

Herf, Jeffrey. *The Jewish Enemy: Nazi Propaganda during World War II and the Holocaust.* Cambridge, MA: Harvard University Press, 2006.

Hilberg, Raul. *The Destruction of the European Jews.* 3 vols. New York: Holmes & Meier, 1985.

———. *Sources of Holocaust Research: An Analysis.* Chicago: Ivan R. Dee, 2001.

———. *Perpetrators, Victims, Bystanders: The Jewish Catastrophe, 1933–1945.* New York: Harper Collins, 1992.

Himka, John-Paul. "Ukrainian Collaboration in the Extermination of the Jews During the Second World War: Sorting Out the Long-Term and Conjectural Factors." In *The Fate of the European Jews, 1939–1945: Continuity or Contingency?* edited by Jonathan Frankel, 170–89. New York: Oxford University Press, 1997.

———. *Galician Villagers and the Ukrainian National Movement in the Nineteenth Century.* London: St. Martin's, 1988.

———. "The Veracity of Testimony: Roza Wagner's Story of the Lviv Pogrom of the Summer of 1941." *Holocaust and Modernity (Голокост і Сучасність)* 2, no. 4 ([Kiev] 2008): 43–80.

Hundert, Gershon David, ed. *The YIVO Encyclopedia of Jews in Eastern Europe.* 2 vols. New Haven, CT: Yale University Press, 2008.

Israel, Yosef. *Rescuing the Rebbe of Belz: Belzer Chassidus—History, Rescue and Rebirth.* Brooklyn, NY: Mesorah Publications, 2005.

Kaienburg, Hermann. "Jüdische Arbeitslager an der 'Straße der SS.'" *Zeitschrift für Sozialgeschichte des 20. und 21. Jahrhunderts* 11 (1996): 13–39.

Kassow, Samuel D. *Who Will Write Our History? Emanuel Ringelblum, the Warsaw Ghetto, and the Oyneg Shabes Archive.* Bloomington: Indiana University Press, 2007.

Katz, Kalman. *Memories of War.* Caulfield North, Victoria, Australia: Eskay Press, 1995.

Khonigsman, Yacov. *Janower Lager (Janower Zwangsarbeitslager für Juden in Lemberg).* Kurzer historischer Essay. Lviv: Lwower Gesellschaft der jüdischen Kultur Namens Scholom-Alejchem, 1996.

Klier, John, and Lambroza Shlomo, eds. *Pogroms: Anti-Jewish Violence in Modern Russian History.* New York: Cambridge University Press, 1992.

Kogon, Eugen. *Theory and Practice of Hell: The German Concentration Camps and the System behind Them.* New York: Farrar, Straus and Cudahy, 1950.

Krawchuk, Andrii. *Christian Social Ethics in Ukraine: The Legacy of Andrei Sheptytsky.* Toronto: Canadian Institute of Ukrainian Studies Press, 1997.

Kruglov, Aleksandr I. *The Losses Suffered by Ukrainian Jews in 1941–1944.* Kharkov: Tarbut, 2005.

Kubica, Helena. *The Extermination at KL Auschwitz of Poles Evicted from the Zamość Region in the Years 1942–1943.* Oświęcim: Auschwitz-Birkenau State Museum, 2006.

Kunert, Andrzej, ed. *Polacy-Żydzi, Polen-Juden, Poles-Jews: 1939–1945: Selection of Documents.* Warsaw: Oficyna Wydawnicza Rytm, 2006.

Kurek, Ewa. *Your Life Is Worth Mine: How Polish Nuns Saved Hundreds of Jewish Children in German-Occupied Poland, 1939–1945.* New York: Hippocrene, 1997.

LaCapra, Dominick. *Writing History, Writing Trauma.* Baltimore: Johns Hopkins University Press, 2000.

Langer, Lawrence. *Admitting the Holocaust: Collected Essays.* New York: Oxford University Press, 1999.

Leff, Laurel. *Buried by The Times: The Holocaust and America's Most Important Newspaper.* New York: Cambridge University Press, 2005.

Lehmann, Rosa. *Symbiosis and Ambivalence: Poles and Jews in a Small Galician Town.* New York: Berghahn Press, 2001.

Levi, Primo. *The Drowned and the Saved.* New York: Vintage, 1989.

Levin, Dov. *The Lesser of Two Evils: Eastern European Jewry under Soviet Rule, 1939–1941.* Philadelphia: Jewish Publication Society, 1995.

Litman, Jacob. *The Economic Role of Jews in Medieval Poland: The Contribution of Yitzhak Schipper.* Lanham, MD: University Press of America, 1984.

Longerich, Peter. *"Davon haben wir nichts gewusst!": Die Deutschen und die Judenverfolgung 1933–1945.* Munich: Siedler, 2006.

Lukas, Richard C., and Norman Davies. *Forgotten Holocaust: The Poles under German Occupation, 1939–1944.* 2nd ed. London: Hippocrene Books, 2001.

Magocsi, Paul R., ed. *Morality and Reality: The Life and Times of Andrei Sheptyts'kyi.* Edmonton: Canadian Institute of Ukrainian Studies, University of Alberta, 1989.

———. *A History of Ukraine: The Land and Its Peoples.* Toronto: University of Toronto Press, 1996.

Megargee, Geoffrey P. *War of Annihilation: Combat and Genocide on the Eastern Front, 1941.* Lanham, MD: Rowman & Littlefield, 2006.

Melamed, Vladimir. *Evrei vo L'vove: XIII–pervaia polovina XX veka.* Lviv: TEKOP, 1994.

———. "Organized and Unsolicited Collaboration in the Holocaust: The Multifaceted Ukrainian Context." *East European Jewish Affairs* 37 (August 2007): 217–48.

Mendelsohn, Ezra. *The Jews of East Central Europe between the World Wars.* Bloomington: Indiana University Press, 1983.

Mick, Christoph. "Ethnische Gewalt und Pogrome in Lemberg, 1914–1941." *Osteuropa* 53 (2003): 1810–29.

Paldiel, Mordecai. *The Path of the Righteous: Gentile Rescuers of Jews during the Holocaust.* Hoboken, NJ: Ktav, 1992.

Paul, Gerhard, and Klaus-Michael Mallmann. *Die Gestapo im Zweiten Weltkrieg: "Heimatfront" und besetztes Europa.* Darmstadt: Primus Verlag, 2000.

Pinchuk, Ben-Cion. *Shtetl Jews under Soviet Rule: Eastern Poland on the Eve of the Holocaust.* Oxford: Basil Blackwell, 1990.

Podol's'kyi, Anatolii [Anatoly Podolsky]. "The Reluctant Look Back: Jewry and the Holocaust in Ukrainian Remembrance." In "Impulses for Europe: Tradition and Modernity in Eastern European Jewry," special issue, *Osteuropa* ([Berlin] 2008): 271–78.

Pohl, Dieter. *Nationalsozialisten od Judenverfolgung in Ostgalizien 1941–1944: Organisation und Durchführung eines staatlichen Massenverbrechens.* Munich: Oldenbourg, 1997.

———. "Ukrainische Hilfskräfte beim Mord an den Juden." In *Die Täter der Shoah: Fanatische Nationalsozialisten oder ganz normale Deutsche?* edited by Gerhard Paul, 205–34. Göttingen: Wallstein, 2002.

Potichnyj, Peter, and Howard Aster, eds. *Ukrainian-Jewish Relations in Historical Perspective.* Edmonton: University of Toronto Press, 1988.

Prusin, Alexander V. *The Lands Between: Conflict in the East European Borderlands, 1870–1992*. Oxford: Oxford University Press, 2010.

———. *Nationalizing a Borderland: War, Ethnicity, and Anti-Jewish Violence in East Galicia, 1914–1920*. Tuscaloosa: University of Alabama Press, 2005.

Rosenblatt, Paul C. *Bitter, Bitter Tears: Nineteenth-Century Diarists and Twentieth-Century Grief Theories*. Minneapolis: University of Minnesota Press, 1983.

Rosenfeld, Alvin H. "Anne Frank and the Future of Holocaust Memory." Joseph and Rebecca Meyerhoff Annual Lecture, USHMM, Washington, DC, October 14, 2004, published March 2005: 3, 14. Available online at www.ushmm.org/research/center/publications/occasional/2005-04-01/paper.pdf (accessed May 10, 2010).

Roskies, David G. *The Literature of Destruction: Jewish Responses to Catastrophe*. Cambridge, MA: Harvard University Press, 1986.

———. *Against the Apocalypse: Responses to Catastrophe in Modern Jewish Culture*. Cambridge, MA: Harvard University Press, 1984.

Rossino, Alexander B. *Hitler Strikes Poland: Blitzkrieg, Ideology, and Atrocity*. Lawrence: University of Kansas, 2003.

Rozett, Robert, and Shmuel Spector, eds. *Encyclopedia of the Holocaust*. Jerusalem: Yad Vashem, 2000.

Sandkühler, Thomas. *"Endlösung" in Galizien: Der Judenmord in Ostpolen und die Rettungsinitiativen von Berthold Beitz, 1941–1944*. Bonn: Dietz, 1996.

Schroeder, Dominique. "Motive-Funktionen-Sprache: Zu Tagebüchern als Quellen der Konzentrationslagerforschung." In *NS-Zwangslager in Westdeutschland, Frankreich und den Niederlanden: Geschichte und Erinnerung*, edited by Janine Doerry et al., 93–104. Paderborn: Ferdinand Schöningh, 2008.

Seton-Watson, Hugh. *Eastern Europe between the Wars, 1918–1941*. Cambridge, UK: The University Press, 1945.

Shapiro, Robert Moses, ed. *Holocaust Chronicles: Individualizing the Holocaust through Diaries and Other Contemporaneous Personal Accounts*. Hoboken, NJ: Ktav, 1999.

Snyder, Timothy. *Bloodlands: Europe between Hitler and Stalin*. New York: Basic Books, 2010.

———. "The Causes of Ukrainian-Polish Ethnic Cleansing 1943." *Past and Present* 179 (2003): 197–234.

———. "'To Resolve the Ukrainian Question Once and for All': The Ethnic Cleansing of Ukrainians in Poland, 1943–1947." *Journal of Cold War Studies* 1 (spring 1999): 86–120.

———. *Sketches from a Secret War: A Polish Artist's Mission to Liberate Ukraine*. New Haven, CT: Yale University Press, 2005.

Spector, Shmuel. "Jews in the Resistance and Partisan Movements in the Soviet Ukraine." *Yad Vashem Studies* 23 (1993): 127–43.

———. ed. *The Encyclopedia of Jewish Life Before and During the Holocaust*. Vol. 2. Jerusalem: Yad Vashem, 2001.

Strom, Yale. "The Last Klezmer: Leopold Kozlowski, His Life and Music" (film on Peremyshliany). New Yorker Films release. Mäelström Films, 1994.

Struve, Kai. "Ritual und Gewalt—Die Pogrome des Sommers 1941." In *Synchrone Welten: Zeitenräume jüdischer Geschichte*, edited by Dan Diner, 225–50. Göttingen: Vandenhoeck & Ruprecht, 2005.

Sword, Keith. *Deportation and Exile: Poles in the Soviet Union, 1939–48*. New York: St. Martin's Press, 1994.

————. *The Soviet Takeover of the Polish Eastern Provinces, 1939–1941.* New York: St. Martin's Press, 1996.

Tec, Nechama. "Diaries and Oral History: Some Methodological Considerations." *Religion and the Arts* 4, no. 1 (2000): 87–95.

————. *When Light Pierced the Darkness: Christian Rescue of Jews in Nazi-Occupied Poland.* New York: Oxford University Press, 1986.

Weinberg, Gerhard. *A World at Arms: A Global History of World War II.* Cambridge: Cambridge University Press, 1994.

Weiss, Aharon. "Jewish-Ukrainian Relations in Western Ukraine During the Holocaust." In *Ukrainian-Jewish Relations in Historical Perspective*, edited by Howard Aster and Peter J. Potichnyj, 409–20. Edmonton: Canadian Institute for Ukrainian Studies, 1988.

White, Elizabeth. "Majdanek: Cornerstone of Himmler's SS Empire in the East." *Simon Wiesenthal Center Annual* 7 (1993): 3–21.

Wieviorka, Annette. *The Era of the Witness.* Ithaca, NY: Cornell University Press, 2006.

Witte, Peter, and Stephen Tyas. "A New Document on the Deportation and Murder of Jews during 'Einsatz Reinhardt' 1942." *Holocaust and Genocide Studies* 15 (winter 2001): 468–86.

Yelisavetsky [Elisavetsky], Ster, ed. *Katastrofa ta opir ukraïns'koho evreĭstva (1941–1944): narysy z istoriï Holokostu i oporu v Ukraïni.* Kiev: National Academy of Science of Ukraine, Institute of Ethnic and Political Studies, 1999.

Yones, Eliyahu. *Smoke in the Sand: The Jews of Lvov in the War Years, 1939–1944.* Jerusalem: Gefen Publishing House, 2004.

Young, James E. *Writing and Rewriting the Holocaust: Narrative and the Consequences of Interpretation.* Bloomington: Indiana University Press, 1990.

Zabarko, Boris, ed. *Holocaust in the Ukraine.* The Library of Holocaust Testimonies. London: Vallentine Mitchell, 2005.

Żbikowski, Andrzej, ed. *Friedrich Katzmann: Rozwiązanie kwestii żydowskiej w Dystrykcie Galicja/Lösung der Judenfrage im Distrikt Galizien.* Warsaw: Instytut Pamięci Narodowej, 2001.

Żeromski, Stefan. *Sułkowski: tragedya.* 2nd ed. Kraków: "Książka," 1910.

Ziemke, Earl F. *Stalingrad to Berlin: The German Defeat in the East.* Washington, DC: Office of the Chief of Military History, U.S. Army, 1968.

CHRONOLOGY OF EVENTS RELATED TO THE DIARY

1900

Birth of Tadeusz Jankiewicz.

ca. 1910

Birth of Samuel Golfard, probably in Radom, Poland.

1920

June 2, 1920: Birth of Jacob Litman in the Warsaw District of Poland.

1939

September 1939: German (September 1) and Soviet (September 17) troops invade Poland, beginning World War II. In the course of the military campaign, units of the German army, SS, and police commit atrocities against civilians. Of the sixteen thousand Poles executed by German units in September 1939, at least five thousand are Jewish. Subsequently, Poland is taken off the political map: some parts of German-controlled Poland become annexed to the Reich, while others are incorporated into an area designated the Generalgouvernement, established in October 1939. The Soviet occupation of eastern Poland extends to Galicia, with Lviv (Lwów) and Peremyshliany coming under Soviet domination (see map 2, p. xxvii).

October 1939: Jacob Litman leaves Nazi-occupied Warsaw. At this time or in early 1940, Samuel Golfard and his sister also leave Nazi-controlled Poland, heading to Volhynia and then to Peremyshliany in the Soviet zone of occupied Poland (present-day Ukraine).

December 1939: Jacob Litman arrives in Peremyshliany. Soviet housing authorities place him in the Jankiewicz household.

1941

June 22, 1941: Germany and its allies invade the Soviet Union; motorized SS and police forces, particularly the *Einsatzgruppen* (mobile killing units) of the Security Police and *Sicherheitsdienst* (SD, or Security Service), begin mass shootings of adult male Jews and other so-called racial and political enemies. Invasion precipitates pogroms in Lithuania, eastern Poland, western Ukraine, and Romania.

July 1, 1941: German forces occupy Peremyshliany, whose population includes some 2,600 Jews. Pogroms continue in Lviv, resulting in the deaths of three to four thousand Jews, and are followed by the murder of more than 2,500 Jewish men by *Einsatzgruppe* C and its Ukrainian auxiliaries.

Germans with Ukrainian assistance lock religious Jews into the local synagogue in Peremyshliany and set it on fire. The son of Rebbe Aharon Rokeach (Belzer rebbe) and another ten Jewish leaders die in the flames.

July 25–27, 1941: With German approval, Ukrainians led by members of the Organization of Ukrainian Nationalists and local militias launch another pogrom, known as the Petliura Days, named for Symon Petliura, a Ukrainian political leader assassinated in 1926 by a Jewish anarchist. More than one thousand Jews are brutally assaulted and killed.

Late July 1941: German *Einsatzgruppen*, Waffen SS, police, and their collaborators in Ukraine begin systematic and total annihilation of Jewish communities in areas occupied east of Volhynia and Galicia. German SS, police, and military forces have been killing Jewish men in the Soviet Union since the invasion began in late June, but in late July they expand their targets to include women and children.

August 1, 1941: The German occupation administration in eastern Galicia is transferred from the German military to the Generalgouvernement. Galicia District, with Lwów (renamed Lemberg) as its administrative center, becomes one of five districts in the Generalgouvernement, Nazi-occupied Poland.

German authorities in Peremyshliany order the establishment of a *Judenrat* (Jewish Council) to administer the registration and marking of Jews with white armbands bearing the Star of David. German authorities order the confiscation of Jewish valuables (gold and silver) under penalty of death.

Jacob Litman and Samuel Golfard meet at the house of Dr. Jacob Katz.

September 29–30, 1941: German military, SS, and regular police forces shoot more than 33,000 Jewish men, women, and children in the Babi Yar ravine on the outskirts of Kiev, Ukraine.

October 15, 1941: German authorities in the Generalgouvernement issue an order that any Jews who leave "the district assigned for their residence" without permission will face the death penalty, as will any persons who knowingly give shelter to these Jews.

October 1941: In Peremyshliany, famine strikes Jews who are unable to secure food outside of town in the countryside (peasants have stopped bringing food to town). Germans demand exorbitant sums of money as Jewish "contributions" to the regime.

October 15, 1941: Senior SS and police leaders begin to establish what will become a network of fifteen labor camps, including Iaktoriv (Jaktorów) and Kurowice, to complete about 160 kilometers of road construction on Thoroughfare IV in eastern Galicia. The undertaking is jointly managed by the SS and police, Organisation Todt, and private German firms. About twenty thousand Jewish men and women are sent to these camps.

October 23, 1941: Jewish emigration from the German Reich is banned. An earlier November 1940 regulation banning Jewish emigration from the Generalgouvernement is later applied to Galicia District, including Peremyshliany.

November 1, 1941: Construction of the killing center Bełżec begins.

November 5, 1941: A detachment of German Security Police (sent from Ternopil) and regular police (from the Warsaw District), who are assisted by local auxiliaries, murder an estimated 450 men (aged eighteen to sixty) in the forest bordering Peremyshliany. Among those killed are the father and brother of Rita Honig, who later becomes the wife of Jacob Litman.

December 8, 1941: Mass murder of Polish Jews, Sinti and Roma, and Polish and Soviet prisoners of war using sealed gas vans begins in Chełmno (Kulmhof), in the Warthegau District of German-annexed Poland. Killing operations at this site continue until July 14, 1944, murdering more than 150,000 men, women, and children.

Jews from Peremyshliany are assigned to nearby labor camps.

1942

January 20, 1942: Senior German government officials meet at the Wannsee Conference in Berlin to discuss implementation of the "Final Solution," the plan to murder an estimated 11 million Jews in Europe. Participants also discuss the use of Jews on labor projects in eastern Europe, especially for road construction, as well as the fate of Jews in mixed marriages and their partly Jewish children.

February 15, 1942: The first transport of Jewish prisoners arrives at the Auschwitz I camp, destined for death by Zyklon B gas.

March 17, 1942: Mass gassings at Bełżec camp begin, with Jews from Lublin as the first victims. Its gassing operations continue until December 1942 as part of "Aktion Reinhard," a Nazi campaign to kill all the Jews of the Generalgouvernement.

May 1942: German authorities murder about one hundred patients in Peremyshliany's local hospital.

June 1942: Gestapo chief Heinrich Müller establishes Sonderkommando 1005 to hide traces of mass graves. In the summer of 1942, a handful of SS men test out methods of corpse disposal at Chełmno (Kulmhof) extermination camp.

July 19, 1942: Heinrich Himmler orders "resettlement" (elimination) of the entire Jewish population of the Generalgouvernement by the end of 1942 ("Aktion Reinhard"), with only some vital Jewish labor retained and confined to special designated camps (*Sammellager*). The clearing of all Jewish ghettos produces labor shortages for enterprises tied to German war production; military officials protest and are able to limit the scale of some of the deportations temporarily.

August 1942: Jews from neighboring Hlyniany and Svirzh are brought to the Peremyshliany ghetto.

August–September 1942: Almost three thousand Peremyshliany ghetto inhabitants are deported to Bełżec and gassed upon arrival. Samuel Golfard's sister is among the deportees.

October 1942: Surviving Jews of Peremyshliany are concentrated in the ghetto, while additional Jews from surrounding localities are sent there during the following month.

November 10, 1942: Higher SS and Police Leader Friedrich-Wilhelm Krüger orders the sealing of Jewish ghettos and residential districts in the Generalgouvernement, including in Peremyshliany. As of December 1, no Jew is allowed to leave or remain outside the ghetto without police permission, and any non-Jews who shelter, feed, or hide Jews are also subject to the death penalty. At this point 254,989 Jews have already been deported from eastern Galicia, mostly to the Bełżec killing center.

December 5–7, 1942: Another massacre occurs in the Peremyshliany ghetto; twenty-four hundred Jews are deported to the Bełżec killing center, while six hundred are killed in the ghetto during the "*Aktion*."

December 30, 1942: Ukrainian Greek Catholic priest Omelian Kovch is arrested for helping Jews and taken from Peremyshliany to the Janowska camp in Lviv.

1943

January 15–16, 1943: Approximately two thousand Jews are massacred in Jaryczów Nowy, located some fifteen miles northwest of Peremyshliany.

January 30, 1943: Three Jewish families (the Alwaglows, Zimmers, and Hochbergs) from the town of Janczyn (Ianchyn, today Ivanivka), less than ten miles southeast of Peremyshliany, are taken to Lviv and shot.

January 31, 1943: The Germans are defeated at Stalingrad.

February 10–11, 1943: Massacres occur at the Velyki Mosty (Mosty Wielkie) labor camp and ghetto north of Lviv. Half the Jewish laborers are shot, and the ghetto is liquidated. In total, some two thousand Jews, mostly women and the elderly, are murdered.

February 18, 1943: In a speech at the Berlin Sportpalast, Reich Propaganda Minister Joseph Goebbels declares "total war" and reiterates Germany's determination to proceed with anti-Jewish measures.

February 26, 1943: The Chuprynosiv (Czupernosów) camp is liquidated; quarry workers are escorted to town, forced on to trucks, and taken away to a camp in Pluhiv (Płuhów), beyond Zolochiv (Złoczów).

March 1943: Eleven Jews in hiding are discovered and shot in Ciemierzyńce, a village near Peremyshliany.

Late March–early April 1943: Numerous massacres occur in Lviv, Zhovkva (Żółkiew), Berezhany, and Zolochiv (Złoczów).

March 21, 1943: The subcamp in Peremyshliany is established. Jews are marched to a quarry from the camp, which is under the control of SS-Unterscharführer Karl Kempka.

April 9, 1943: In the Zboriv (Zborów) massacres, some twenty-three hundred Jews are arrested, forced to dig pits, and shot by a German police unit under Hermann Mueller, assisted by the German gendarmerie and Ukrainian police.

Hundreds of Jewish laborers, including women and girls, are killed during the night shift at the clothing factory of Firma Schwarz & Co. near Lviv, which employs three to five thousand Jews; the action may be a retaliation for the murder of an SS officer in the Janowska camp.

April 13, 1943: Security Police from Lviv, assisted by the German gendarmerie and the Ukrainian police, liquidate the ghetto in Bibrka (Bóbrka), a village about twelve miles from Peremyshliany, massacring some twelve hundred Jews. This is one of the last Jewish communities destroyed in the region.

April 19, 1943: The Warsaw Ghetto Uprising, an armed rebellion of Jews, begins when German police and troops start the final liquidation of the ghetto. The revolt continues until May 16 and is only suppressed when German Waffen SS and police units thoroughly search, burn, and raze the ghetto, street by street.

May 10, 1943: The labor camp at Velyki Mosty (Mosty Wielkie), run by the German army under the command of a Viennese officer named Krupa, is liquidated and most of the workers are killed.

May 22–23, 1943: The Peremyshliany ghetto is liquidated. A few hundred German police (Schutzpolizei) surround the ghetto. Aided by a Jewish demolition unit, they begin a systematic search for Jews in hiding, seize property, and raze buildings. For more than one week, massacres occur in the ghetto and in the nearby forest. A company of the 1st Battalion, Police Regiment 23, shoots an estimated 2,000 people.

May 23, 1943: An official German announcement is made in Peremyshliany that the town is "free of Jews."

June 28, 1943: The Peremyshliany labor camp, where Jacob Litman and Samuel Golfard are prisoners, is liquidated: 250 women are shot and 200 men are sent to the Kurowice camp. This is possibly also the date of Golfard's failed attempt to shoot a German commandant, which results in his own death.

July 1943: Jacob Litman is transferred to the Kurowice camp but soon rescued and brought to a hiding place in the forest.

The Red Army decisively defeats the Wehrmacht in the Battle of Kursk, an important rail hub city. The first war crimes trial is held in Krasnodar (in southern Russia) by Soviet authorities, with charges brought against eleven auxiliaries attached to an *Einsatzgruppen* unit.

Operations to conceal traces of mass murder are completed at Bełżec, and the last transport of Jewish prisoners is sent to the Sobibór extermination camp.

July 10, 1943: The Allied invasion of Sicily (Italy) begins.

July 22, 1943: The Iaktoriv (Jaktorów) camp is liquidated.

July 23–August 1, 1943: The Kurowice camp is liquidated.

August 1943: During an uprising in the Treblinka extermination camp, hundreds of prisoners manage to escape from the killing center in eastern Poland. Few remain alive at the end of the war.

October 1943: Several prisoners kill eleven SS officers and guards in an uprising at the Sobibór extermination camp in eastern Poland. Half of the approximately six hundred prisoners manage to flee (less than a quarter of them survive the war, mainly in hiding).

November 6, 1943: The Red Army recaptures Kiev.

1944

January 6, 1944: The Red Army advances into western Ukraine, entering Berdychiv.

April 15, 1944: The Red Army retakes Ternopil.

June 6, 1944: The Allied invasion of France begins (D-Day).

July 23, 1944: The Red Army enters Majdanek, a killing center and concentration camp on the outskirts of Lublin.

July 1944: The Soviet offensive in Galicia begins.

July 20–24, 1944: The Red Army arrives in Peremyshliany. Forty Jews come out of hiding and return to the town.

August 1, 1944: The Warsaw Uprising begins, coming over a year after the Warsaw Ghetto Uprising and staged by the Polish Home Army to liberate the city from Nazi occupiers. Unaided by the Red Army, the Polish resistance fights for more than two months before capitulating.

October 7, 1944: A *Sonderkommando*, or special Jewish prisoner detachment, stages an uprising at Auschwitz-Birkenau. The group blows up one crematorium and kills several guards before being killed themselves.

November 25, 1944: With the Germans in retreat, SS chief Heinrich Himmler orders the destruction of crematoria and gas chambers at Auschwitz-Birkenau in an attempt to hide evidence of mass murder at the camp.

1945

January 17, 1945: The Red Army ends the Nazi occupation of Warsaw.

January–April 1945: The SS evacuates more than 250,000 prisoners from Nazi camps in occupied Europe, forcing them on "death marches" to camps in the interior of Germany and Austria.

January 27, 1945: The Soviet army liberates the seven thousand prisoners remaining at Auschwitz-Birkenau.

April 11, 1945: Troops with the U.S. Third Army arrive at Buchenwald concentration camp in eastern Germany, soon after prisoners take over the camp and capture or kill the remaining camp guards.

April 29, 1945: The U.S. Seventh Army liberates Dachau concentration camp near Munich, Germany.

May 8, 1945: VE Day marks the end of the war in Europe.

1946–1947

Jacob Litman makes his way westward to Austria and the displaced persons (DP) camp in Bad Reichenhall, Germany. A United Nations relief unit (UNRRA team #1070) and the Jewish Agency for Palestine employ him at Bayerisch Gmain, Ainring DP Camp.

1949

Jacob and Rita Litman arrive in the United States.

1966–1968

May 31, 1966: Tadeusz Jankiewicz is recognized as Righteous Among the Nations.

The Lemberg war crimes trial takes place in West Germany. Opening in October 1966, the trial lasts for eighteen months. Among the fifteen defendants standing trial for helping to murder Jews in the Lvóv region, Ernst Epple is sentenced to life in prison and Paul Fox is acquitted.

1974

The Main Commission for the Investigation of Nazi War Crimes in Poland (Wrocław District prosecutor) investigates atrocities in wartime Peremyshliany.

1985

November 13, 1985: Death of Tadeusz Jankiewicz.

1991–1992

Bodies are exhumed from mass graves in Peremyshliany's forest, where Samuel Golfard was buried. Local Ukrainian authorities claim the victims are non-Jewish peasants and, in a public ceremony, rebury the remains in a Christian cemetery in town.

1998

The Main Commission for the Prosecution of Crimes against the Polish Nation, Institute of National Memory (IPN), Kraków branch office, reopens investigation into crimes in Peremyshliany and contacts prosecutors in Ludwigsburg, Germany, to collect additional evidence about the murders of four hundred Jews in 1942 and 1943.

2001

Investigation of former German commandants of Kurowice and Iaktoriv (Jaktorów) is opened and closed by German prosecutors, who determine that Ernst Epple and Josef Grzimek have died.

2004

June 27, 2004: Death of Jacob Litman.

2005

May 2005: Polish investigation of crimes in Peremyshliany is discontinued.

Biographies[1]

Aumeier, Julius (1911–?). Deputy camp commander of Iaktoriv (Jaktorów) camp. A Czech German from the Sudetenland, he joined the SS in 1938. Recruited to the Waffen SS in 1939, he was placed on the staff of the SS and police chief for Galicia, Friedrich Katzmann, in October 1941. Appointed head of Jaktorów at the end of 1942, he remained there until the camp was liquidated in July 1943. He was responsible for multiple prisoner shootings and abuses. According to one Jewish testimony, Aumeier shot three Jewish prisoners one day because he discovered his clean clothes had fallen from a laundry line onto the dirty ground. Aumeier was held in U.S. custody in 1945 but later released. He settled in Bavaria and worked as a farmhand. In the 1960s a West German court acquitted him for lack of evidence.

Dorn (first name and dates unknown). A German gendarme with the local stationary police in Peremyshliany who distinguished himself as a corrupt boozer and plunderer. He participated in anti-Jewish massacres and shot five Jews who were hiding in the office of the Jewish Council. He may have served with two other regular police stationed in town during the war, Willi Seeman and Bruno Sämisch.

---

1. Additional biographical information on the German SS and police perpetrators in eastern Galicia is available in Pohl, *Nationalsozialistische Judenverfolgung in Ostgalizien*, 411–22, and Thomas Sandkühler, *"Endlösung" in Galizien: Der Judenmord in Ostpolen und die Rettungsinitiativen von Berhold Beitz 1941–1944* (Bonn: Dietz, 1996), 426–59.

Epple, Ernst (1908–1976). After attending primary school, he worked in a cotton mill near Reutlingen as a machine operator. He married in 1931 and had three children. Epple joined the SS in 1936 and was assigned to the 35th Infantry Regiment when the war broke out. In November 1939 he was sent to noncommissioned officer's school for the Waffen SS in Breslau (Wrocław). After completing an eight-week course, he was assigned to the 8th SS-Totenkopfstandarte (regiment) in Kraków, with the rank of SS-Unterscharführer (sergeant). Active in the areas of Lublin and Chełm in 1940, he also trained *Volksdeutsche* units as a member of the SS and police in Lublin. He was promoted to SS-Scharführer (squad leader) in July 1940. Assigned to the SS and police for the Lviv district in October 1941, he was charged with creating and managing the Kurowice forced labor camp. On March 4, 1942, Epple was awarded the War Service Cross 2nd Class in recognition of his "tough" work at the camp. In the fall of 1942 he was transferred to an SS replacement and training battalion in Arolsen, Hesse, Germany, and in early 1943, he was assigned to a Waffen SS unit near Munich. At the war's end he was in Silesia and taken into Soviet custody on May 9, 1945. Held in a series of Soviet camps, Epple was released around Christmas 1949. He returned to the Stuttgart area to work as a crane operator in a factory in Reutlingen. He was arrested while at work on August 18, 1960, and sentenced to life in prison by the Stuttgart State Court in 1968.

Fox, Paul (1912–?). Son of a German mason and Polish mother from Tarnowitz, Upper Silesia. He joined the Nazi movement in the 1930s and worked as a coal miner. In April 1937 he joined the SS, and after the beginning of the war he was assigned to the "ethnic German" auxiliary police (Hilfspolizei) operating in the area by Tschenstochau (Częstochowa) and Radom. In August 1940 he was appointed chief of a labor camp in Lublin, and from there he was sent on November 19, 1941, to the office of the SS and police leader for Galicia, Friedrich Katzmann. Fox was tasked with the establishment of forced labor camps along Janowska Street. He moved from camp to camp until he ended up as the deputy commandant of the forced labor camp of Iaktoriv (Jaktorów), reporting to Josef Grzimek. In the late summer of 1942 he was assigned to a Waffen SS unit in Weimar, Germany, at the Buchenwald camp. He completed training as a driver and was placed in an SS tank division that saw military action in Belgium. With the rank of SS-Sturmmann (private first class in the SS), he was captured by the Americans on the western front but released. From June 1946 until his arrest in March 1963, Fox worked as a hewer in a West German coal mine. The Stuttgart State Court tried and acquitted him in 1968.

Fuglevych, Ivan (1927–). Began working at the barbershop in Peremyshliany after graduating from primary school in 1942. The shop was located at the edge of the ghetto on the main street (Pieracki Street, now Galicia Street), directly across from the *Judenrat*'s office. Since the Germans wanted to get rid of the Jewish barbers, they forced the Jews to train young Ivan in the trade. Two of the Jews who trained Fuglevych were named Scherer and Fechter. By autumn 1943, no Jewish barbers were left. Fuglevych was curious about what was happening to the Jews and secretly went to the forest killing site, where he saw the mass graves. He recalled that in the summer of 1943 he overheard German and Ukrainian policemen in the barbershop speaking about "one brave Jew" who dared to shoot a German commandant; they were referring to Samuel Golfard. Fuglevych provided his testimony to the author (July 2005, October 2010) and to the Litman family (summer 2008).

Golfard, Bronia (dates unknown). The youngest of Samuel's sisters, who was alive in Radom in January 1943. She sent him a care package of clothing. Her nickname was Belutka. She may have died in the Radom ghetto, been shot in the nearby forest, or numbered among those deported from Radom to Treblinka in 1943 or Auschwitz in 1944.

Golfard, Mania (Maniusia) (?–1942). Samuel Golfard's younger sister and "next of kin." Mania fled with Samuel to Volhynia in 1939 and to Peremyshliany in July or August 1941. After living with the family of Jacob Katz for some months, they were forced into the Peremyshliany ghetto. In August 1942 Mania was deported to Bełżec, where she died.

Golfard, Pola (1927–?). Samuel Golfard's younger "middle sister," who was a sickly child. He mentions nursing her before the war when she was ill. No additional information about her has been found.

Golfard, Samuel (Samek) (ca. 1910–1943).[2] A man who grew up in the Radom district of Poland with three younger sisters: Mania, Pola, and Bronia. He fled with his sister Mania to Volhynia in late 1939, where he found refuge until the German attack on the Soviet Union starting on June 22, 1941. He arrived in Peremyshliany in July and found shelter with the family of Dr. Jacob Katz (where he met Jacob Litman). Litman described him as social, well-spoken, urbane, suave, and witty, with a lean figure, high forehead, copper-blond

---

2. On the uncertainties surrounding his name and biography, see pp. xv–xx.

hair, mustache, and left-liberal convictions. Samuel Golfard was sent to the Iaktoriv (Jaktorów) labor camp some time in late spring or summer 1942. His sister Mania was able to bribe the Jewish Council to release him from the camp, perhaps by exchanging him with another Jew from the ghetto. Samuel secured a job as a scrap collector from January until April 1943, perhaps for the German Equipment Works (DAW). This "privileged" position gave him the chance to secretly write the diary. After the Peremyshliany ghetto was liquidated in May 1943, Samuel hid at the *Nebenlager* (labor camp) for three weeks. At this time, he planned his escape to the forests in Czupernosów with Jacob Litman and also secured a small pistol. On the eve of their escape, the *Nebenlager* was surrounded by German SS and police, and prisoners were forced to line up outside. Even before being separated from the laborers, Golfard pulled out his pistol. He aimed it at the German commander, but the pistol misfired or failed, and the Germans responded with a hail of bullets, killing him and several prisoners near him. Litman buried Golfard in the Brzezina Forest at the edge of Peremyshliany.

Grzimek, Josef (1905–1950). Joined the Nazi Party in 1930 and the SS in 1932. He was assigned to an SS cavalier battalion in Breslau (Wrocław) in November 1939. In February 1942 he became chief of the forced labor camps of Iaktoriv (Jaktorów), Zolochiv (Złoczów), Iarychiv (Jaryczów), Kamyonka Buska (Kamionka Strumiłowa), and Rava Ruska (Rawa Ruska). Transferred to the command staff of the Janowska camp in Lviv on February 19, 1943, Grzimek subsequently went on to command the camps in Szebnie. In March 1944 he arrived in Płaszów, where he was deemed a "suitable" successor to the brute Amon Goeth, made famous in the film *Schindler's List.* Captured and extradited to Poland in 1947, he received a death sentence on January 29, 1949, at a public trial in Warsaw, and was later executed.

Jankiewicz, Helena Swoboda (?–1979). The wife of Tadeusz Jankiewicz, whom he married in 1924. Helena assisted in the rescue of Jacob Litman and aided other Jews in Peremyshliany. She was the daughter of a prosperous farmer of Czech descent, and her brother was the local forester who arranged hiding places for Jews in the forest.

Jankiewicz, Tadeusz (1900–1985). According to Jacob Litman's testimony, "a tall man with a high forehead and bony face that made him appear stern. Actually, he was a serious, no-nonsense, hardworking and reliable person whose thoughtfulness was not obvious or easily detected. Before Poland's capitulation, he worked in some executive capacity at the local bureau of taxation and continued to work at the same place under the new regime of the Soviet Union. Thus, he was one of the very few, if any, Polish officials who was not deported to Siberia right after the Red Army invaded. His responsibilities as a tax assessor and knowledge of the entire territory often kept him in the surrounding villages."[3] Jankiewicz nursed Litman back to health after he contracted typhoid fever. He paid a Ukrainian peasant a few bottles of vodka to get Litman out of the Kurowice camp in July 1943, and he prepared a hiding place for Litman in the forest. Jankiewicz brought food to the Jewish refugees in the forest. He also helped Samuel Golfard, who gave him his diary for safekeeping. After the war, Jankiewicz sent the diary to Jacob Litman. Yad Vashem declared Jankiewicz one of the Righteous Among the Nations in 1966. He died in Lubaczów, Poland, in 1985.

Katz, Dr. Jacob (?–1943). A married man with two children and a respected lawyer in Peremyshliany who had completed his degree at the University of Vienna. He was barred from practicing law under the Soviets, so he taught math at the Jewish high school (where Jacob Litman also worked). His house on the main street was among the few located outside the ghetto and was the place where Samuel Golfard and Jacob Litman met in August 1941. Later, in May 1943, after the ghetto was liquidated, Litman saw among the bodies of Jews strewn on the marketplace a "crouched little figure . . . a round bald head stooped on its bent knees," his dear benefactor and senior colleague, Jacob Katz. No information could be found about the fate of his family.

Katzmann, Friedrich (Fritz) (1906–1957). Worked as a carpenter and joined the Nazi Party and SA in the 1920s. He joined the SS in 1930 and quickly rose through the ranks after the Nazis came to power in 1933. He was recognized in his personnel file as "a convinced National Socialist whose entire life and activity are aligned according to the principles of the [Nazi] worldview." After serving on the staff of the SS and police office in Radom in 1939–1940 (where he led the "outstanding pacification measures" against Polish and Jewish intelligentsia), Katzmann was promoted to SS-Brigadeführer (lieutenant general) and appointed SS and police leader for the Galicia District in mid-October 1941. He aggressively carried out the murder of the Jews in his district and was promoted again to SS-Gruppenführer (major general) on January 30, 1943. After the war, he took on the false name Bruno Albrecht and settled near Darmstadt,

---

3. Jacob Litman, *Autobiography* (unpublished manuscript, 1997), 19.

West Germany. He was not publicly linked to his wartime role until his death in 1957.

Kempka, Karl (1902–1946). An SS-*Unterscharführer* (sergeant) who joined the Nazi Party in 1932. As of January 1942, Kempka worked in the SS and police office at the forced labor camp in Lavrykivci (Ławrykowce). From there he was assigned to the Kurowice subcamp near Peremyshliany, and after it was liquidated, he helped manage the forced labor camp of Janowska in Lviv.

Kovch, Omelian (1884–1944; also known as Emilian Kowc). A Greek Catholic priest who attended seminary in Lviv and graduated from the College of Sergius and Bachus in Rome. Prior to and during World War I, he was active in Galicia, helping Ukrainian refugees and serving as a military chaplain. In 1922 he became a parish priest in Peremyshliany and was noted for extending a hand to members of all faiths. During the Nazi occupation, Kovch baptized Jews and provided them with Christian identification papers. Local German secret police discovered this and arrested him on December 30, 1942. Later, in August 1943, he was deported to Majdanek, where he continued to minister to prisoners and died on March 25, 1944. In September 1999, the Jewish Council of Ukraine named Kovch a Righteous Ukrainian, and on June 27, 2001, Pope John Paul II beatified him.

Litman, Jacob (1920–2004). A friend of the diarist who arrived in Peremyshliany from Warsaw in December 1939. Because of wartime housing shortages, Soviet authorities ordered Litman to live in the Jankiewicz household. He worked as a teacher in the Jewish junior high school and was subjected to antisemitic allegations and torture by Ukrainian police in the summer of 1941, after the Germans arrived in Peremyshliany. He survived the first roundup of Jewish men while hiding in the pantry of Jacob Katz's home in November 1941, but was later forced to move into the Peremyshliany ghetto. In 1942 he labored in the quarry in Chuprynosiv (Czupernosów), then was transferred in May 1943 to the *Nebenlager* (subcamp) and assigned to the construction of a new granary near the railroad station in Peremyshliany. As of June 1943, he was placed in the *Totenbrigade* (burial brigade) in the Brzezina Forest. After burying Samuel Golfard, he was among those transferred to the Kurowice labor camp. At the end of the summer of 1943, he escaped with the help of Tadeusz Jankiewicz and fled into the forest. Shot by a German during a raid of their hideout, he recovered and was liberated by the Red Army in July 1944. Litman married Rita Honig, another survivor from Peremyshliany, whom he met in the forest. Before emigrating to the United States in 1949, the Litmans worked at the Bayerisch Gmain (Germany) displaced persons home for orphaned Jews and the Yehud ha-Macabi Children's Center, where they taught Hebrew in preparation for the children's emigration to Palestine (Israel). In the United States, Litman secured a teaching position in Utica, New York, where the couple's first two children, Julius and Anita, were born. The family later moved to Union, New Jersey, where Jacob Litman became the principal of Temple Beth Shalom's Hebrew School. Their third child, Robert, was born there in 1956. Jacob completed a doctorate in education at New York University and worked for the American Association for Jewish Education (now known as JESNA) until his retirement in 1985. Rita Honig Litman passed away on April 26, 2008.

Ludwig (first name and dates unknown). A notorious Security Police (Sipo) leader in the Zolochiv (Złoczów) branch office and head of the forced labor camps in Zolochiv in early 1943. Samuel Golfard refers to Ludwig as the SS chief from Lviv who lorded over the massacre and deportation of twenty-four hundred Jews in December 1942 and January 1943.

Rokeach, Aharon (1880–1957). The fourth rebbe of the Belz Hasidic dynasty. Rokeach led the movement from 1926. During the war he sought temporary refuge in Peremyshliany and suffered the loss of his son in the July 1941 massacre at the synagogue.

Sämisch, Bruno (May 1890–?). Posted to the gendarme office in Peremyshliany from November 1941 until April 1942. He participated in the November 1941 massacre of six hundred Jews. After the war he confessed to East German interrogators that he beat and robbed Jews when they were gathered at the local school and escorted to the killing site in the forest. His superior in Peremyshliany was Fritz Romocki; his colleagues in the gendarmerie included Friedrich Bartelt, Mehlig, Tharun, and Willi Seeman.

Seeman, Willi (dates unknown). A German gendarme in Peremyshliany during the war, originally from Upper Silesia. He participated in the mass shooting of six hundred Jews. Seeman allegedly killed the Jewish man Chaskiel featured in the wartime photograph reprinted in this book on p. 85. The Ukrainian barber Ivan Fuglevych remembered Seeman as the gendarme who beat his mother. The gendarmes were responsible for the executions of smaller groups of captured Jews (twenty-five or fewer persons). The killings occurred every two or three days in the Brzezina Forest in early June 1943, according to Jacob Litman's testimony.

Warzok, Friedrich (1903–?) A trained mason who in 1931 joined the Nazi Party and SS, in which he was to attain the rank of SS-Hauptsturmführer (captain). Before arriving in eastern Galicia, he was assigned to a police regiment in Warsaw and led the 4th Sonderdienstkompanie in Lublin. He joined the staff of the SS and police of Galicia in October 1941 and was named commander of the forced labor camps in the Zolochiv (Złoczów) district, including Lyashky (Lacki), Pluhiv (Płuhów), Zboriv (Zborów), Iaktoriv (Jaktorów), Sasov (Sasow), and Brody. He remained there until June 1943, when he took over command of the Janowska forced labor camp in Lemberg (Lviv). There Warzok tormented, beat, extorted, and shot prisoners. He pocketed huge sums of cash, gold, diamonds, and other valuables, which he brought with him as he oversaw a "death march" evacuation of prisoners to the Neuengamme concentration camp in March 1945. With the stolen valuables and a false identity, Warzok successfully fled to Cairo. It is not known when or where he died.

Wöbke, Karl (1910–?). A native of Leipzig who served as an SS-Oberscharführer (sergeant) and Jewish affairs adviser in the Office of the Commander of the Security Police and Service, Lemberg (Lviv). He personally participated in the roundup of about forty thousand Jews brought to the Janowska camp in August 1942 prior to their deportation to the Bełżec gassing center, as well as the murder of individual Jews. In November and December, Wöbke arrived in Peremyshliany to lead two anti-Jewish actions. With his SS subordinates, he shot sixty Jews in the hospital who were suffering from typhus. He was also seen shooting a boy who tried to flee in front of him, leaving him dead on the ghetto street. Wöbke was sentenced to nine years in prison at the Lemberg Trial in Stuttgart, West Germany. Because he was ill and had already served more than two-thirds of his sentence during the investigation, he was released in 1968.

INDEX

Page numbers that appear in boldface refer to the Biographies. Place names are in Ukrainian, unless spelled differently in Golfard's Polish-language diary. Polish and German variants are provided as cross-referenced terms.

"actions," 41, 45, 46, 54–5, 57–64, 79, 80, 91, 93, 104–6, 114–16, 126. *See also* deportation(s); mass shooting(s)
Aktion Reinhard, 17, 105
Allies, 26, 62, 74, 81–2, 106–7, 108–10
Alwaglow family, 75
antisemitism, 1, 5–7, 16, 20, 33, 98, 101
Appelfeld, Aharon, 10–11
aristocracy, Polish, 28
Armia Krajowa (Home Army, AK), 26
Aufbau, 117, 118
Aumeier, Julius, **161**
Auschwitz, 1, 50, 64
Aussiedlung. See deportation(s)
Austro-Hungarian Empire, eastern Galicia under, 4–5, 31, 33–4
Autobiography (Litman), 124, 125, 130–1

Babi Yar massacre, 3
Bartelt, Friedrich, 167
Bauer, Otto, 98, 99, 100
Bełżec, 11, 15, 16–18, 47, 56–8, 59, 98, 111, 112, 115–16
Bełzer rebbe. *See* Rokeach, Aharon

Berger, Karolina, 134–5
Bóbrka, 54, 59, 92
Boryslav, 15, 40
Brack, Victor, 17
Brzeżany, 60, 88
Brzezina Forest, 44–5, 52–3, 86, 121, 127–8, 164, 167
bystanders, 20, 97, 111, 114, 122

Casablanca Conference, 74
Chaskiel, 85, 167
Chmielnicki, Bohdan. *See* Khmel'nyts'kyi, Bohdan
Chortkiv, 15
Christian clergy, 75–6
Ciemierzyńce, 85, 86
collaboration: Golfard on, 24, 25, 82–3, 93, 94; by Jews, 24–5, 79, 83, 93; in killing operations, 16; by local non-Jews, 16, 19–24, 94; by Poles, 20, 94; postwar punishment for, in eastern Europe, 120–1; by Ukrainians, 3–4, 19–24, 39–43, 53, 82, 89, 94, 112, 114, 121. *See also* Jewish Council(s);

Jewish police; Ukrainian militias;
Ukrainian police
communism and communists, 6–7, 41,
110
Cossacks, 30, 34, 83
Czerniaków, Adam, 25
Czupernosów, 127, 164; labor camp,
78–80, 126, 166

deportation(s): to Bełżec, 16, 17, 18,
47, 57, 98, 114–16; in December
1942, 58, 61; from eastern Galicia,
Katzmann Report on, 104–6; for
German colonization, 64; of Mania
Golfard, 11, 18, 47, 50, 51, 54–5; from
Peremyshliany ghetto, 47, 54–5, 57–8,
61, 86, 88, 98, 111, 114–16, 126;
"selection" for, 19; in spring 1943, 79,
80–1, 86, 88, 126; in summer-autumn
1942, 47, 54–5, 57–8, 98, 111, 114–16
diary writing, 7–14
documents: on Tadeusz Jankiewicz as
rescuer, 131–5; by Jacob Litman, 123–
31; postwar, 116–23; wartime, 97–116
Dontsov, Dmytro, 5
Dorn, 61–2, **161**
Drohobych. *See* Drohobycz
Drohobycz, 15, 40, 80
Durchgangsstrasse IV (Thoroughfare IV), 19,
66, 103, 121
Dziunia, testimony, 121–3

eastern front, Golfard on, 63, 74, 81–2
Einsatzgruppen, 3, 17, 126
elites, Polish, 28, 30, 35–6, 37
Epple, Ernst, 66–7, 91, 111–14, 116, 117,
119–121, 122, 123, **162**
executions: in Ciemierzyńce, 85;
gendarmes' role in, 84, 85, 167; at
Jaktorów labor camp, 68–70, 112; in
Kimierz, 84–5; in Kurowice, 112–14,
122, 123; in Lwów, 75; number of Jews
killed by, 2, 15; around Peremyshliany,
77, 85–6, 92–3, 128, 167. *See also* mass
shooting(s)

Fechter, 163
forced labor, 16, 19, 46–7, 98, 100–5, 125,
126, 166
forests: executions in, 24, 44–5, 53, 86,
120, 127, 167; as hiding place, 19, 24,
75, 77–8, 84, 127, 133–5, 164, 165,
166
Fox, Paul, 47, 51, 67–8, 70, 71, 73, 116,
119, 121, **162**
Frank, Anne, diary of, 9
Frank, Hans, 22, 44
Fuglevych, Ivan, 12, 13, **163,** 167

Gabel, Arthur, 57
Galicia: (*See also* peasants, of eastern
Galicia; Poles; Ukrainians, of eastern
Galicia; *specific towns*); Austro-
Hungarian rule of, 4–5, 31, 33–4; and
Bełżec, 17–18; end-of-war violence in,
23; ethnic communities in, 28, 30–7,
38, 82–4; ethnic warfare in, during
German occupation, 110; "Final
Solution" in, 15–19, 98–106; German
administration in, 45, 98; German
invasion of, 3–4, 15–16, 38–9;
historical background of, 28–33;
history of Jews in, 28–33, 34–5, 38;
Holocaust in, 3–4, 7, 14–26, 98–106;
interwar, 31–3; Jewish refugees in, 28,
38; Jews hiding in forests of, 19, 24,
75, 77–8, 84, 133–5, 164, 165, 166;
massacres of prisoners by NKVD in,
40; number of Jews killed in, 18, 100,
105, 119; pogroms in, 3–4, 15–16,
20; Polish rule of, 28–33, 83–4;
postwar expulsions from, 38; Soviet
occupation of, 6–7, 23, 28, 37, 38,
40; Soviet propaganda in, 110–16;
western, 32.
Galicia District. *See* Generalgouvernement
Gareis, Hanns, 98, 99, 100
Gavrylivna, Anna. *See* Liakher, Faina
Gelin, Gisela Gross. *See* Gross, Gisela
gendarmes, 23, 44, 45, 47, 61–2, 84–5, 86,
121, 127–8, 161, 167

Generalgouvernement, 16, 22, 44, 45, 98;
"Final Solution" in, 15–19, 98–106;
map of, 27
German Democratic Republic, 85, 121
German Order Police, 126
Germans: colonization by, 31, 64, 84; as
gendarmes, 44, 45, 47, 61–2, 84–5,
86, 121, 127–8, 161, 167; Golfard on,
52, 74–5, 94; knowledge of Holocaust,
107; postwar trials and investigations of,
116–21
Germany: Allied bombing of, 106–7,
108–10; invasion in Peremyshliany,
38, 39; invasion of eastern Galicia,
3–4, 15–16, 38–9; invasion of Soviet
Union, 2–3, 22, 63, 74, 81–2; North
Africa campaign, 74; postwar trials
and investigations in, 100, 116–21;
propaganda by, 106–7; in western
Poland, 28
ghetto(s), 16; Bóbrka, 54, 59, 92;
conditions in, 16; economy of, 79;
Jewish Councils in, 24–5; Kraków, 86;
liquidations, 16, 17, 18–19, 24, 58, 59,
86, 88, 92, 105, 106; Lwów, 18, 51,
63, 86, 106; Radom, 50; Warsaw, 8,
25, 79; Złoczów, 87, 88, 90–1. *See also*
Peremyshliany ghetto
Goebbels, Joseph, 72, 74, 107, 109
Goering, Hermann, 72, 74, 108, 109
Goeth, Amon, 86, 164
Goldberg, Lieba Pfefer, 134
Golfard, Bronia (Belutka), 52, 62–3, **163**
Golfard, Mania (Maniusia), **163**;
deportation of, 11, 18, 47, 50, 51, 54;
Samuel Golfard on, 50–1, 52, 54–5, 62,
87; and Samuel Golfard's release from
labor camp, 47, 164
Golfard, Pola, 52, **163**
Golfard, Samuel (Samek), **163–4**; beating
of, 70–1; on collaboration, 24, 25,
82–3, 93, 94; on death, 10, 14, 77,
85–9; death of, 12–13, 101, 124–5,
128, 130–1, 163, 164; description
of, 125; final weeks of, 13–14, 127,

164; on Germans, 52, 74–5, 94; and
Jankiewicz family, 77, 95, 123, 132; on
Jews, 10, 65, 72, 82–3; at labor camps,
19, 46–7, 67–72, 78–9, 164; on Poles,
63–4, 77, 83–4, 94; response to killings,
9–10, 11, 78, 86–7, 89–90; response
to loss of Mania Golfard, 11, 50–1, 52,
54–5, 62, 87; on Ukrainians, 24, 30–1,
82–3, 94; on war, 25–6, 63, 72, 74–5,
81–2
Golfard, Samuel, diary of, 1, 7, 8, 9–14,
123; and Anne Frank's diary, 9; as
historical source, 14–26; literary
tradition of, 7–9; Litman's introduction
to, 124, 125–9; motivations for, 9, 11,
49; reappearance of, 123–4, 132; saving
of, 165; as "suicide note," 10, 13–14;
text of, 49–95; writing of, 11, 164
Golliger family, 59
"Golliger gang," 59, 61, 93
Gross, Gisela, 41, 42, 45, 57
Gross, Lucy, 36–7, 42, 43, 45
Grzimek, Josef, 51, 112, 120, **164**

Habsburg Empire. *See* Austro-Hungarian
Empire
Hasidism, 28, 34, 53, 167
Heydrich, Reinhard, 3, 17
Hildebrand, Friedrich, 80
Himmler, Heinrich, 16–17, 22, 57, 64,
66, 84
Hitler, Adolf, 28, 80–1, 112, 115–16;
anniversary of tenth year in power, 72,
106–7, 108–10
Hochberg, Frida (Freda), 75, 133–4
Hochberg, Izio (Yehuda), 75
Hochberg family, 75
Höfle, Hermann, 18
Holocaust: Allies and, 26, 62; in eastern
Galicia, 3–4, 7, 14–26, 126; "Final
Solution" in eastern Europe, 3, 15–19,
106, 107, 112; "Final Solution" in
eastern Galicia, 15–19, 98–106;
Golfard's diary as source on, 14–26;
Jewish diaries of, 7–14; killing centers,

1, 17, 64; killing methods in, 1, 2, 7, 15, 17–18; knowledge of, 107; in Peremyshliany, 37–47; and pogroms, 1, 3–4, 43–4; in Poland, 14–26; Soviet propaganda on, 110–16; in Ukraine, 1–4, 7, 14–26, 57

Home Army (Armia Krajowa, AK), 26

Honig, Rita. *See* Litman, Rita Honig

Honig family, 30

Horodenka, 15

Hrushka camp. *See* Jaktorów labor camp

Iaktoriv labor camp. *See* Jaktorów labor camp

Ianchyn. *See* Janczyn

Institute of National Memory (IPN), 120

intelligentsia, eradication of, 6, 16, 25, 28, 32, 40, 165

Italy, 74

Ivanivka. *See* Janczyn

Jaktorów labor camp, 19, 46, 51; administration of, 51, 66, 105, 116, 120, 161, 162, 164, 168; executions in, 68–70, 112; Golfard at, 19, 46–7, 51, 67–72, 164; liquidation of, 51, 78; photographs of, 65, 73

Janczyn, 75

Jankiewicz, Helena Swoboda, 39, 77, 95, 131, 133, 134, **164**

Jankiewicz, Tadeusz, 129, 131–5, **164–5**; Golfard on, 77, 95, 133; as rescuer, 20, 39, 75, 77, 123, 127, 128, 131–5, 165, 166

Janowska labor camp, 66, 75, 87, 92; administration of, 76, 162, 164, 166, 168; liquidation of, 75–6

Jaryczów Nowy, 63

Jaworów, 59, 67

Jedwabne, 20

Jewish Council(s), 24–5; Golfard on, 78, 80, 88–90, 93; of Peremyshliany, 44, 46–7, 54, 55, 58, 88–9, 93

Jewish diaries, of Holocaust, 7–14

Jewish "militia." *See* Jewish police

Jewish police, 46, 59, 79, 80, 88, 92, 93; of Peremyshliany ghetto, 54, 55, 58–61

Jewish refugees, 18, 28, 38, 44, 75

Jews: and antisemitism, 1, 5–7, 16, 33; conversions to Christianity, 76, 81, 166; in German propaganda, 106, 107; Golfard on, 10, 65, 72, 82–3; hiding in forests, 19, 24, 75, 77–8, 84, 133–5, 164, 165, 166; history of, in eastern Galicia, 28–33, 34, 38; numbers killed, 1–2, 15, 18, 100, 105, 119; of Peremyshliany, 28–31, 33, 34, 35–8; resistance by, 10–15, 78, 93, 105–6; under Soviet occupation, 6–7, 37; in Soviet propaganda, 110–11; and Ukrainian nationalism, 5–6, 24

Jordan, Gerhard von, 58, 88

Judenrat (Judenräte). *See* Jewish Council(s)

Kahane brothers, 54

Kalinski, Zbigniew, 123

Kaplan, Chaim, diary of, 8–9

Kapos, 79

Katz, Jacob, 57, 82, 125, **165**, 166

Katzmann, Friedrich (Fritz), 19, 66–7, 98–101, **165–6**

Katzmann Report, 100–6, 119

Kempka, Karl, 67, 121, 127, **166**

Kempner, Robert M. W., 118–20

Khmel'nyts'kyi, Bohdan, 30–1, 83

Khmel'nyts'kyi uprising (1648–1657), 30–1, 83

Kiev, 3

Kimierz (Kimirz), 84–6

Kirschner family, 121, 123

Kovch, Omelian (Emilian Kowc, Kowcz), 20, 41, 75–6, **166**

Kraków, 45, 58, 86, 91

Krosienko, 81

Krüger, Friedrich-Wilhelm, 58, 100, 102

Kurowice, 121–3, 129; labor camp, 46, 65–7, 71, 78, 112–17, 121–3, 126, 129, 162, 166

labor camp(s), 1, 19, 66, 100; administration of, 66–7, 161, 162, 164, 166, 168; avoiding assignment to, 79; Czupernosów, 78–80, 126, 166;

and *Durchgangsstrasse IV,* 19, 66, 103;
Golfard in, 19, 46–7, 67–72, 78–9,
164; Himmler's inspection of, 66; Jews'
behavior in, 72; in Katzmann Report,
101, 102–3; Litman in, 166; Mosty
Wielkie, 80; near Peremyshliany, 46,
66–7; Płaszów, 86; Pluchów, 79–80;
Ukrainian collaboration in, 23–4; in
Złoczów district, 66, 168. *See also* forced
labor; *other specific labor camps*
Lachodów, 77
Lacki labor camp, 66, 168
Laufer, Lucy, 89
Lebensraum, 2
Lemberg. *See* Lwów
Lemberg Trial, 76, 116–17, 119–21
Liakher, Faina, 45
Lichtenberg, Judah, 54
Lipski family, 84
Litman, Jacob, **166–7**; accounts by,
123–31; arrest and torture of, 39–42;
on German invasion and aftermath,
38–40; and Golfard, 82, 125–30, 164,
165; on Golfard, 13–14, 38–9, 46–7,
123–31, 163–4; Golfard on, 78–9;
and Golfard's diary, 123–9, 132; and
Jankiewicz family, 39, 75, 77, 128,
132–4, 164, 165, 166; and Katz, 165,
166; on Kovch, 76; on Peremyshliany,
interwar, 35; on Peremyshliany ghetto,
46–7, 125–6; photograph of, 124
Litman, Julius, 124, 129–30
Litman, Rita Honig, 124, 166–7
Losacker, Ludwig, 98, 99–100
Lublin, 64, 162
Ludwig, 58, 88, **167**
Luts'k, 40
Lviv. *See* Lwów
Lwów: attacks on Poles in, 6; cemetery, 63;
eradication of Jews in, 17; historical
background, 4–5; Jewish refugees in, 28;
massacres by Germans in, 58, 64, 86;
massacres by NKVD in, 40; pogroms in,
3–4, 15, 22, 31; Ukrainian nationalists
in, 4–5, 22. *See also* Janowska labor
camp

Lwów ghetto, 18, 51, 63, 86, 87, 103, 106
Lyashky labor camp. *See* Lacki labor camp

Mach, Alexander, 81
Majdanek, 64, 166
Mann, Hans, 45
mass shooting(s), 1, 15; at Babi Yar, 3; at
Kimierz, 84–5; at Lwów, 3–4, 58, 86;
at Mosty Wielkie, 80; number of Jews
killed by, 2, 15; in Peremyshliany, 44–5,
52–3, 121; in Peremyshliany ghetto,
58–62, 126, 127–8; in Peremyshliany
Nebenlager, 128–30; and pogroms,
43–4; in Ukraine, 1, 3–4, 21. *See also*
executions
Mehlig, 167
Melamed, Vladimir, 121–3
Mendel, David, 54
Mosty Wielkie labor camp, 80
Mussolini, Benito, 74

nationalism: Golfard on, 37, 82–3; Polish,
32–3; Ukrainian, 4–6, 21–4, 31, 32,
33–34, 40, 83, 111
Nebenlager (subcamp), 93; in
Peremyshliany, 127–9
Neumann, Hans-Georg, 98, 99, 100
NKVD, 6, 40, 121

Operation Barbarossa, 3, 22; pogroms
during, 3–4, 15–16
Organization of Ukrainian Nationalists
(OUN), 5, 22

peasants, of eastern Galicia: Golfard on, 24,
30–1, 83–4, 85, 94; hiding of Jews by,
77–8; historical background, 4–5, 6, 24,
28, 30–1, 83; in pogroms, 43; Polish,
83–4, 94; uprisings by, 83. *See also*
Ukrainians, of eastern Galicia
Peremyshliany, 28–37; ethnic relations
in, history of, 28–37; executions in
and near, 77, 85–6, 92–3, 128, 167;
German administration in, 45; German
invasion period in, 37–44; German
occupation of, 37–47; Golfard in, 38–9,

46–7, 163–4; historical background, 28–33; interwar, 34–7; Jews of, 28–31, 33, 34, 35–8; labor camps near, 46, 66–7; mass shooting of Jewish men in, 44–5, 52–3; massacre of prisoners by NKVD in, 40; pogroms in, 4, 15–16, 40, 41–4, 53, 82; postwar expulsions from, 38; postwar investigations concerning, 120–1; Soviet occupation of, 28, 37, 40; synagogue destruction in, 30, 41, 42, 53

Peremyshliany ghetto, 45–7, 58; "actions" in, 45, 46, 54–5, 57–63, 80, 87, 91, 92, 106, 114–16, 126; conditions in, 45; creation of, 45, 58; deportations from, 47, 54–5, 57–8, 61, 86, 88, 111, 114–16, 126; Jewish Council of, 25, 44, 46–7, 54, 55, 58, 88–9, 93; Jewish responses in, 46, 61, 62, 65, 72, 86, 126; laborers taken from, 46–7, 65; liquidation of, 46, 58, 126; mass shooting in, 58–62; massacre of hospital patients in, 46, 168; Soviet propaganda on, 110, 111, 114–16

Petliura, Symon, 5, 22

Piast political party, 83

Pizem, Rubin, 38

Płaszów labor camp, 86, 164

Pluchów (Płuhów), 79–80, 168

plundering, 42, 43, 79, 82, 100, 105

Podolia, 40

Podusów, 92–3

pogroms: during German invasion, 3–4, 15–16, 22, 40, 41–4, 52–3, 82; Golfard on, 52–53, 82; and Holocaust, 1, 3–4, 43–4; in Jaryczów Nowy, 63; during Khmel'nyts'kyi uprising, 30, 83; in Lwów, 3–4, 15, 22, 31; in Peremyshliany, 4, 15–16, 40, 41–4, 52–3, 82; by Poles, 20, 31; prewar, 1, 30, 31, 34; by Ukrainians, 3–4, 20, 22, 30, 41–2, 82

Poland: eastern Galicia under, 4, 5, 28–33, 83–4; "Final Solution" in, 15–19, 64; German colonization in, 64; German invasion of, 2, 28; German occupation

of, 15–19, 64; ghettos in, 16; Holocaust in, 14–26; Jewish Councils in, 25; pogroms in, 20; postwar trials and investigations in, 100, 120; Soviet occupation of, 6, 37; Ukrainian minority under, 4, 5, 28, 30–2, 82, 83. *See also* Galicia, eastern; *specific towns*

Poles: anti-Jewish acts and pogroms by, 20, 31, 94; of eastern Galicia, 28, 30, 83–4; as elite, 28, 30, 35–6, 37; under German occupation, 20, 28, 63, 64; Golfard on, 63–4, 77, 83–4, 94; peasants, 83–4, 94; of Peremyshliany, 35–8; persecution of, 1, 6, 23, 63–4; as rescuers, 20; under Soviet occupation, 6, 23, 37, 165

police: Jewish, 46, 54, 55, 58–61, 79, 80, 88, 92, 93; Schupo (Schutzpolizei), 81; Security Police (Sipo), 3, 44, 47, 167; Ukrainians in, 20, 22, 23–4, 45–6, 47, 121, 127. *See also* gendarmes

Polish resistance, bulletins by, 26, 91

Polish-Ukrainian War (1918–1919), 31–2

Polonization, 32–5, 83

postwar trials and investigations, 100, 116–21, 164, 168

press reportage: Allied, 108–10; Jewish American, 117–18, 119–20; Polish underground, 26, 91; Soviet underground, 110–16

prisoner massacres, 40

propaganda: British, 108–10; German, 106–7; Soviet, 110–16

property confiscation. *See* plundering

Prosvita, 33, 121

Przemyślany. *See* Peremyshliany

Pyasetsky, Petro, 84

Radom, 28, 50, 163, 165

Radomyshl, 40

Rajchman, 69, 71

Rajchman family, 69

Raubvogel, Lucy. *See* Gross, Lucy

refugees, 28, 38, 44

Reich Commissariat Ukraine, 22

religious communities, in eastern Galicia, 28, 30

rescuers, 20, 45, 84, 131; characteristics
   of, 131; Golfard on, 20, 77–8; Helena
   Jankiewicz as, 39, 77, 131, 134, 135,
   164; Tadeusz Jankiewicz as, 20, 39, 75,
   77, 95, 123, 128, 131–5, 165, 166;
   Kovch as, 20, 41, 75–6, 166; Swoboda
   as, 77, 132, 164
resettlement. *See* deportation(s)
resistance: Golfard on, 11, 14, 72, 93;
   Golfard's final act as, 12–13, 124–5; by
   Jews, 11–15, 25, 78, 93, 105–6; near
   Peremyshliany, 89, 90, 93; Polish, news
   bulletins by, 26, 91
Righteous persons, 131
Ringelblum, Emmanuel, 8
Ringelblum Archive, 8
Rokeach, Aharon Belzer rebbe, 41, **167**
Rokeach, Moishe, 41, 53
"Rollbrigade," 59
Rollkommando, 59
Romocki, Fritz, 167
Rosenberg, Alfred, 22
Rotfeld, Dr., 54
Rothenberg, 67
rumors, 18, 26, 30, 43, 47, 56, 57, 59, 62,
   76, 107, 126
Russia: tsarist, 83. *See also* Soviet Union

Sądowa Wisznia, 59, 67
Sämisch, Bruno, 85, **167**
Scheer, Paul Albert, 17
Scherer, 163
Schindler's List, 86, 164
Schneider, Frederick, 57
Schulze, Willy, 80
Schutzpolizei (German Protective Police,
   Schupo), 81, 92
Schwartz (Szwartz) factory, 87
Schwarzbart, Samuel, 5
SD. *See* Sicherheitsdienst
Security Police (Sipo), 3, 44, 47, 167, 168
Seeman, Willi, 85, **167**
"selection" for deportation, 19, 79
self, eradication of, 10–11
Sheptytsky, Kliment, 20
Sheptytsky brothers, 75

Shukhevych, Roman, 24
Sicherheitsdienst (SD), 3, 58, 80, 88
Sikorski, Władysław, 26, 91
"simulants," 68–9
slavery, 19, 21, 80
Slovakia, 80–1
Sobibór, 17
Sokół, 36, 84
Soviet Union: invasion of, 2–4, 22;
   massacres of prisoners by, 40; occupation
   of eastern Galicia, 6–7, 23, 28, 37, 40;
   propaganda leaflets on Holocaust, 110–
   16; punishment of collaborators by, 121;
   and Ukrainian nationalists, 5, 6, 40, 111.
   See also eastern front
Sovietization, 6, 37
SS, 22, 23, 66, 76, 98
Stalin, Josef, 28
Stalingrad, battle of, 63, 74
Stanimierz, 77
Stanisławów, 58, 67, 80
Staub, Ervin, 11–12
Stryj, 40, 80
Sujba, 84
Sułkowski, 49
Świrz, 69, 71, 84
Swoboda, 77, 128, 132, 164
synagogues, 30; burning of, 41, 42, 53

Tarbut, 36–7
Tarnopol district, 81
testimonies. *See* documents
Tharun, 167
Thoroughfare IV *(Durchgangsstrasse IV),* 19,
   66, 103, 121
Totenbrigade (burial squad), 127–8
trains, escape from, 60, 61
Trawniki labor camp, 23
Treblinka, 17
Trofimayak brothers, murder of, 39–40
Tychyna, Pavlo, 111
typhus, 63, 80, 87, 168

Ukraine: and *Durchgangsstrasse IV,* 19;
   German occupation of, 1–4, 7, 15–16,
   19, 22; in German thinking, 2, 17,

21; Holocaust in, 1–4, 7, 14–26, 57; Holocaust research in, 1–2, 108; modern-day, approach to Holocaust in, 21, 24; pogroms in, 3–4, 7, 15–16, 32; prewar background, 4–7; punishment of collaborators in, 111, 121; western, end-of-war violence in, 23. *See also* Galicia, eastern

Ukrainian Insurgent Army (UPA), 23, 24

Ukrainian military units, 22, 23

Ukrainian militias: anti-Jewish acts by, 3, 4, 22, 38–39, 67, 70, 71–72, 75, 83, 84, 92, 93–4. *See also* Ukrainian police

Ukrainian nationalism, 4–6, 21–3, 24, 31, 32, 33–4, 39–40, 83, 111

Ukrainian police, 21, 22, 23–4, 45–6, 47, 111, 112, 121, 127. *See also* Ukrainian militias

Ukrainian-Polish War (1918–1919), 31–2

Ukrainians, of eastern Galicia: antisemitism among, 5–7; under Austro-Hungarian rule, 33–4; casualty figures for, 21–2, 23, 40; collaboration in anti-Jewish acts by, 3–4, 19–24, 39–43, 53, 82, 89, 94, 111, 112, 114, 121 (*See also* Ukrainian militias; Ukrainian police); Germans' treatment of, 21–2, 23; Golfard on, 24, 30–1, 82–3, 94; historical background of, 4–6, 24, 28, 30–4; massacre by Soviets, 40; nationalist, 4–6, 21–4, 31, 32, 33–4, 40, 83, 111; in Peremyshliany region, prewar, 28, 30, 33, 35, 36; under Polish rule, 4, 28, 30–1, 32, 82, 83; as rescuers, 20, 45, 75–6, 78, 84; under Soviet occupation, 6, 23, 40, 111, 121; Soviet wartime propaganda and, 111, 112, 114

underground press: Polish, 26, 91; Soviet, 110–16

UPA. *See* Ukrainian Insurgent Army

Vinnytsia, 110

Volhynia, 5, 37–40, 110

Volksdeutsche (ethnic Germans), 21, 30, 64, 84–5, 86, 121, 162, 167

"W" insignia, 80, 87

Waffen-SS. *See* SS

war crimes trials and investigations. *See* postwar trials and investigations

Warsaw, 58

Warsaw ghetto, 8, 25, 79

Warsaw Uprising, 50

Warzok, Friedrich, 66, 76, 88, 101, 120–1, **168**

Washington Post, 108–10

Wendt, Otto, 45

Wirth, Christian, 17

Witos, Wincenty, 83

Wöbke, Karl, 61, 119, **168**

Wojciechowski family, 84

World War II: Allies in, 26, 62, 74, 81–2, 106–7, 108–10; German invasion of Galicia, 3–4, 15–16, 38–9; German invasion of Soviet Union, 2–3, 63, 74, 81–2; Golfard on, 25–6, 63, 72, 74–5, 81–2; Jews' knowledge of events in, 25–6, 107–8; propaganda in, 106–16; Soviet occupation of Galicia, 6–7, 23, 28, 37, 40

Wyspiański family, 84

Yad Vashem, 20, 123, 131, 132

Yiddish language, 35–6

Zamość, 64

Zborów, 81, 91, 168

Żegota (RGŻ, Polish Council to Aid Jews, Relief Council for Jews), 26, 91

Zhytomyr, 17, 40

Zimmer family, 75

Zionism, 33

Złoczów, 15–16, 45, 47, 50, 58, 77, 78, 79, 84; "actions" in, 54, 57; ghetto massacre, 87, 88, 90–1; massacre by Soviets, 40

Złoczów district, 45; labor camps in, 66, 88, 164, 167, 168

Żółkiew, 86, 87

Zolochiv. *See* Złoczów

About the Author

Wendy Lower, historian, research fellow in the eastern European history section of Ludwig-Maximilians-Universität in Munich. Dr. Lower's recent publications include "Male and Female Holocaust Perpetrators and the East German Approach to Justice, 1949–1963," *Holocaust and Genocide Studies* 24 (spring 2010): 56–84; *The Shoah in Ukraine: History, Testimony, Memorialization* (2008), coedited with Ray Brandon; and *Nazi Empire-Building and the Holocaust in Ukraine* (2005).

Ingram Content Group UK Ltd.
Milton Keynes UK
UKHW011256270323
419233UK00002B/2

9 780759 120785